A JOURNAL OF CONTEMPORARY WRITING

IRISH PAGES

DUILLÍ ÉIREANN

IRISH PAGES is a biannual journal (Spring-Summer, Autumn-Winter), edited in Belfast and publishing, in equal measure, writing from Ireland and overseas. It appears at the end of each six-month period.

Its policy is to publish poetry, short fiction, essays, creative non-fiction, memoir, essay reviews, nature-writing, translated work, literary journalism, and other autobiographical, historical, religious and scientific writing of literary distinction. There are no standard reviews or narrowly academic articles. Irish-language and Scots writing are published in the original, with English translations or glosses. IRISH PAGES is a non-partisan, non-sectarian, culturally ecumenical, and wholly independent journal. It endorses no political outlook or cultural tradition, and has no editorial position on the constitutional question. Its title refers to the island of Ireland in a purely apolitical and geographic sense, in the same manner of The Church of Ireland or the Irish Sea.

The sole criteria for inclusion in the journal are the distinction of the writing and the integrity of the individual voice. Equal editorial attention will be given to established, emergent and new writers.

The views expressed in IRISH PAGES are not necessarily those of the Editors. The journal is published by Irish Pages Ltd, a non-profit organization.

Submissions are welcome but must be accompanied by return postage or an international reply coupon. No self-addressed envelope is required. Reporting time is nine months. If work is accepted, a copy on disk may be requested.

Your subscription is essential to the independence and survival of the journal. Subscription rates are £16stg/€26/$45 for one year. Visit our website at www.irishpages.org for a subscription form or to order online. Credit cards are welcome.

IRISH PAGES
129 Ormeau Road
Belfast BT7 1SH

Advisory Board
William Crawley
John Gray
Maureen Mackin
Bernard O'Donoghue
Daniel Tobin

Legal Advice: Elliott Duffy Garrett, Belfast

*IRISH PAGES is designed by Alicia McAuley Publishing Services
and set in 12/14.5 Monotype Perpetua. It is printed in Belfast
by Nicholson & Bass.*

*This issue has been generously asssisted by Foras na Gaeilge
and the Arts Councils of Northern and Southern Ireland.*

Foras na Gaeilge

ISBN 978-0-9935532-5-7

IRISH PAGES

CHRIS AGEE, *Editor*

CATHAL Ó SEARCAIGH, *Irish Language Editor*

STEPHEN DORNAN, *Scots Language Editor*

SEÁN MAC AINDREASA, *Managing Editor*

STEPHEN ELLIOTT *Editorial Assistant*

EDITED IN BELFAST
VOLUME 9, NUMBER 2

IRISH PAGES
DUILLÍ ÉIREANN

VOLUME 9, NUMBER 2

CONTENTS

Israel, Islam & The West

"The world has turned into a big Ulster ..."
Seamus Heaney, *circa* 2012

IN OTHER WORDS: FROM THE PERSIAN

FROM THE HOLOCAUST ARCHIVE

FROM THE HISTORICAL ARCHIVE

The Patron of This Issue

JEWISH VOICE FOR JUST PEACE (IRELAND)
GLÓR GUÚDACH AR SON SÍOCHÁIN CHÓIR

FRIENDS AND SUPPORTERS OF *IRISH PAGES*

Anonymous (Glasgow)
Gerry Bell
Vincent Browne
Paddy Bushe
John Cassidy
Manus Charleton
Charles Coventry
Donnell and Alison Deeny
Joe and Geraldine Duffy
Gandolfi Fish (Glasgow)
Elliot Duffy Garrett
Jack Gillespie
Joseph Hassett
Philip Haughey
Marie Heaney
Brialn Mac Call
Tom Mac Intyre
Enda McDonough
Robert McDowell and Manfred McDowell
John McGinley
John McMahon
Colette Ní Ghallchóir
Joe Prendergast
Gillian Reynolds
Carolyn Richardson
Tony Skelton
Anne Smith
Timothy Vignoles
David Woods

Subscribe online at www.irishpages.org

Near the Shankill Road, Belfast
By Mark Cousins
2015

"And this place, built on mud and sand, salt and sweet,
is a small place — isn't it? There's plenty of reading here —
you could read me like a book."

(from I am Belfast)

MY TIME IN LATRUN

Under the Green Line — as dawn rose.

I spent part of the summer of 1982 in Palestine and Israel working on a dig run by the French Archaeological Mission in the Middle East. Our beautiful stone headquarters and surrounding encampment was on the hill by the monastery of Latrun, just inside the Green Line within the West Bank, literally a stone's throw from the Jordanian trenches surrounding a crusader fort – facing the ruins of an ancient Byzantine church (a reputed site for the New Testament Emmaus), and overlooking the scene of a famous tank battle between the Arab Legion and Israeli forces, the broad plane below now dotted with kibbutzim. The fieldworkers were Palestinian and the centre staff Israeli, but the *lingua franca* was mainly French in the field, and English off-duty. I still remember entirely in French the terminology of our dig near Beit Shemish, in Israel Proper – we were excavating a hill-city of the period "ancien bronze": 3000-2000 BC, before the "Jews" and "Arabs" there, so-called, were even a twinkle in anyone's eyes.

My stay was, of course, an eye-opener in every direction – a "blessed breaker," in particular, of the accepted Israeli narrative. I got my first feeling for poetic Islam as the dawn rose blue and mauve over the exquisite Palestinian drumlins as the bus drove our large sleepy crew to the site. We listened on the radio in our various holes – mine turned out to be a four-thousand-year-old midden – to the news following Ariel Sharon's methodical and brutal expeditionary invasion of Lebanon. From my various vantage points at Latrun, Beit Shemish and Jerusalem, the whole cocktail seemed a classic occupation, so I was surprised by the degree to which the Palestinian fieldworkers and Sephardic kitchen staff interacted and related in a way both civil and intimate – something, I imagine, that obtains very much less now.

One afternoon out of the blazing heat I spent an enjoyable half-hour chatting with Michael, the Mission's Israeli Ashkenazi manager, in the cool of his office, a cornucopia of shade and leaves outside his window – for this was still the pre-air-conditioning period. He wore khaki shorts and a green floppy sun-hat (known in Hebrew, I am told) as "an idiot's hat," and an Uzi lay nonchalantly over the papers of his desk. A moment after, I stepped out in the dusty struggling vineyard next to the Mission and began up the hill.

Suddenly a Palestinian about my age – 26 – stepped out of a row of vines and stood before me. He was clearly extremely poor, with ragged trousers, an unbuttoned work-shirt, and ripped sandals. He looked at me intensely – and said only one thing: *Palestine, Palestine, Palestine*, pointing towards the reddish soil, before vanishing seconds later back into the vines. In the cultural transitions covered by those three minutes, I received an image of the tragic pattern of the West Bank – the European involvement, the Israeli occupation, the Palestinian dispossession – that has not left me as the catastrophe has deepened and accelerated. In that microcosm, the macrocosm of Palestine-Israel was given its full symbolic force.

After the dig, I went to the then-small resort of Eilat on the Red Sea and spent a week lolling on the beaches and snorkelling the amazing Arabian reefs with the other European and North American backpackers. When I got back to Belfast, I stopped into the Crown Bar en route home and bumped into an acquaintance with a paramilitary past (even present?). He looked at my suntan and glared at my brief explanation. Had I heard?

The Israeli Defense Forces had stood by while the Palestinians of Sabra and Shatila – 1948 refugees and their descendants – had been massacred by its Lebanese proxies.

The Editor

THE ONE-STATE SOLUTION

Dervla Murphy

Sharing the land of Canaan.

How best to promote the one-state solution? In 2009, when Mehdi Hasan wrote, "There is no longer a two-state solution to the Israel-Palestine conflict" I myself had just reached the same conclusion, having lived for months on the West Bank and in Israel. But many of the Palestinians' foreign friends find it hard to accept this. As Mehdi has recently observed, "Most of the West's leading politicians and pundits – especially of the liberal/left variety – refuse to acknowledge this inconvenient truth." My arguing in favour of one-state often prompts accusations of "deserting to the Zionists" – even now, in 2015, when the "inconvenient truth" becomes daily more apparent.

Clearly, BDS is by now unnerving Net. & Co. but unfortunately the campaign doesn't yet link itself directly to one-state, as the ANC's BDS movement did. That link is surely needed; a campaign to "End the Occupation" is by now irrelevant. The demand must be for one-person-one-vote, equality before the law, everyone "sharing the land of Canaan." One-state must come to be seen, internationally, as a stabilizing solution in that tiny fraction of the Middle East known as Palestine/Israel. And there's no time to waste. The Palestinians are not, in general, temperamentally disposed to support any sort of extremism, yet a proportion of the young will of course be driven (or are being driven) towards IS by Zionism's implacable brutality and injustice.

Some 15 years ago, as the Second Intifada was ending the Oslo Accords humbug, the Palestinians and their friends should have dropped two-states. Ever since, repeating that futile demand has been playing the Zionist/US game. President Obama, remember, has been no more concerned about the Palestinians than his predecessor. As illegal settlements expanded, Washington made hypocritical noises about "freezing settlements" while "peace" talks continued – and, predictably, the EU nodded agreement. Meanwhile, most of the Palestinians' foreign supporters failed to see that they were being hoodwinked. This is understandable, given the international media's reluctance honestly to explain or analyse the situation. For example, the true nature of the Palestinian Authority (PA), as it has developed, is left opaque. It was established by the Oslo Accords in 1993 and involves Mahmood Abbas's Fatah administration collaborating with Zionism to "strengthen Israel's security." In 2006, when Hamas beat Fatah in a free and fair election, the "international community" hastily condemned the winners as "terrorists." Ever since, the PA has been an increasingly docile creature of Israel. Its leader is still referred to as "President Abbas" though his mandate was allowed to expire without comment in January 2009; had the required presidential election been run then, he would certainly have lost to an Hamas candidate.

No one of my generation expects to see the curtain coming down on this tragedy. I used to say, "Maybe my grandchildren will be around to celebrate..." Now, oddly enough, I dare to hope, "Maybe my daughter will..." One-state does seem closer now than it did a generation ago. Not because last March Netanyahu made an histrionic eve-of-poll declaration about "no two-state solution" but because of the speed at which regional sands are shifting. In September 2014 Khalil Shikaki noted in *Harper's Magazine* – "A new development is something we observe among the younger half of the adult Palestinian population – people between the ages of eighteen and thirty-four – and that is the solid support they have for a one-state solution." Also, there's a rising level of unease, among thinking Israelis, as they witness the corrupting effects, throughout their society, of the military occupation of the Palestinian territories.

It's important to remember that a significant minority of Israelis are pro-Palestinian. For decades, many groups (lawyers, doctors, rabbis, journalists, academics, human rights advocates) have been bravely active on the Palestinians' side. Most of them see that two-states is dead. Literally, they *see* it. On the West Bank, the settlers and their linking apartheid roads (Israeli traffic only) and the expanding Military Zones, have stolen the landmass necessary to form a viable state. That is the fact on the ground. It's pointless to go on protesting against the settlers' defiance of international law and the IDF's contempt for the Geneva Conventions. Israel's powerful allies have consistently given in to them so that's where we're at. Now we can only help the Palestinians by demanding one-state.

This solution will of course deprive the Zionists of their *Jewish* state, a grotesque concept in the 21st century. Israel has always claimed to be a "democracy" – while reserving numerous privileges for the pretend members of one religion. "Pretend" because most Israelis are not observant Jews and the 19th-century founders of political Zionism were secular colonialists – though happy to ride on Judaism's bandwagon. Netanyahu's declaration of intent last March was awarded undeserved exclamation marks by some headline writers, then was unconvincingly retracted a few days later having served its electoral purpose. In reality he had merely admitted the obvious: those who manufactured Israel *never* intended to share their (twice) "Promised Land" with anyone. Yet since 1967 it has suited their purposes to go along with elaborately staged "peace talks," usually mediated by US officials acting as dishonest brokers. Meanwhile, to serve certain geopolitical interests, the UN's effectiveness as an enforcer of international law and an upholder of human rights has been repeatedly exposed to ridicule. The world notices that those countries wielding Security Council vetoes can always ensure their clients' immunity.

Recognising Palestine as a "State" is increasingly discussed as a way of helping to secure justice and peace but this is no more than gesture politics. And actually it harms the cause because it blurs reality – and therefore aids Zionism's propagandists. A few years ago joyful crowds turned out on the West Bank to celebrate most countries having voted in the UN General Assembly to recognise Palestinian "statehood." Yet this vote, though touching as a measure of global sympathy, was otherwise meaningless – could do nothing to lessen the daily miseries endured by Palestinians on the West Bank, on the Gaza Strip, within Israel itself and throughout the Diaspora. Abdel Bari Atwan, a distinguished Palestinian political journalist born in a refugee camp, explains:

> ...there are two types of statehood: the "declaratory" and the "constitutive." The former requires that, in order to declare itself a state, the entity must have a clearly defined territory, a permanent population and a government capable of exercising authority over the population, its territories and its resources. The 1933 Montevideo Convention also determined that declaratory statehood is independent of recognition by other states. Constitutive statehood, by contrast, requires recognition by existing states; but this has proved untenable, since there is no official international body with the authority to recognise states on behalf of the entire world community (the UN cannot do this).

Thus the Palestinians cannot achieve statehood, given the death of the two-state solution. And to recognise something that cannot exist seriously confuses the situation. Incidentally, Avi Shlaim has something relevant to say about the state of Israel. Until his recent retirement, he was Professor of International Relations at St Anthony's College, Oxford, and in a lecture given to the Society for Asian Affairs, on 20 October 2010, he said:

> My conclusion may come to you as a shock but it is not a conclusion I have reached lightly. Israel has become a rogue state. In the academic literature, three criteria for a rogue state are usually put forward. One, a state that habitually violates international law; two, a state that either possesses or seeks to develop weapons of mass destruction; and three, a state which resorts to terror. Terror is the use of force against civilians for political purposes. Israel meets all three criteria and therefore, in my judgement, it is now a rogue state. It is because Israel behaves like a rogue state that it is well on the way to becoming a pariah state.

One-state campaigners must take into account Zionists' paranoia about their right to possess *all* the land of Palestine. This illusion is often defined as a mental illness but it's *real* and always one has to make allowances for it. Political Zionism's founders, however secular, were *Jews*. Therefore they spoke on behalf of people who were peculiarly disadvantaged in Christian Europe. The Holocaust was not something unspeakable that happened because Hitler was very nasty. Its roots are plain to be seen in two millennia of Christian-inspired anti-Semitism. This is where Martin Kemp's diagnosis of triple guilt (the West's, the Israelis', the Arab States') is of huge importance. He has pointed out that this whole conflict is a psychological rather than a political problem. But of course it is also, and increasingly, another of the problems created by Capitalism Rampant.

The corporate oligarchy now running the world is against one-state. It favours a situation in which millions of stateless, impoverished Palestinians have no one to defend them while multinational entrepreneurs set up Industrial Parks on illegally held Palestinian land. Fat-cat profits must not be limited merely to grant justice to Palestinians – and to the countless Israelis who are thin cats and likely to get thinner if the recent take-over of the Knesset by extremists is allowed to go unchecked. Or is the Knesset not very important? Perhaps by now our political leaders (in any country) don't matter much, having long since furtively sold their soul – substitutes to the highest corporate bidder.

Peace in Northern Ireland was given space to grow when the paramilitaries – Orange and Green – and the British Army realised no one could win, militarily. Then came prolonged negotiations – between hard-liners, as the "moderates" faded into the background... And consider the U.S. input: George Mitchell did a very good job, in collaboration with paramilitary leaders and British and Irish politicians. Imagine the changed atmosphere in the land of Canaan if a US administration defied AIPAC *et al.*, stopped playing the two-state game and resolutely backed one-state.

The above essay is the last chapter of Dervla Murphy's forthcoming volume, Jordan From Afar.

One of Ireland's most celebrated non-fiction and travel writers, Dervla Murphy was born in 1931 in Cappoquin, Co Waterford. She left school at the age of fourteen to care for her invalid mother. She has since journeyed across five continents and 54 countries, and many of her subsequent books reflect and dissect her global travels by bicycle and foot. She is the author of twenty-one travel books, including Full Tilt: Ireland to India With a Bicycle *(1965, Eland),* A Place Apart *(1978, John Murray),* Race to the Finish? The Nuclear Stakes *(1982, John Murray),* Tales From Two Cities *(1987, John Murray),* One Foot in Laos *(1999, John Murray), and* Between River & Sea *(2015, Eland), as well as her autobiography,* Wheels Within Wheels: The Makings of a Traveller *(2010, Eland). She has a particular interest in the Middle East and her forthcoming book is* Jordan From Afar *(2017). She continues to live in Lismore, Co Waterford.*

MITILINI HARBOUR

Gerard McCarthy

Acts of submission.

When the plane landed in Athens airport, I was soon outside with the inevitable confusion. I was helped by a few others to find the way to the platform of the metro that took me in. As it came in near the city centre, it crowded with Athenians. Many got off at Syntagma Square. I waited for the next stop, Monastiraki. Outside on the street I asked a man with the one word, *Athinas?* He pointed to the street, and I walked the short distance to the Attalos hotel, gladly relieved to have forded the first part of the journey. The welcome from the man at the desk was cordial. He gave me the card to my small good room. I visited it briefly before heading up to the roof-top bar where I drank a beer and sat looking out at a building on a hill, wondering was it the Acropolis, until I turned around and saw another hill that was the Acropolis, indubitably; the Parthenon was lit on top of it. I sat on, drinking in the powerful sight of it, and I was still sitting there at midnight when the manager announced that the bar was closing.

I had been in Athens a few times before. The first time had been in 1980, at a time of personal crisis, under a siege to my fragile sense of identity, overshadowed by the question: how to go on from there; how to live? Decades later, in 2016, having reached a stage when I wondered might I not ever see Athens again, I was glad to be back. I returned to my room and, after all the nerves, slept peacefully and sometimes deeply.

The next morning I headed off walking with the image of the Acropolis periodically in front of me, memories stirring. Then, when I was underneath it, the place came back to me when I saw it. But the ticket office was shut. There was a notice saying that the Acropolis was closed as part of a strike of public services. I loitered around the entrance as various groups of people came along and were disappointed. I purchased in a stall a frozen lemonade and nursed it as it gradually melted. I sent texts home to fond figures of the world that had grown up around me and within me since I first stood there. I was about to leave to go down when I heard a man mention that the new Acropolis museum was nevertheless open. The man in the stall confirmed it. I walked on down to it: a new airy building, more spacious than required for the amount of artefacts currently inhabiting it.

The atmosphere was friendly and congenial, and the assistants were helpful. One of them pointed me towards an exhibit I had seen in the guidebook: a votive offering in a cranny on a pillar from the sanctuary of Asclepius: a pair of eyes. I had a snack outside in a balcony café. Sitting there with the incontrovertible reality of the Acropolis rearing above me, it was easy to see why the artefacts dubiously appropriated by the British during their colonial heyday should be returned by them forthwith.

I wandered along a road that I had a vague memory of leading to a hotel I stayed in years before, but I didn't find it. I passed a man who was playing a stringed instrument. I wondered was the music Syrian as I gave him a few coins, and I sat secluded in trees listening to the music, drawn once again to the lure of the Near East. The streets emerged into familiarity as I made my way to Syntagma Square. I crossed it to the parliament building. It was with a feeling of inevitability that I went in to the national gardens, remembering 1980. As I sat there I remembered the orange trees, but had no intimation of the desperation that I had felt way back then. That time had become so remote as to be hardly real any more. I imagined what my thirty-year-old self might have thought if he had passed that way, his youthful eyes seeing the figure of his fate as an elderly man dozing on a park bench. Beyond the imaginings, the incontrovertible: how one has actually lived.

My thoughts moved to contemporary concerns. I returned to Syntagma Square where a friendly bus driver directed me to the bus stop for the airport. There was a notice giving the times. I was about to take out a pen to make a note when a couple came along, and the man took a photograph of the timetable, giving me the example that I followed. I then made my way circuitously back to Monastiraki metro station where I saw that the earliest metro to the airport would be suitable to my purposes the next morning. Back in the roof-top bar as the day darkened the lights came on again on the acropolis. I heard the chanting of a demonstration, and could see a crowd on a street nearby. I went down immediately, but caught only the periphery of what seemed a modest demonstration that the city took in its stride. I thought, despite the crises, democracy is unquenchable in its birthplace.

The next morning I was up and out early. I walked along as I had the morning before, and soon I was at the open entrance of the Acropolis. Familiarity once again re-surfaced as I climbed the steps leading up to the Parthenon. It still looked like a building site, which it has been, it seems, for most of modern times; but the spirit of the place came through again, until the crowds arrived and took over the foreground. I sat a long while, inarticulately imbibing the atmosphere of it, gaining no clearer understanding of the world of those for whom it was perhaps the most important part: the sanctuary of the gods, while, down below, Socrates was loitering in the market-place, acting as midwife at the birth of secular rationality, until he was indicted for impiety.

I headed back down to the world below, into the ancient agora. I made first for the museum, and the stoa of Attalos. I sat outside underneath the stoa, close to a bust with the grave preoccupied face of the emperor, Antoninus Pius, Marcus Aurelius's adoptive father. I went walking, lingering. It came as a surprise to recognise the large area of scrub ground and trees. I moved very slowly. At one stage I was standing and saw a slow movement on the ground. It was a tortoise. It stopped, looking round at me, before it carried on its patient journey. I climbed to the temple of Hephaistos, and sat on a bench close by it. It was shaded from the sun by a tree, and afforded a good unimpeded view of the Acropolis. I sat for what seemed a couple of hours there in reverie, wondering wordlessly about the ethos of the Acropolis. I fell asleep a few times, waking once to the words: "a beautiful lost thought." Those words were all that remained.

That night was a night of short fitful sleep, with numerous wakings, before the call from reception at five o'clock. Soon, I was down, handing the man my card, and I headed out on the street. It was still alive, with a mixture of people who were still lingering in their night, and others just beginning their day. There were a few stall-holders who seemed as if their day never ends. I went down into the metro station and began my journey to the airport. On the way I had a series of minor mishaps of no lasting consequence; suffice to say that I was bothered and bewildered by the time a woman behind a desk casually and calmly handed me my boarding card. I made my way to the gate with my fellow passengers, two of whom were men flamboyantly dressed in Arab clothes. A bus took us out onto the tarmac, and stopped at a propellored plane. It rose mistily into the sky. I could make out little of the Mediterranean until it began to descend, and I caught my first sight of the island of Lesbos.

I had never been on Lesbos before. The images in my head were all from the news reports over the previous year of boats landing, filled with refugees. They came in their hundreds of thousands; thousands were drowned. It was called Europe's refugee crisis. The islanders welcomed them and helped them, assisted by volunteers. There was a while when

Europe rose to the challenge, particularly Germany that took a million refugees during the course of 2015. There was a lull in the arrivals during the winter. But soon after, by the beginning of 2016, the flow was beginning to build again, and again there were dramatic scenes on the news. I was particularly struck by a video I saw on the "no comment" series on Euronews, one evening in January, after I had booked my flight to Athens; there was a boat filled with Afghan refugees being rescued by a team from Medecins Sans Frontiers and Greenpeace. Amidst the *ri ra* and *ruaille buaille*, a woman was soothing her crying baby by gently tapping its mouth in a maternal gesture of great tenderness. As winter gave way to spring, it was beginning to appear as if the flow of refugees in 2016 would surpass that of the previous year. Fences began to be erected at the borders of countries north of Greece. The gates of Europe were closing. The main refugee camp, at Moria, on Lesbos was turned into a detention centre. By the time I arrived there in early April, the European Union had made a deal with Turkey, using it as a buffer, without putting under too close a scrutiny the tactics that Turkey was using. NATO ships began patrolling the Eastern Aegean. The passage of boats across the narrow straits was almost quelled. One flank of Europe's refugee crisis had been assuaged. The crisis of the refugees continued elsewhere.

———

The plane landed at Mitilini Airport, right beside the coast. Soon, most of my fellow passengers had departed in hired cars or taxis. I loitered for a while before crossing the road to a bus shelter where a woman and a man were already separately waiting. The wait was a long one but I didn't mind, as I stood there taking in my new situation. The airport was quiet in front of us. The sea was directly behind us. On its sparse rocky shoreline, I could see what looked like the remnants of two dinghies, along with some flotsam and jetsam scattered along the shore. Eventually, a bus appeared from the direction of Mitilini, turned and came back to us. The driver had a modest friendly air. The atmosphere was parochial. As we approached Mitilini, he drove off up a hill through suburbs and, in a circuitous route that included reversing turns, he picked up his quota of passengers, many of whom knew one another. We returned to the coast road, and soon Mitilini harbour appeared in front of us. In the middle of the waterfront I could make out the hotel I had booked: the Hotel Lesvion. We passed it and the bus stopped shortly after. A woman came up behind me who told me that was the last stop. She introduced herself as Jenny, a Catholic from Wales, and she invited me to come with her for tea to her church which was just around the corner. I went with the flow. After all the nervous imaginings about my arrival in Lesbos, I could never have imagined the utter eccentricity of the individual experience that presented itself. She opened up the small church and brought me to a side room where she served me tea and savouries that she had bought, and she talked lengthily, meanwhile apologising for doing so. We spoke of course about the refugees, and of the Pope's visit to the island the following week. She told me of a mass that was to be said by a bishop in the church the following Monday. I said that I would probably attend.

After checking into the hotel, I went wandering, along the harbour, past the docks for the ferry boats, and out beneath the battlements of the old castle of Mitilini on the hill above me. There was a refugee encampment behind a beach underneath it. There was a van marked canteen, and a sign saying "No Border Kitchen." I exchanged greetings with a few young Asian men on a wall, one of whom said "kalimera," then corrected himself with a laugh, saying "kalispera." I tapped my chest apologetically and ridiculously, saying "English, English." I was standing looking out into the harbour when there was a slight movement behind me: it was a young boy of perhaps seven or eight; he held out his hand begging in a way that showed that he hadn't been reared to it. I dismissed him and immediately he retreated. But then I looked back and saw him joining a young pregnant woman who was obviously his mother, and an infant in a pushchair who was presumably his brother. I went back to them and handed the boy my miniscule donation.

I had been told that during the height of the refugee influx there had been people sleeping all around the harbour, including right in front of my hotel. But by the time of my visit the populace of Mitilini seemed to be taking it all in their stride. The streets were crowded, and the atmosphere was voluble and noisy. The cafés and bars were crowded with Saturday evening proceedings. I went into a place that had an element of fast-food about it. Outside I saw some young girls running, exuberantly playing. One of them came in and asked for something from my plate, until the proprietors shooed her away.

There was a scattering of other people down at breakfast, including a few Greek soldiers. Afterwards, as I sat out on the balcony with my coffee, one of the soldiers came out for a cigarette, and greeted me with a hesitant good morning. On the street below, a band of soldiers marched past to the slow beat of a drum. They had disappeared by the time I went out after them. There was a Hellenic coast-guard boat moored in front of the hotel. Close by it was a rescue boat that had the poignant human presence of life-jackets scattered around its deck. I walked as far as an Orthodox church. It was closed, but the porch was open, and a woman was there before me, lighting a candle which she then stuck into a bed of sand that was there for the purpose. I did likewise.

I headed out to the marina. There was a club-house with a sign that said marina yacht club. From my vantage point in the doorway, the atmosphere, the company and the décor were indistinguishable from a similar gathering in a yacht club in Ireland. I left behind their hubbub and carried on out the pier. The waters were choppy enough in the harbour, and choppier beyond it. On the pier there was a group of more than a dozen people beside a boat marked, "International Maritime Rescue." They were dressed accordingly. A mini-bus came along and took most of them away. There were just two men left, and I plucked up the modest courage to approach them. In voices that sounded German they confirmed that the crossings had hugely diminished following the deal between the EU and Turkey. Their communication was formal and reticent. I commented on the weather, saying it would have been rough for a crossing, and the older man spoke of a swell warning that had them on dry land for the day. I retreated past the yacht club, back to a small pier at the edge of the inner harbour. It was crowded with groups eating and drinking. I chose a bar and ordered beer. I sat outside directly beside the water where a couple of small fishing skiffs were bobbing up and down in front of me. A young refugee boy came along selling tissues. At first he immediately retreated to my refusal, and then when I bought I could see the relief on his face that showed his shyness matched mine. There was a woman and man at a table beside me, who seemed to be deeply unhappy, who, after words, had become silent. Two men were in voluble conversation at a table behind me. Musicians for a while struck up at a nearby crowded table. A pale delicate child came down briefly and looked into the water.

As I went out past the ferry terminal, there was a huge ferry tied up there that had a notice that it was to head off that night to Athens. There were two young Asian men in the shade of a vehicle parked on the quay, scrutinising the deserted gangplank with an intensity that they seemed to try to hide as I passed. At the end of the pier I sat awhile beneath a covered pavilion. Across at the other side, where I had been earlier, I could see

Sunday sailors in their small yachts sailing seemingly thoughtlessly around the mouth of the harbour. On my way back I could see the No Border Kitchen encampment on the beach, from where the inhabitants must have watched the comings and goings of the ferries. Along the rocks beneath the pier there were numerous pieces of detritus of their own much more fragile voyages: the remnants of a dinghy, lifejackets and rings, and nautical bits and pieces. I passed a man and woman who were employed cleaning the environs of the pier. They had a sweeping brush, and a big bin on wheels. Amidst the detritus in the bin, all my eyes were able to fix on was the sight of a single shoe.

Later, I went wandering again, back out the pier in the darkness. There was a handful of stars in the dark sky, and a crescent moon. The wind was still up. The water was like a living thing. The dark water: I could only make out its dark undulations as I stood there looking across at the glimmering beyond it of the lights on the coast of Turkey. Somewhere out there in the dark water was the boundary between Europe and Asia that will always remain invisible, by night and by day.

I came back past the ferry terminal, and the municipal tourist office that I never saw open. There was a British naval boat moored at the quay, with its notice: Border Force: those two words that historically have gone too often together. I thought of the contrast between the present migration of refugees and the migration of the European colonial powers over the past few centuries: how the European entry into the rest of the world characteristically began with invasion, was followed by the subduing of the inhabitants by force of arms, and afterwards the drawing of borders. I thought of the images of the refugees making landfall on Lesbos, defenceless and vulnerable. I remembered the video I had seen in January: the image of the woman and her child that transcended every national boundary.

The next morning, I walked out the road past the No Border Kitchen encampment. As I approached it I heard shouting. It was explained when I saw some of the young men enthusiastically playing football. I passed the gate with its sign welcoming the visitor. As I carried on out the road with the ramparts of Mitilini castle above me, I met four young men. One of them, a cheery one, said hello and held out his hand. I shook it and the hands of his companions. He asked my name and my country. He introduced me to each of his companions. Emboldened, I asked them their country. He told me that they were all from Pakistan, and I thought I detected a vulnerability in his face and voice when he said it.

I went into a restaurant on the near side of the harbour. I ordered fish, with a Greek salad and wine. The fish were small, their names beyond me; it seemed clear that the way to eat them was head and all. I baulked at the heads, aided by my accomplices, three cats that congregated beside me, until they began to squabble with one another as cats do, until two of the waiters came rushing over and shooed them away. Afterwards I walked out the jetty where there were small boats with outboard motors. A few men were foostering in theirs. I watched one in particular, who came along with his daughter of about ten. He began briskly and with purpose tackling the rope that tied the boat to the jetty. But it went on and on and his daughter became increasingly resignedly impatient, her hand clenched underneath her chin as his brisk work went on interminably. At the end of the jetty there was a group of elderly men in a kind of cabooche, who perhaps while away their days of retirement there. Close by me there was a car with its passenger seat inclined backwards, and a man who looked an invalid, his fingers preoccupied with his worry beads. There was another man banging an octopus repeatedly on the ground, while a woman sat by, waiting. I decided I would wait until the man with the girl had set off. Eventually, the man had finished with the rope, but spent a further while trying to start his outboard engine, until finally it fired, and they headed off out on the silkily calm water. It was a beautiful early evening, with still clouds in the blue, the sunlight filling everything in deep luminous colour, and I saw clearly the magic of the Mediterranean.

As I came back I heard the calls of men playing a game amidst old boats that seemed to be in dry dock. They were four refugees, playing volleyball with an improvised net, probably two or three generations of the one family. They were entering enthusiastically in to the game. As I passed them I heard a baby crying, and then, amidst the semi-dereliction of the scene I saw a small camp where the family must live, and I caught a glimpse of the baby's mother, rocking, comforting it. I passed on by, and returned to the church to attend the mass that was to be said by the bishop. I entered the small space and was one of a small congregation of about two dozen. A priest came out who didn't look like a bishop to me. He had a wide mouth, set as if in a sombre view of the passage of life, until he sang in a voice that was surprisingly sweet. He gave a long vigorous sermon, all in Greek as the mass was. When the consecration came it was the Welsh woman, Jenny, who sounded the bell, three times for the bread and three times for the wine. At the end she told me that the priest was not the bishop, that the latter was taken up with meeting envoys from the Vatican, in preparation for the Pope's visit at the end of the week. She told me also that the priest's sermon had been about the refugees, and the necessity to be kind to those who had landed on the shores of Lesbos. I thanked her for her kindness to me.

Back out again along the pier was in darkness. A man came near me, with a torch on his head, positioning himself for fishing. The water was still silkily calm. I thought how it would have been a night much better than the previous one for heading out in a fragile craft. A powerful boat came from the inner harbour and passed out into the dark sea. I couldn't tell what kind of boat it was, but I guessed that it was not fish but human souls they were after. The passage of the boat set off undulations in the water that lasted for a long while after it had gone out of sight. Again there were stars in the clear sky, and a crescent moon. The lights of Mitilini were brighter in their nearness than the lights of Asia.

What filled the hearts of those refugees who looked across at our lights on such a night? With what longing must those thousands of eyes have looked across the narrow straits before embarking on their hazardous journey? Their setting-out must have been an act of submission, the distant lights of Europe glimmering in front of them: an uncertain voyage, out there on a small craft in a huge sea, their fate in its hands. I thought of the meagre challenges of my own journey, compared to the hugeness of theirs, and of all the millions who have similarly set out already this millennium. How can we do them justice?

Back at the hotel, as I was going up past the lounge, I saw seated around a few tables put together a group of clerics who must have been the Vatican envoys. They were in the company of the bishop, and I recognised the priest who had said mass earlier. I bought a bottle of beer and drank it out on the balcony. Outside under the crescent moon I thought, at that particular late juncture, there was no place I would rather be than Mitilini harbour.

The next morning before leaving, I loitered for a couple of hours out on the pier, gazing around, in to the harbour and across the water towards the coast of Turkey. There was a boat stationary off the shore that might have been the one of the British navy, and a small fishing boat plying up and down close by it. I sat a long while watching and listening to the water against the pier. Behind it, I could see on the hill the ramparts of the castle. The No Border Kitchen refugee camp was quiet beneath it. It looked idyllic: a quiet encampment, behind the beach. The battlements above it were the only portend in that image of the external world that was about to visit. A couple of weeks later, I saw a report on the internet of the closure of the camp, and the transfer of its residents to the detention centre at Moria. There was phone footage of a resigned procession of young men, being marshalled out of the camp onto a bus by the police.

A bus brought me early back to the airport. Before I went in I crossed the road and sat close to the bus shelter of the first morning. Down on the shore I examined the detritus that was still scattered there: along with the remains of the dinghies I could see a few rubber tubes, an abandoned coat, and what looked like a woman's party dress that will never be worn again.

The flight was hardly more than a half an hour before we were landing in Athens. Back in the Attalos hotel, I had been given a room out the front with a balcony. I visited the balcony for a little while before heading back to the roof-top bar. I sat with a bottle of beer, at a table with an unimpeded view of the Acropolis. The bottle of beer was followed by another. Two American men behind me were talking about medical work with the refugees. One of them had just arrived in Athens, and the other was briefing him, mentioning Piraeus, Idomeni, and Lesbos. I took them to be doctors working for some NGO. Impressed by their commitment, I would have liked to join their conversation, but my native shyness inhibited me. Then, before they left, they came up close by me, taking photographs of the Parthenon, and I, influenced by solitude and alcohol, asked them what did they think of its significance. One of them mentioned the dawn of western culture. I, in my inebriation asked might that building on the hill have been the setting for a priestly bureaucracy who, without fellow feeling, ruled the people below heartlessly. I had meant it as a contrast to the heart of their work, but they seemed taken aback by my intrusion, and very speedily they melted away inside into the hotel.

I headed back out the street to Monastiraki. I purchased a souvlaki, admiring the speed with which the small man produced the package that he handed to me. I crossed the road into the square, and did what I had intended to do: I purchased small lights that their sellers were catapulting into the warm Athenian night air. The one from whom I made my purchase said he was from Bangladesh. I told him my memory of buying the same toy in Rome from one of his compatriots, and he and some of his fellows laughed in recognition that that truly would be the case. I thought of the solidarity of the refugee and the economic migrant as I walked back to the hotel with a can of beer I had bought, which I consumed out on the balcony above the loud crowded street, before I came in to the room and closed the door on my final night in Athens.

The next morning, as I checked out, the man behind the desk asked me how were things in Ireland now. He said he didn't believe anything he heard on the news about the economic crisis, either in Greece or anywhere else: that those who have money hold onto their money, regardless. My flight home was not until the evening. I left my bag in the hotel and took the metro to Piraeus. A ferry had just docked. There were groups of Eastern people standing around on the quay. There was a quickened atmosphere about the place. Some police were in attendance, a few with riot shields. A policeman was interviewing two young Asian men who seemed as if they had alighted from the ferry. They had no baggage with them, but I surmised that all they had to smuggle was themselves. A family of refugees passed, and boarded a bus, along with others. A group of Syrian boys and girls walked by. One of the girls was pointing out and laughing at a young Greek couple kissing at the edge of the quay. I came across an encampment of refugees on a grassy island beside the road. I noticed one young family who seemed oblivious to traffic passing around them; they were engaged with one another as if they were in their own private domestic space. The man was entertaining an infant as the woman, doing some domestic task, was smiling over at them as she talked to him. I noticed her perfectly formed white teeth, and her rasping cough.

I was back on the metro to Monastiraki when a woman suddenly emerged from behind me. She had a baby in her arms and she was inarticulately begging. I took her to be Syrian; she had the fluid poise of women from that region: our Near East. Taken by surprise I found myself refusing, as everyone else was doing. She immediately disappeared like a ghost, silently, and immediately I regretted my refusal. I held a small donation in my hand hoping that she would return but she didn't. I looked for her at Monastaraki, but I couldn't find her.

A few hours later I flew home, from the South-Eastern periphery of Europe to its far North-Western shores. A few days later, Pope Francis was visiting Lesbos. I happened to be back on another island: in the old schoolhouse on Collan More, in Clew Bay. The school had been open for just seventy years, from 1887 until 1957. The old classroom was now a living room. The voices of the children singing out their lessons were now stilled in the silence of its stones. The nearby ruins of the islanders' houses remained a testament to the desertion of the island, most of whose families had set off as economic migrants, across the Atlantic or the Irish Sea. It was only when I returned to the mainland that I saw images of Pope Francis's visit to Lesbos. He was accompanied by Patriarch Bartholomew of Constantinople, and Archbishop Ieronymous, of Athens. After they visited the camp at Moria, their motorcade made their way to the harbour of Mitilini. Standing at the edge of the quay, Francis made his speech. He expressed his admiration for the generosity of the Greek people, sharing the little they had with those who have lost everything. He said that refugees and migrants, rather than simply a statistic, are people first of all with faces, names and individual stories. He said that it is only through service to others that we can get beyond ourselves. He said that Europe is the homeland of human rights, and that whoever sets foot on European soil ought to sense this, and thus become aware of the duty to respect and defend those rights. He remembered those who set out on the journey, but had foundered, unable to reach the shores of Europe. The ceremony concluded with Francis joining his companions as each of them threw a wreath into the waters that had carried so many, and in which so many had drowned. God rest them.

Gerard McCarthy works as a social worker in the West of Ireland. His first published essays, "Old Istanbul," "Old Jerusalem," "Home from Andalucia," "The Road to Granada," and "The Silence of Seamus Heaney's Father," appeared in earlier issues of Irish Pages.

IN IRAN
(fictions)

—

Sheila Llewellyn

The Sufi weave.

YALDA

I've just fixed up a lift to Shiraz. We can stay with my uncle there for the Yalda celebrations, then go on to Persepolis. Someone from the Consulate is travelling south tomorrow and we can go with them. If we leave it any later, we might not get there at all, there's a rumour that they're going to stop all internal travel.

I call in to Jahan's in the bazaar on the way home, and buy a gift box of pistachios arranged in the petal shapes of a Tabrizi rose. Five slightly open-shelled nuts clustered upright in the centre and a red-ribboned bow set diagonally across the corner of the cellophane box top. We sit about on the floor cushions, eating the nuts after dinner. Sara, as usual, is wide-eyed and delighted when I mention the trip is definitely on.

"Arash," she says, "you are a magician." Damian rolls his eyes but I can see he's just as pleased.

I decide to keep the mood light, so I put Gogosh on, blasting out her pop rhythms and sing-along lyrics. The other two groan in mock protest. Everyone's favourite, Gogosh, with her mini skirts and the western cropped hair and striking make-up. As I listen this time, it occurs to me that she will probably be banned soon.

"We'll visit my uncle for Yalda," I tell Sara, "and celebrate the re-birth of the sun after the Winter Solstice."

"Does it mean I have to get up early?" Damian and the breaking dawn are strangers.

"You don't have to get up at all, we stay awake through the night." He seems happy enough with that and he and Sara join in with Gogosh's ya-ya-yas, then burst out laughing. It's the first time I've heard them laugh out loud for days.

"Thank Christ for that!" says Damian, as Gogosh fades away. He gets up and puts *Kind of Blue* on, helps himself to a vodka and settles back against the cushions, his eyes closed. A memory of us lying together, gazing up at the California sky, flashes into my head – then slowly fades away.

We listen to *Kind of Blue* one more time.
They are precious to me, these two people.
Stay together, friends. Don't scatter and sleep.

———

It is tense around Shiraz, but my uncle won't talk about it. "Remember, Arash, the walls have mice and the mice have ears," he says. He would say that to me when I was little and came to spend the summers with him. It would always make me laugh, but in the night, I'd listen out for the mice.

The evening of the Winter Solstice, the neighbours come round. They light tiny candles in the courtyard. This year, there'll be no torches, no bonfires. The curfew has seen to that. Sara helps my aunt do the Yalda food: eggplant stew; *ab-goosht* with beef; slices of watermelon; pomegranates with angelica powder, the fresh fruit chosen specially for its red flesh to fight off the dark.

We talk through the night and someone beats out quiet rhythms on a tonbak while the men take it in turn to recite poetry. A few lines from Ferdowsi, but mostly Hafez, it is always Hafez at Yalda in Shiraz. When the dawn breaks, we stand in the courtyard. More Hafez. But my uncle also recites something from Sa'di. He's never done that before.

> *With all my pains, there is still the hope of recovery.*
> *Like the eve of Yalda, there will finally be an end.*

He recites the poem, his voice cracking a little as he sees the sun come up.

PERSEPOLIS BLUE

I ran my hand over a line of carved Cappadocians, their stone flesh warmed by the brittle December sun. Arash was ahead of me and turned round, his face in three-quarter profile, looking like he could have just stepped down from the Apadana frieze itself.

"You seem dazed," he said, waiting for me to catch him up. Damian followed on behind us, clicking away, determined to photograph everything.

"This place ... it makes my head spin." My finger traced the fold of a Persian's fluted crown, over two-thousand-five-hundred-years old. "I came out to Iran thinking I'd find Persia. But all I've found is Iran, till now." Dust motes displaced by my touch floated in the sunlight.

"Don't let it fool you too much." Arash leaned towards the frieze to examine a lock of curled hair delicately chiselled behind the ear of an Assyrian. "All of this lot also had to pay tribute to an Emperor, remember. This one just happened to be Darius."

"Come on," said Damian, taking hold of my hand, "let's show Sara how our present Shah of Shahs did it," and he set off towards the western edge of the site.

———

"Behold Tent City." Arash gestured towards the area in front of us where the Shah had held his celebrations in 1971. Twenty five years of his Peacock Throne.

"That's it? That's Tent City?" I'd been expecting something from a *Shanameh* miniature – golden medieval fantasies with scalloped edging and fluttering pennants. All I could see were forlorn rows of shabby pavilions, their covers bleached to a patchy ochre, stretched out in the shape of a five point star, bordered with crumbling concrete walkways and scrappy cypress trees.

Damian nodded. "The whole thing was an illusion. They're prefabs – steel skeletons. Shah-style prefabs, mind you – gold-plated taps, marble floors and Persian rugs. Now long gone, needless to say. They draped the outsides in blue and gold fabric so they looked like tents."

"Sounds as vulgar as anything Darius ever did to show off his power," I said.

"That was the point, the Shah showing off his power," Damian nodded. "Two hundred million dollars' worth of pure Hollywood. The whole spectacle out-DeMilled Cecil B. De Mille. The French made a packet – Jansen designed the 'tents', Maxim's supplied all the food."

"They all played the game," said Arash. "The French, the British, the Americans, they all came to pay false homage, then went home with their oil and arms contracts."

It was strange to hear Arash talking politics, like he'd suddenly put on a shirt that wasn't his colour.

"I bet no one back in '71 thought it would come tumbling down," I said. Arash shook his head.

"Darius. Xerxes. The Shah. All Emperors think they're invincible."

A bird, big enough to be a buzzard, circled high above, his eye probably on some small creature scuttling among the prefabs below.

"What will you do if the Shah falls?" As soon as I said it, I wished I could stuff the words back.

Arash moved closer to Damian and rested an arm on his shoulder. "All this – from Darius to Tent City – it's what we were…it's what we are." He shrugged. "It's Persia and it's Iran. If the Shah goes, we'll have to work out what comes next. I can't help to do that if I leave, can I?"

For once, Damian had nothing to say.

Arash stroked Damian's neck and smiled at me. "This corner feels a bit too much like Iran."

The bird had lost interest and flapped off in the direction of Shiraz. We picked our way back through the ruins of Xerxes's Palace, to the Apadana portico. Arash took a photo of Damian squinting into the sun, gazing up at a capital of addorsed griffins, their two heads outlined against the backdrop of the sky – a sky of lapis lazuli, shading down through palest blues to smudgy white merging into the horizon across the plain of Marv Dasht.

"Persepolis blue," Arash said, "that's what we should call a sky like this."

We stopped for lunch. Damian and I lay on a huge stone slab and Arash perched on the crumbling remains of a bell-shaped column base. He passed chicken and cucumber salad over to us. Damian raised himself on his elbow and helped himself to a chunk of flat bread.

I had this sensation of being outside of myself, floating above the three of us, a buzzard's-eye view. Living figures on a moving frieze, surrounded by ancient columns with mythical capitals and Princes frozen in stone. I thought, "I want to keep this moment just like it is. I want to suspend it in my memory and remember this time and place for the rest of my life."

I lay flat, breathed in and closed my eyes, the image of us imprinted on my eyelids. I must have dozed off. When I opened my eyes again, Damian and Arash were on the other side of the site. I wandered across to them with Damian's camera, but he didn't want it. They weren't saying much, just leaning close into each other, Damian looking serious and thoughtful, both of them gazing out over the plain. Way in the distance, blue smoke curled into a bluer sky.

I left them to themselves, and passed the time taking close-ups of the lion and bull panel on the Apadana. The sculptor had caught the split second after the lion had grabbed the bull's flank – the foot bones and the tendons in the front paws carved at full stretch, pulling back on the hooked-in claws, the tension in the jaws bearing down to anchor teeth into the bull's backbone. And the bull, whipping round as he felt the weight and the pain, his arched neck echoing the line of the lion's dipping head. I was transfixed by the violent beauty of it. Over two thousand five hundred years ago, someone else must have stood here and probably felt the same.

Damian and Arash came over. Damian fingered the ribbed fur of the lion's mane, murmuring something about lions and the power of Kings. We drifted back to our lunch table among the columns. Arash poured a last glass of wine into our plastic tumblers, then rummaged about in his shoulder bag. He brought out two small parcels and came across to the slab to sit with us.

"I thought I'd get Yalda, Christmas and New Year over in one go." He handed the one wrapped in marbled paper to Damian. "You stroked it like a cat when you were holding it in the bazaar," he said, as Damian undid the paper. It was a copy of Rumi's poems, tooled in gold and bound in red Morocco leather. Arash had written something inside but Damian kept it to himself. They looked at each other. Arash nodded. Damian lay back down on the slab, the book on his chest.

My gift was rolled up in a small square of amethyst silk. A silver bracelet. Dangling from it, a long-tailed bird with a high feathered crown, each tiny shaft delicately picked out in filigree. A hoopoe. Leader of the Conference of the Birds. For a moment, I was back in Tabriz, the three of us sitting round on floor cushions, the stove in the corner pop-popping as Arash read to us:

> Once, in the dim old days, all the birds of the world assembled in
> solemn onclave, to consider a momentous question...

Din Attar's story of the thirty birds of Persia. The Hoopoe, the Huma and the Nightingale. And all the tiny birds full of fear with tears in their eyes. Wandering through the valleys of Bewilderment and Stupefaction. Searching for the truth.

We sat together on the slab, Arash in the middle, lost in ourselves. A shrill screech in the distance cut into the quiet. I wondered if the buzzard had sneaked back and caught its prey among the ruins. Damian got up and started to pack away the remains of the food. Arash and I gathered up everything else and stuffed it into plastic bags.

The heat had gone from the sun and I shivered. The Apadana columns cast long shadows, the griffins facing east and west, etched as blurry outlines in the dust of the Palace floor.

THE PAPAKH HAT

Tanks clatter past at six, heading from the barracks to the town centre. I roll over and try to squeeze another half-hour. A second convoy rattles the skylight, waking me up for good. The day begins much like any other has for the last few months in Tabriz. The door edges open and Arash appears in his grey Berkeley sweats, backing in with coffee mugs. He's been up since five. Best time to write, he says. But he potters mostly, getting the stove going, washing dishes. He has that Iranian blue-black hair and as he bends down to put the mugs on a pile of books next to the bed, a lock of it falls forwards, glinting like gunmetal in the thin light.

I start where I left off at three in the morning. "Have you changed your mind?"

"Not really." He sits down on the bed and tries to stroke my cheek.

I turn my head away and he drops his hand onto my shoulder. I turn back. "Let me get you out, please." The whine in my voice makes me feel sick.

"How many more times, Damian?" He reaches to stroke my face again and this time I let him, breathing in the scent of lemons. He once said, "You either drink Tabrizi tea through a lump of sugar at the back of your teeth, and end up with no teeth, or you don't drink it at all." So he drinks lemon tea instead and that's another of his morning routines, slicing up lemons.

I put my hand over his. "People we know have disappeared. They'll come for you next."

"I'm not important enough. I'm a part-time poet and I've never been on a demo in my life."

He stands up. "I have to go to work. I'm late."

Late for what, exactly? I want to say, but don't. The library at the American Consulate has long been closed, but he still goes in every day. Someone needs to be there to guard the books, he says. I've given up going to the University – no students left to teach, Professors leaving the country, or trying to. I spend most days reading Arash's translations of Rumi – I'm supposed to be the Sufi expert, but he knows more than I ever will.

He walks towards the door, then turns and looks back at me, his head on one side in that birdy way he has. "I'll see you later. We'll talk."

Waves of misery roll through me as he goes out and I lie there, heavy-limbed and helpless.

My hand searches his side of the bed. There's too much empty space.

He will never leave Tabriz. I know this. The revolution has already started in a raggedy sort of way, though no one is admitting it, and he's a target whoever ends up in power. SAVAK will come for him – its' well known the Shah's Secret Police hold a special hatred for poets. Rumours have made their way from Teheran about what they do to them there. Or the revolutionaries will take him. His year in Berkeley, his librarian job at the American Consulate – the fundamentalists will say he's too "western-stricken." But it's for being with me they'll despise him most. Somewhere, he'll be on someone's list as one of their abominations.

I lie on my back, staring through the skylight at the snow-heavy clouds. Back in Berkeley, I had a room at the top of an old apartment block. The room was tiny but the roof was mainly taken up with an oversize window as large as the poster of Miles Davis dwarfing most of one wall. Saturday mornings, we'd laze in bed listening to *Kind of Blue,* gazing up at a block of California cobalt. At night, the city lights bleached out the stars. "But I know they're there," I'd say to Arash.

When he knew I was serious about following him back to Tabriz, he said he'd find me a place. "And I'll make sure it's got a skylight," he said.

———

"Damian." His voice cuts in from far away.

I open my eyes to a square of iron-grey Tabrizi sky.

"Damian," Arash says again, softly. He's standing in the bedroom doorway, his face drained of colour.

"What are you doing back so soon?"

"I found this." His voice sounds reedy.

He isn't really standing, he's slumping against the door jamb, clutching some sort of hat in his hands. I jump out of bed, go over to him and we manage to stumble across to the kitchen. I sit him down, but he won't let me take the hat from him.

He'd found the body in a shop doorway. His quickest way to the Consulate is past the prison. Everyone tries to avoid it if they can since SAVAK took it over for their Headquarters. When Arash reached the shops next to the prison entrance, there the body was.

"I thought he was sleeping. But his head didn't look right, it was lying too flat on the ground." He hunches over, clutching the hat on his knees. "They're leaving bodies out now, as a warning. They'd tossed his hat near his feet. The street was deserted, but I was sure I was being watched."

The hat twitches in his hands. "I snatched it and ran."

I reach across and this time, he lets me take it. It is a *papakh,* with a narrow, brimless crown, a squashed version of a Cossack hat. Astrakhan wool. Expensive. I edge it round on the pads of my fingers, staring at the scroll-work patterns made by the dark, tight curls of a young lamb's fleece. Most of the whorls of wool are clogged, smeared brown.

"Maybe someone will recognise it, maybe we can find out who he was," Arash says. He just about makes it to the sink before he throws up.

Both of us are shaky for the rest of the day. In the evening, I make barley soup but we just dabble in our bowls and spoon a few beans around. For once, we don't have any music on and the only sound is the pop-popping of the stove. We stretch out on the floor cushions, our backs against the wall, both trying to read. I have the book of Rumi poems Arash gave me for my birthday, a fine copy bound in red Morocco leather. Arash had laughed when he'd handed it to me, saying I'd stroked it like a cat when I picked it up in the bazaar.

But the words dance around on the page and I give up.

Arash has his notebooks and his translations. He keeps taking his glasses off, putting them on, dropping his hand back down on the page. I reach across and stroke his fingers.

"What are you working on?" If I can get him to talk, it might help.

"I can't concentrate." He takes his glasses off again and massages the bridge of his nose with his thumb and forefinger. "I'm struggling with a complex pun in a Rumi poem."

"You're always struggling with a complex pun in Rumi." I smile at him. "What's this one?"

He puts his glasses back on and looks down at his notes. "*Ma ku*, two words, means 'Where are we?' in Persian. But *maku*, one word, means 'a weaver's shuttle.' A poet from Teheran has had a go at it, and sent me a version." He takes a loose sheet of note paper from the back of his notebook. It's covered in small, neat handwriting and is annotated down one side.

"Read it to me, I need soothing." I know he likes reading to me.

His voice wavers at first, then grows stronger.

A bright weaver's shuttle flashes back and forth,
east-west, *Where are we? Ma ku? Maku?*
Like the sun saying, *Where are we?*
as it weaves with the asking.

He once told me Din Attar had written that writing poetry was like stringing pearls on a necklace. "That's one beautiful necklace your Teheran poet has made there," I say, when he finishes reading. I think of asking him how many Teheran poets he's had contact with, but I hold back.

"It's much better than my version, I think." He takes his glasses off again and closes his eyes. "I've been working on it for weeks, but it's a slow job." He opens his eyes and manages a weak smile. "It might be a pearl too difficult to pierce in the time we've got left."

The time we've got left. I can't help myself. "I can get you out." And off we go again.

"I've lived less than half a mile from the poet Shariyar's house for all my life," he says, "apart from my year at Berkeley and that half-killed me – it probably would have done if I hadn't met you. Whatever happens to me, it'll happen here."

There's a resignation I've not heard before in his voice. And fear. He's as frightened as I am, I realise. If he stays, they'll take him and try and break him and he's feared this all along.

Later, the night sky clears and we lie watching the stars. "We are living on the lip of insanity," he says, allowing the tears to come. All I can do is hold him to me, like a lute.

———

The tanks go past at six as usual, but we are both in bed, both awake. He gets up, says he's going into work, says he needs to keep things normal. I resist picking up on "normal," my anxiety will make it come out wrong. At least take a taxi, I say, no, he says, he won't go past the prison, he'll take another route, he needs to walk. I get up with him and he seems content to sit and let me fuss about, slicing lemons for his tea, making coffee.

The *papakh* is still on the kitchen table where we left it. He touches it, but doesn't pick it up.

"When I get back," he says, "we'll go to the bazaar – maybe ask around. Someone will be missing him," and as he goes, he smiles at me, an achingly sad smile.

I drink my coffee, stare at the hat, come to a decision. I'll take it to the bazaar myself, find out what I can, it will please Arash. I put the hat in a plastic bag, then hide the bag in my shoulder satchel under some of Arash's Rumi books. I feel a pulse of excitement on doing this, then a skitter of nerves. If I'm stopped, I've no idea how I'd explain the *papakh* under the poetry.

I turn into the Square and see a tank parked in front of the main entrance to the bazaar, its gun pointed outwards. People walk round it, never looking directly at it, speeding up as they go past. I find myself doing the same.

I call on Arash's cousin, Ervand, the spice seller. The Tabrizis can't live without their spices however bad things get and he has a constant daily flow of customers who tell him the latest news.

He's wearing a *papakh* himself, a poorer version than the one in the bag, made of coarse wool. It frames his shrewd Tabrizi face. It has a worn patch on the left side where he has a habit of rubbing it with his finger. When Arash and I first used to visit him, his eyes would flicker over me lightning fast and I'd think he knew everything there was to know about me, about us. But now he hardly looks me in the face at all, and when he does, all I see is anxiety. I pass the plastic bag over the palette of cinnabar reds and ochre yellows of his stall display and ask if he's heard anything. He peers in the bag, gives me a long look. Invites me through to the back for Tabrizi tea.

He doesn't mention the hat I showed him. Instead, he tells me about his sister's children, twin girls aged seven, and a son, aged five. They were playing in the *kucheh*, the narrow lane that separated their house from their neighbours across the street. The neighbours' children were with them, playing the circle game of the Chain Weaver Uncle who weaves chains of friendship for children. He and Arash, he says, used to play it when they were little.

In this game, they sing the song about the day the Chain Weaver Uncle does not come to see them. The children are worried about him, so they bring him presents and they clasp each other's hands to make their own chain, as a present for him. The children in Ervand's *kucheh* join hands and choose his nephew to go into the centre of the circle. They all dance round him, singing this song. But then a neighbour comes out and says they shouldn't be singing songs about making chains and they shouldn't be making themselves into chains and putting chains around people.

Ervand tells me this story, shaking his head in a "kids will be kids" sort of way, his eyes constantly scanning the beaded doorway behind me, his fingers tapping the bag with the papakh hat in it. Then he gives the bag back to me. Even in the bazaar, it seems, even in our great beehive of gossip, fear has struck everyone selectively dumb.

I make my way out. There's been a fresh snowfall. It lies on the tank, blurring the lines of its turret and gun barrel, softening it into a mound of vanilla ice cream with a long-handled spoon.

But it's still a tank.

I get home, take out the hat, put it on the table and pour a vodka. Wait for Arash.

Six o'clock, I begin to feel uneasy. He's always home by four. When I used to go to work, I'd rely on him to be around when I got home.

Eight o'clock, I go downstairs, open the door, look up and down the street. It's deserted. Someone throws open the top shutters across the way and there is a quick blast of state television, then silence as the shutters bang shut again.

Nine o'clock. Curfew. He's never been out after curfew.

I can't just sit there. I decide to clear out the cupboard. Arash has been moaning about how untidy it is. I take everything out, wipe down the shelves, put things back where they should be. Then I start on the fridge. There isn't much in it, we've been living on soup this past week or on fruit and fresh yoghurt when either of us remembers to buy it. At the back, I find a saucer of sliced lemons, the flesh already drying out, the rind beginning to curl. A pain lurches against my ribs, followed by a wave of dizzying panic. I put the lemons in the bin.

I sit there trying to steady myself, then I hear a shout from up on the roof and the panic turns to a surge of relief. All this time, and I never thought to check the roof. Maybe he came home early and went up to clear the snow, maybe he's had a fall and knocked himself out and he's been lying there, getting colder and weaker.

I run upstairs and push the roof door open. But the shout isn't from our roof, it's from next door's. "Allahu Akbar!" echoes round, followed by something I can't make out. It drifts across from a house on the left, then from one over on the right, and then many voices, point and counterpoint, rising to a crescendo in the darkness, coming from all directions. Shadows float into a group on the roof opposite – men, children, women in chadors – our neighbours, punching the air in a football salute to the rhythm of the chant. It takes a while for me to work out the translation. I'm not sure, but it sounds like "Death to the Shah!"

The nearest they've got to that before is "Death to the Dictator!" This is new. This is specific.

I go downstairs, sit back down at the table. I pick up the hat, stroke a spot where there's only the silkiness of the fleece. When he gets home, I'll have to tell Arash I've had no luck at the bazaar.

I wake up at the kitchen table, my head on my arms. It is past six in the morning, but I haven't heard the tanks, haven't felt the rumble. The first thing I see is the hat. I decide to try Ervand again. But not at the bazaar, this time. I go to his house, down the same *kucheh* where the children played the game of The Chain Weaver Uncle.

Ervand's hand shakes as he hands me a glass of tea. "There's a rumour," he says, rubbing the worn patch of his hat. "Just a rumour, you understand."

I don't speak.

"They say the solders in Tabrizi Barracks have refused to fight against the people. They will no longer drive the tanks out against the people. This is the first time this has happened. Anywhere."

"Have you heard anything about Arash?" I look at him.

Ervand shakes his head. No words. The face is as mask-like as ever, but the eyes are different. It's not anxiety in his eyes now. It's fear.

It's like the fucking Via Dolorosa. I go from Ervand's house down the *kucheh* to the American Consulate, then Arash's flat, then the British Consulate and end up at the American Consulate again. There's a new guy on the front desk tonight. They used to have Iranians on duty there all the time, but this guy is American, polite but cool. I tell him I'm Irish, and this helps me get past him to the corridor of Attaché offices at the back, where I get to speak to another American, tall and thin with sad eyes. He's busy sorting documents into two boxes, one labelled "incinerator."

I tell him the same story I've been telling all the others: Arash is their librarian, he's not come home, do they know anything? He doesn't stop what he's doing but gives me a patient look. People are disappearing all the time he says. Doesn't matter what side you're on. The Shah's people are getting out while they can. The fundamentalists and God knows what other rival factions are settling old scores with each other before they take power. Arash isn't on any side, I say, he never takes sides. The man stops sorting the papers for a moment and looks at me with those sad eyes. Well now, sir, that's the most dangerous place to be. Who's going to protect him? he says. And he goes back to filling the boxes.

———

I've forgotten to stoke up the stove, that's usually Arash's job, so the place is freezing. I stay in the kitchen with my coat on and make tea, cut up some lemons, bob the slices round the glass with my finger. I breathe in the scent of them and feel Arash's hand on my cheek. The papakh hat is still on the kitchen table. It is already beginning to give off a slightly fetid smell of rotting matter. I can't stand looking at it any more. I wrap it up in a plastic bag and decide to put it away in the bottom drawer of the chest in our bedroom.

As I open the drawer to stash the hat away, I spot the red cover of my Rumi poems tucked under some other papers at the back. I leave the hat on the floor and pick up the Rumi. The translation from the Teheran poet is tucked in the front. Arash must have slipped it in there before he set off for work. Across the top, in his almost too perfect Latin script, Arash has written:

Ma ku? Where are we?

Sheila Llewellyn was born in Manchester and grew up in England, British Guyana and the West Indies. She has degrees from the University of Manchester, Oxford, The Open University and Queen's University Belfast. For many years, she worked as lecturer, government adviser and teacher-trainer in Africa and Asia, including for the British Council in Iran and Singapore. Her short stories have appeared in various magazines and anthologies, most recently The Glass Shore: Short Stories by Women Writers from the North of Ireland *(Liberties Press, 2016). In 2003, she returned with her husband to Northern Ireland, where she now works as a psychotherapist in post-traumatic stress disorder. She lives in Enniskillen.*

IN OTHER WORDS: GHAZELS OF HAFEZ

Mario Petrucci

All grief has an end.

Hafez
Khwāja Šamsu d-Dīn Muhammad Hāfez-e Šīrāzī
(Shiraz, Iran, 1325 – 1390)

TRANSLATOR'S NOTE

There's a great deal of room in contemporary literature for translations of Hafez that capture and invigorate secular readers. Indeed, once one steps beyond Rumi, one could well argue that the major classic poets of Hafez's period and place remain somewhat under-represented. Publishing modern, vibrant versions of Hafez in English, now, also makes a palpable contribution to literary diversity and inclusivity, raising subtle topical issues concerning the true breadth and quality of communication between East and West.

HAFEZ 370

Holy traveller – we have cut a new path to the highest garden. There, fresh wines pour to our heart; together, we disperse time's petals,
                                            inwardly, split sky's dome.

Armies may shed loving blood, raise towers of grief; yet the cup-bearer and I shall relieve the earth of such hordes, peeling them up and away
                                            by a corner.

Wine isn't given, always, full bitter-strength: at times, a draught is thinned with rosewater. Wind's censer spins few heads with intense rose incense.

In your hand, I'm a sweet-strung instrument. Make ever-sweeter songs in me. We dance – palms up, head down – one loving, involuntary body.

Breeze, loft me, as You do all dust, to that high cloudlet of the Beloved.
My speck, unnoticed, might glimpse the Kingdom of lovely ones, dripping
wisdom.

One preens vain intellect; another is the very loom for stuffy gossip. Let
both try themselves before the Just Ruler.

If you're looking for Eden, aspire – to the Tavern.
Drain its wine-jar: plunge into the Lake of Good; forget yourself at
heaven's spring.

Beloved, Your true face is the glow in those far-off faces here convened: a
row of sated roses I sing for, with Love the tune and Love the tapping foot
I put breath to.

Who, among us now, can tell the God-first sense in verse or, across a glib
globe, that weighted, well-placed Word? Reader: join me, in that
necessary, other world.

HAFEZ 12

That simple action, right by God: where is it? And I – without it?
What path etched on the world cannot lead from one nightfall to the next?

Separate from myself, I am far from All: lend no traction to good or wrong.
Deaf to the roadside's Holy bird, even to the evangelist guitar, I limp on.

In temples, I grew guilt-thin. How wearying, to carry hypocrisy's heavy
quilt.
Circling dervish, extinguishing self, where may I glimpse you? Where is it –

God's wine? Our union, with morning, is a drunken memory. My vessel: dry.
Those strong advances – now a simper. The wise chastisements – gone. Why?

Friend, love-luminous, You show nothing to the graceless camps of the
enemy.
They are blown lamps – so let me see that. Sun's waxing face: why that
disguise?

The dust from His sandals, His soul's sweepings, are kohl for my blinking
eyes.
Where are we going? Command me. From here – to where? Where –
exactly?

Yes, a chin's bittersweet dimple took me in. That Eden-apple opened a pit.
Raw heart – why did you flurry into it? Instead of soaring, you flit.

Reader, if you seek here simplistic release or patience – read deeper.
Release – is what? Patience – what? As for sleep – you know where that
leads.

HAFEZ 31

Ah Breath – whether you brush the stones of the Holy Lands
or comb the tree-heads there – rush here with their perfume.

Upon my one soul, it is far better to let fly this blood-bond
and die than miss any word, a single letter, from the Groom.

Air, if your insinuations find no means, if every door is sealed,
at least accost from His stair some dust: collyrium to help me see.

Where now that intent, urgent Self, to merge? Lost. Beggarly.
Asleep, might I yet sense some contour, a shadow of Your outline?

I am trembled willow. A pine-cone blown against by God's Name.
A cone that can grow the Tree entire – this is the form of the heart.

I was bought by Him with no more than a sand-grain, a mote of light;
yet I would refuse all Persia in exchange for one strand of His thought.

Reader: what use? – to be released from the binds and vows of holy Pain
only to find yourself re-bound, awaiting all over – His pleasure – again.

HAFEZ 169

If I pursue You, You turn on me with an almighty
fuss – if I sit down again, You angrily stand up.

On the road, if my passion causes me to flop at
Your feet, Your gust carries the dust off without me.

Yet, if I try a kiss unrequited, some half-way mouth,
then sherbet chastisements pour from Your pout.

The dunes of love, with their crests and slacks, entrap:
where is the desert lion brave enough to enter all that?

If Your deceit lies in the eye of beholders, I'm lost
nonetheless: Your glance turns any reputation to rust.

I try to speak, asking: *Why are You so promiscuous?*
Your answer is to marry, in me, my blood and tears.

Reader: for a long life, be longsuffering – then see
how roundly this cosmos lends itself to trickery.

Let's lay these insistent heads on surrender's block:
to resist is to be on your deathbed tilting at clocks.

HAFEZ 194

I smart for You, I said. You replied: *Grief has its ends.*
I said: Kindle me to Moonbeam. *When the clouds part*, You replied.

I began: Be my full Moon… *No*, You corrected – *Half-moon. Yin-yang.*
I wooed: Will You soon send it? You replied: *Not before I do.*

Once more I tried: See how Your avowed lovers are an epitome
of fidelity. You replied: *From their moony cheek comes poor illumination.*

I said: I'll steer my stare from vain crowds – away – right at You!
You replied: *Night-prowlers remain awake, gain entry by unexpected means.*

I spoke: Your fragrant locks made me nomad to the world – lost to its
                                                                    byways.
You replied: *That myrrh, delectable within you, is also your star.*

I said: This glad air I breathe, stroked by love's leaves, makes me sad enough.
You laughed: *Pleasanter is the breeze from My street corner.*

I spoke again: At Your bluff lip, that sweet drip You dangle... banishes me!
You said: *Attend Me, and your soul is beloved, cherished.*

I said: When will Your heart's heart tender me to rest?
You said: *Desist — why speak of such turbulence while heart-blood is shed?*

I insisted: Surely, You see how brief is Your flood, how long Your ebb?
You whispered: *Be still now. All grief has an end.*

Editor's Note: The "ghazal" (originally from the Arabic) is poetic lyric form composed of a minimum of five couplets — and typically no more than fifteen — that are structurally, thematically, and emotionally autonomous. Each line of the poem must be of the same length, though meter is not imposed in English, in which the ghazal is now widely practiced. The form is ancient, originating in Arabic poetry in Arabia long before the birth of Islam.

Persian lyric poet Hafez grew up in Shiraz. Very little is known about his life, but it is thought that he may have memorized the Qur'an after hearing his father recite passages. When his father died, he left school to work at a bakery and as a copyist. Hafez became a poet at the court of Abu Ishak and also taught at a madrasa, or religious college. He is one of the most celebrated of the Persian poets, and his influence can be felt to this day. As the author of numerous ghazals expressing love, spirituality, and protest, he and his work continue to be important to Iranians, and many of his poems are used as proverbs or sayings. Hafez's tomb is at Musalla Gardens, in Shiraz.

A poet, translator and ecologist with a higher degree in optoelectronics, Mario Petrucci is the author of 14 collections of poetry, including Shrapnel and Sheets *(Headland, 1996),* Bosco *(Hearing Eye, 2001),* Heavy Water: A Poem from Chernobyl *(Enitharmon Press, 2006),* Flowers of Sulphur *(Enitharmon Press, 2007),* i tulips *(Enitharmon Press, 2010) and* Crib *(Enitharmon Press, 2014). His three works of translation are* Catullus: Contemporary Adaptations *(Perdika Press, 2006),* Sappho *(Perdika Press, 2008) and* Xenia by Eugenio Montale *(Arc, 2016). He lives in London.*

POEM & TRANSLATION

—

Marko Vešović & Francis R. Jones

In the beginning was the Camp.

THREE CIGARETTES

At day's end, I went outside to right myself
in black and white. The sun, a coin descending
onto a dead man's eyelids. My God, the speechlessness
all round me, harder to pierce than tank armour.
Life's as brutal as the nightly sound of bootsteps
in the *logor*, the Serbian camp, announcing to
the Muslim captives that a squad of thugs is coming.
I lit a first cigarette, so my eyes could briefly wander,
screened by its smoke, out of this *logor*.
Last night's dream came back again: my hands held a thread,
tied to the hawthorn growing from my father's grave
in the Sandžak, in the gorge called God-Never-Seen.
A thread which can guide you out of hell.
I lit my second. So my soul could float away on its smoke
towards the ghosts from a deaf and grizzled past.
Which whisper to my soul: a single stride between
never-seen and nevermore, that's all there is to your life.
And the world's as grim as the guffaws of laughter
from the blinded in Canto 2 of Kovačić's *Pit*.
And then I lit the last. So I could hold, for a moment,
a star between my middle and index finger. An evening
star. And to give me, through its bluish veil,
a clearer insight into Karadžić's universe
whose *Logos* is the *Logor*.

TRI CIGARE

U smiraj, iziđoh vani da se crnim na bijelome.
Sunce je novčić koji se stavlja
na kapke pokojnika. Svuda božija šutnja
od tenkovskoga oklopa neprobojnija.
Život je strašan kao jeka koraka
što muslimanima, noću, u srpskim logorima
najavljuje dolazak batinaša.
Zapalih jednu da mi, za dimom duvanskim,
oči na koji tren odlutaju iz ovog logora.
Sjetih se sna sinoćnjeg: u rukama mi konac,
privezan za glog, nikao iz groba mog oca
u sandžačkome neviđbogu. Konac po kom se
može iz pakla izići.
Zapalih još jednu. Da mi po dimu duša
odlebdi do utvara iz gluve i sijede davnine.
Koje joj šapću: jedan korak iz neviđenše
u nedođenšu – to ti je sav tvoj život.
A svijet je grozan kao grohotni smijeh
oslijepljenih iz Jame Goranove.
Zapalih i posljednju. Da mi, na tren, zaliči
na zvijezdu, među srednjim i kažiprstom. Zvijezdu
večerenjaču. I da kroz plavičast velić
sagledam, što jasnije, Karadžićevu vaseljenu
u kojoj Logor je – Logos.

Translated, from the Bosnian, by Francis R. Jones

TRANSLATOR'S AFTERWORD

I was asked to translate this poem by Damir Arsenijević of Tuzla University for an article he was writing about poetry, atrocity and memory in modern-day Bosnia. Bosnia is in many ways a post-war state, even fifteen years after the fighting has finished. One fact that makes it so is the missing: those who still lie unidentified in mass graves, and whose killers still deny responsibility for their deeds, as do many of the politicians who sponsored their killing. The article tells how the International Day of Missing Persons on 30 August 2008 was designated in Bosnia "as a day which was to make visible and encourage the idea that the problem of missing persons [...] is the responsibility of us all." Arsenijević adds that, for Bosnian society, "the way ahead, out of the predominant feeling of paralysis, will not happen unless we start openly requesting that those responsible for the execution, burial, and hiding of those who are now missing must be named."

As coordinator of civil-society initiatives at the International Commission of Missing Persons in Sarajevo, Arsenijević organized for 30 August 2008 a display of poems by prominent Bosnian poets, to appear at the Bosnian Parliament alongside works by relatives of missing persons. The International Committee of the Red Cross (ICRC), however, as the exhibition's co-funder, barred two poems: Marko Vešović's *Tri cigare (Three Cigarettes)*, and Šejla Šehabović's *Srebrenica, Potočari, 9.5.2004 (*Vešović, "They want to remove our right to remember," 2008). Arsenijević reports the ICRC representative telling him that these poems were "not good poetry" – because Vešović mentions "Serbian camps" for Muslims, and Šehabović writes about how "četniks" carried out the Srebrenica massacre.

Translators, they say, are the closest readers. Translating Vešović's *Tri cigare* involved intensely analysing the poem's words, exploring its allusions, and giving a best-guess interpretation of its implications. This convinced me that condemning this poem as "not good poetry" rests on a failure to understand the complexities and subtleties of its poetic message. Below I explain why.

Vešović reports that this poem tells of an incident during the siege of Sarajevo. In a lull in the shelling, he was able to slip outside into the snow for a smoke: here the final phrase came into his mind: that in "Karadžić's universe, the *Logos* is the *Logor*." Thus the poem, it's true, explicitly mentions just one side in a conflict where, as in all wars, no party had wholly clean hands: Radovan Karadžić, the Serbian nationalist leader, and the concentration camps in which non-Serbs were tortured, beaten and killed. Even on this superficial level, however, Karadžić's world-view is one of the pivotal, unavoidable facts of the Bosnian tragedy. If highlighting this makes *Tri cigare* a bad poem, then Picasso's *Guernica* is a bad painting for depicting only the Fascist aggression in the Spanish Civil War.

A more fundamental misconception, however, is that a poem only means what it explicitly states. If we examine the allusions and undercurrents that underlie *Tri cigare*, it does not simply accuse one group of hatred, and so stereotype them as the uncivilized Other. As least in my reading, it suggests that any ideology based on irreconcilable difference breeds hatred. Moreover, by alluding to the common origins of Karadžić and the poet, it suggests that the hating Other is perilously close to the self who rejects hatred as a rationale for identity. Paradoxically, when the hating Other views his or her communal roots as a justification for hatred, only by going to these roots oneself can one find "a thread which can guide you" out of the hell of hatred.

The clues which led me to this conclusion are intricately linked to Vešović's poetic craft. Because this works both with the possibilities of his own language and with complex nets of allusion, these were hard to reproduce in English. Hence my interpretations of these clues are worth making explicit here:

> A wordplay in the opening line links the physical fact of escaping into the open air with the poet's duty to communicate – not from outside, like a news report, but from inside, from the self. *Da se crnim na bijelome* literally means "to blacken myself on the white," with allusions not only to self, but also to sunlight and space (in Bosnian-Croatian-Serbian you don't "go brown" but "blacken yourself" in the summer, and you go out not into the "wide world" but the "white world"). More importantly, *crno na bijelome* also means "in black and white." I tried to render this complexity with the English pun *to right [write] myself in black and white*.
>
> In Line 3, *božija šutnja* could mean either "divine speechlessness" or "goddam speechlessness." In my translation *My God, the speechlessness*, I tried to preserve the ambiguous intertwining of positive and negative which I saw as important for the whole poem.

In Line 6, I had to turn the original *u srpskim logorima* (literally, "in Serbian camps") into an explanation of the BCS word (*in the logor, the Serbian camp*), because *logor* was needed for the crucial wordplay in the final line. This highlighting of how the politics of Serbian identity were a key cause of the 1990s Bosnian tragedy is what the ICRC representative objected to. He presumably missed, however, how this was immediately nuanced by the next image: that of Vešović's own identity. Like Radovan Karadžić, Marko Vešović was born in Montenegro: Line 12 places the poet's origins in the *Sandžak* border region with Serbia. In Karadžić's universe ruled by ethnic hatred, therefore, Vešović would also be categorized as an ethnic Serb, which puts him in a privileged position to critique this universe. But Vešović describes his identity, his rootedness in family and place, as something, literally, "by which one can get out of hell" (*po kom se može iz pakla izići*, translated as *which can guide you out of hell*) – unlike Karadžić, who used the self-same rootedness to create that hell.

Even this insight is nuanced, however. In his commentary, Vešović describes how his father was killed in 1949 because of his alleged pro-Soviet views after Tito's break with Stalin – and that the hawthorn tree was growing from his grave when Vešović's family were allowed to give his father a proper burial many years later. Ideological hatred, therefore, is not just something of the war that the poet is experiencing

Similarly, in Line 18 the phrase *Jame Goranove* ("of Goran's Pit") subtly signals that ethnicized hatred is not a Serbian monopoly. Goran Kovačić was a Croatian poet and World War II partisan fighter; his 1943 epic poem *Jama* ("The Pit") tells of the atrocities perpetrated by Croatian fascists against Serbs and Jews. In order to signal that this was a literary allusion, I expanded it to *in Canto 2 of Kovačić's Pit* – but its underlying meaning could not be made explicit in English, particularly as Vešović himself supplies no ready-made interpretations here.

In the final line, Vešović ends his three-cigarette mental journey through the personal and literary roots of his country's hell with a far more complex conclusion than that jumped to by the ICRC representative. I read it as this: hatred is, sadly, an aspect of the human condition. Nevertheless, one of the duties of poets is to expose those who create hatred: those whose founding belief is not St John's *In the beginning was the Word (En arkhē ēn o Logos),* but *In the beginning was the Camp.* And even, or perhaps especially, if those who believe this are not some outside Other, but are those who share the poet's own roots.

Far from stirring up old hatreds, therefore, publishing Vešović's complex but thoroughly humane poem allows us to reflect on the complex nature of such hatreds. And in so doing, it offers a possible way out of the hells that the hatemongers create.

One of Bosnia's most distinguished writers, Marko Vešović was born in Pape, Montenegro in 1945, and has lived in Sarajevo since the sixties. Also a highly respected critic and novelist, and an influential opponent of Serb nationalism, his poems, essays and articles appeared to much acclaim during the siege of Sarajevo. His fifth book of poems is Polish Cavalry *(Planjax, 2002), and his collection of war prose,* Death Is a Master from Serbia *(Bosanska Kniga), appeared in 1994. He continues to live in the city, where he now teaches at the University of Sarajevo.*

Francis Redvers Jones teaches translation studies at the University of Newcastle in the North of England. He has translated extensively from Bosbian-Croatian-Serbian, Dutch, Hungarian and Russian, including the poetry of Mak Dizdar, Ivan Lalić and Vasko Popa. He is the author of 11 books of poetry translation, most recently Camp Notebook *by Miklós Radnóti (Arc, 2000, from the Hungarian),* Against the Forgetting *by Hans Faverey (New Directions, 2004, from the Dutch),* What It Is: Selected Poems *by Esther Jansma (Bloodaxe, 2008, from the Dutch) and* Chrysanthemums, Rowers *by Hans Faverey (LeonWorks, 2011, from the Dutch).*

THE SECURERS OF JUSTICE
(ANTI-JEWISM AS ANTI-MUSLIM)

Rusmir Mahmutćehajić

On the meaning of Muslim.

O believers, be you securers of justice, witness for God,
even though it be against yourselves, or your parents and kinsmen,
whether the man be rich or poor; God stands closest to either.
Then follow not caprice, so as to swerve; for if you twist or turn,
God is aware of the things you do.

Qur'an, 4:135.

Bosnia's current international borders with its three neighbours, Croatia, Serbia, and Montenegro, were largely determined by a series of international treaties between the end of the seventeenth and the end of nineteenth centuries. They demarcate a historical and cultural particularity that has been developing for more than one thousand years. A small country in both territory and population, Bosnia has long been an unavoidable political and cultural factor in international relations.

Throughout its long history, Bosnia has always belonged both culturally and politically to that European synthesis in which so many similarities and differences are brought together, just as Bosnia has always, throughout its existence, been a religiously plural society. Its borders do not introduce a break or discontinuity in the linguistic, religious, and cultural characteristics that are supposed peculiar to the political and cultural identities of Serbia, Croatia, and Montenegro, Bosnia's immediate neighbours. The forms of cultural identity and exchange extend in both directions over those borders.

In reading Evliya Çelebi's famous seventeenth-century *Travelogue*, where he describes this synthesis in the areas which would, by the end of the twentieth century, become the independent and internationally recognised states of Bosnia, Serbia, Croatia, and Montenegro, but which were then all part of the Ottoman Empire, one catches a glimpse of how the principle of the pluralistic state functioned at that time, as people of various ethnic and religious affiliations lived together in cities and other settlements throughout the area.

Muslims and Jews and Christians of both the Eastern and Western communions continue to live in these areas, dotted with the ancient remains of Bosnia's mediaeval culture, as the land's legitimate inhabitants and heirs. With regard to the Muslims, one must stress that the vast majority belong to the local Slavic population and derive the reasons for their belief in the Prophet Muhammad and the sacred tradition which, according to their good news, marks them out as one of the peoples of the Book, from the Christian culture of their own ancestors. Indeed, God says of their Book and of them in relation to His revelation:

> *Alif. Lam. Mim.* That is the Book, wherein is no doubt, a guidance to the conscious who believe in the Unseen, and perform the prayer, and expend of that We have provided them; who believe in what has been sent down to thee and what has been sent down before thee, and have faith in the Hereafter; those are upon guidance from their Lord, those are the ones who are to be saved. (Qur'an, 2:1-5)

Their being what they are introduces no form of cleavage, whether synchronic and diachronic, between these Muslims of Bosnia and their ancestors or their neighbours through Bosnia's history, at least according to their own understanding of their identity. They remain bound to the land and to the heritage of their ancestors, who discovered in what they were as Christians that same consciousness that they give form to as Muslims, preserving an absolute diachronic continuity in their ideas of God, the world, and humanity. Consequently, they remain an integral part of the religiously plural society of Bosnia.

There is no discontinuity between the graveyards and the cultic places of the Muslims of Bosnia and those of their Christian forbears. There is not a single town or settlement in which their identity involves denying the right of others to different identities. This is why, in principle, Bosnian towns normally contain churches *and* monasteries *and* mosques *and* synagogues, as well as other religious foundations belonging to the various communities, foundations that have been passed on, built-up, preserved, and developed over centuries. (Certain readers may find it unclear as to why such stress is being put on the Christian ancestry of the Muslims of Bosnia. Whoever they were, whether this or that group of Eastern or of Western Christians, members of the Bosnian Church, orthodox or heretic, what is emphasised is that they were Christians.)

Muslims find the principal reasons for recognising the right of Jews and Christians, as other and different, to be precisely what they are, in their own being Muslims in the first place. Their acceptance, support, and protection of difference are not by-products of goodwill, rational assessment, necessity, or toleration. For Muslims, it is God's will that there be a variety of ways to achieve full humanity and the revelation they accept as their Book tells them that salvation is also guaranteed to the members of the other religious communities, in fact to "whoso believes in God and the Last Day, and works righteousness – their wage awaits them with their Lord, and no fear shall be on them, neither shall they sorrow" (Qur'an, 2:62).

In so many different places and periods, it is this coexistence of monasteries, churches, synagogues and mosques that bears witness to religious plurality and the one God guarantees their inviolability as places in which His name is uttered (Qur'an, 22:40). The inviolability of religious plurality is itself derived from the divine revelation and guaranteed by it. Insofar as national differences, which entail linguistic differences, different genealogies, and separate areas and dynamics of development, are simply realities of our world, then truth must necessarily also take on many forms.

In this motley, no one has or can have advantage or disadvantage, which is to say none have the *a priori* role of collective ruler over others or of collective subject to others, as is clear from God's call to the people of the Book, revealed in the Recitation: "People of the Book! Come now to a word common between us and you, that we serve none but God and that we associate not aught with Him, and do not some of us take others as Lords, apart from God" (Qur'an, 3:64).

Each of us has the capacity to be noble, regardless of our collective identity, but it does require consciousness of God (Qur'an, 49:13). Grounds for this view are to be found in the sacred Muslim tradition. Any sacred tradition may be realised or denied, given clear expression or obscured. Which possibility is realised depends on the individual self, as is clear from God's revelation to the Prophet, the Praised, in the Recitation: "O believers, look after your own souls. He who is astray cannot hurt you, if you are rightly guided. Unto God shall you return, all together, and He will tell you what you were doing" (Qur'an, 5:105).

In our secular dramas determined by the forms of identity, exclusion and alienation, Muslims, whose aim is to realise their own highest potential in a relationship to God through His apostle, cannot bear witness to the path they themselves are on while denying recognition to the other paths of self-realisation, as that very variety is God's will. None of our collective identities overrides or relativises our moral responsibility as individuals. The realisation of the self is an individual responsibility, regardless of who, where, and when that individual is.

To be Muslim, in the full meaning of the term, entails recognition of this variety of paths towards God, while taking responsibility for one's own self and one's own path. This is exemplified by the oath of Sultan Mehmet the Conqueror to the Bosnian Franciscan Andjeo Zvizdović, confirmed to him in writing in 1463, which includes the following text:

> Let no man hinder or disturb either these or their churches. Let them live in my dominion, and let those who have fled be free and safe, let them return and live without fear in my dominion, in their monasteries, and let neither my Highness, nor my Viziers, nor my officials, nor my subjects, nor any of the inhabitants of my dominion, nor any man meddle in their affairs or attack or insult them, or endanger their lives, or their property, or their churches. And even if they would bring some man from foreign parts to my state – let them be permitted to do so.

At the end of the seventeenth and beginning of the eighteenth centuries, when the borders of the Ottoman Empire in the north shifted south and those in the south shifted north to approximately the current international borders of Bosnia and the territories that remained outside them became part of the Habsburg Empire or the Venetian Republic, the Muslim populations of these areas without exception faced three options – flight, conversion, or extermination. These were the solutions imposed in every occupied or lost community.

There was a concerted effort to eradicate everything Muslim, whether person or thing, alive or dead, from these occupied territories. Mosques were sacked or converted into churches, while all forms of material culture (schools, dervish lodges, bathhouses, graveyards, etc) were erased. Even when Muslims, faced with the three options, did accept baptism to ensure their survival, they could still be murdered or expelled. A case in point took place in 1689, in Lika. Even when they did negotiate an agreement to go, leaving behind all their property for the conquerors, the refugee columns could nonetheless be massacred and annihilated.

During the nineteenth century, Muslims in areas to the east of contemporary Bosnia suffered a similar fate. When the Serbian rebels of that century captured villages or towns, Muslims who did not manage to escape were likely to be killed, including children, women, and the elderly, in ways that not infrequently involved terrible savagery. There was no safety for them in offers of baptism or immigration. This was how both Muslims and every trace of their material culture disappeared from all the cities east of Bosnia, in spite of all Evliya Çelebi's references to them, so that today their having ever existed and their destruction and silence with regard to them that has fallen are a constant source of horrified confusion.

These evident horrors have been crowned by one even more terrible, as the persecution of Slavic Muslim populations during the seventeenth, eighteenth, nineteenth centuries in all the areas that border contemporary Bosnia continues to be presented in overcompensating historical constructions as liberation and the national emancipation of Croats and Serbs. As a result, the descendants of those who fled into Bosnia to escape the slaughter of their kin are now taught that these crimes were sacred acts of liberation from internal and external evil. The criminals are presented as national heroes, their victims as cruel villains from whom the Christian world was to be defended (Tomaž Mastnak, *Crusading Peace: Christendom, the Muslim World and the Western Political Order*, 2002).

There can be no doubt that the Ottoman conquest was traumatic for the Christian inhabitants of the Balkans, who were subject to various forms of oppression or discrimination over the ensuing centuries. The images of a golden age of interfaith tolerance under Ottoman rule are sometimes painted in overly positive colours. On the other hand, co-existence between communities and individuals of different faiths, Muslims, Jews, and Christians, was not just possible, but guaranteed by the imperial authority. No European society during the Renaissance and early modern period provided the same security to large Muslim populations as the Ottomans did to Jews and Christians of all denominations, while the position of Jews and Christians not of the established denomination under Christian rule was often as bad if not worse than under the Ottomans. The ideology and practice of cleansing the Balkans of the Muslim stain were less native growths due to the suffering of the Christian peoples under the Ottomans than imports from the Habsburg and Venetian West, where they had served as ideological and material motivators for the reconquest of the Hungarian lands and Dalmatia.

What does this concept of national emancipation and the creation of national states so characteristic of the period after 1700 mean without reference to what determines a people as unique, normally understood in terms of ethnic origin, language, history, religion, and territory? There have never been homogenous peoples and never will be. Consequently there cannot be territories that belong solely to them, irrespective of the rights of others who happen to live on those territories.

When national homogeneity is, nonetheless, ideologically asserted, the need arises to define the "other" and the "different," who are assumed not to be of the same race, language, or history and who consequently do not belong on the given territory. All European movements for national self-determination and emancipation share this trait. According to the usual teleology of the awakened nation, these "others" incarnate everything that stands against the good. Nation-building is defined by its opposition to these evil "others," as the struggle against them is identified with the struggle for liberation and emancipation of the nation.

For most European nationalisms the most important different "others" were the Jews. Their transnational presence and their link to a transcendental God meant the ideology of national emancipation could posit them as insoluble otherness. For more than 1000 years, European peoples were conscious of being members of a Christian Commonwealth, with particular reference to two enemies – an external one determined in theology and in human terms as brute force and given the names of *Arab*, *Agarian*, *Ishmaelite*, *Saracen*, or *Turk*, and another, theologically subversive, internal one, with the same, but falsely interpreted, sacred tradition, who had denied, betrayed, and murdered the Christ and had infiltrated the very flesh of Christianity like a disease.

For the articulation of the Southeastern European Slavic national identities, the Muslims were allocated the role given the Jews in the formation of other European nationalisms. Through the constructed image of the "Turk," Slavic Muslims were identified wholesale with the incarnation of evil, of force, of infidelity, and of a constant threat against all things holy and Christian. This anti-Muslim construction brought together all the fantasies and all the experiences of the Crusades and merged them with the resentments of an oppressed peasantry, who made little distinction between their foreign Ottoman rulers and their Slavic Muslim compatriots. Slavic Muslims, consequently, found themselves increasingly placed in a position of ambivalence. They were identified with this image of the Turk as the external enemy of everything Christian, but also with betrayal, conspiracy, and internal disease under the sign of infidelity and apostasy.

In 1848, Europe was shaken by revolution and counterrevolution and the tightly wound emotions and programmes of national liberation, all of which added fuel to the fire in the bellies of the Serbian youth gathered around the Belgrade Lyceum. Their anti-Muslim feeling, informed by the principle "baptism, expulsion, or death," was in turn integrated into their revolutionary rhetoric. According to the eminent Serb historian and nationalist, Milorad Ekmečić, "they chanted the contemporary song: 'Turk, eat up your bacon or take the mountain road'" (*A Long Movement of Slaughter and Ploughing*, 2008).

Nearly all attempts to modernise the societies of the Balkans have involved certain assumptions regarding how to deal with the "Muslim question." Even if not always expressed in the radical form of "baptize, expel, or murder," the solution has retained essentially similar characteristics. Any proposed emancipation of the Muslims has regularly been supposed to entail a rejection of their culture, whether through Serbification or Croatization, even if only in order to affirm loyalty to the Communist party and state. They have been required to put aside any aspect of their behaviour that expresses their cultural identity or any attachment to it, culminating in the demand that they themselves deny, reject and destroy the cultural characteristics that mark them out as Muslim.

This process has involved the destruction of graves, the adoption of Christian features in the funerary ritual, the destruction of traditional houses and towns, the denigration and banning of traditional clothing, the introduction of cultural forms foreign to the Muslim heritage, the destruction of mosques, madrasahs and mektebs and their replacement by buildings out of all harmony with the older urban fabric, the destruction of libraries and archives, and the introduction of a whole range of anti-Muslim aspects into school curricula, etc. Once modernisation had been accepted as a general goal for social development, it became possible to blame Muslims for simply existing by establishing them as the ideological contrary of that ideal.

Repeatedly emphasising the perennial guilt of Muslims, while at the same time recognizing the Communist order's successes in modernising Yugoslav society, but passing neatly over the horrors of Nazism, in his recent history of Serbia's national trauma, Ekmečić concludes: "It was only among the Albanian and Bosnian Muslims that social modernization failed. It was suffocated by the demographic explosion". So, the mere fact that, after more than three centuries of baptism, murder and exile, the remnant of this people continues to have children is alarming and unacceptable for Serbian ideologues. Where this leads has been made clear by Ekmečić himself, who has declared on the Republika Srpska channel of Bosnian television in 2011 that "if Yugoslavia cannot exist as a civil state [i.e. a state based on citizenship rather than a single homogenous nationality], then neither can any of its successor areas." In this way, their eradication is justified in advance. Only their disappearance as a people will satisfy the historical necessity of the homogenous nation.

This ideological creation of that primordial Pan-Serbian integrity for which others are simply "grey ethnic areas," considers the baptism, expulsion, and murder of Muslims both necessary and desirable. During the Second World War, Stevan Moljević would give this necessity yet another outing in his writings in *Homogena Srbija* (*Homogeneous Serbia*) while contemporary Serb historian, Veselin Djuretić, sums up the unfinished nature of the destruction of the Muslims and their integration within Yugoslavia, in the following way:

> During the formation of the new Yugoslav state, the Serbs didn't just subordinate their national goals to supra-national goals, they subordinated their own social and political organization to that option. Because of this folly, they were unable to accomplish what it was their task as a people to accomplish: they did not achieve homogenization even of the ethnic area that had been liberated during the anti-Turkish and anti-German wars. Whole areas that had been untouched by Karadjordje's rebellion, like those which were not caught up in the rebellion in Montenegro, Herzegovina and Bosnia, remained incoherent in terms of nationality. They remained grey ethnic areas, in which social experiments of various sorts would later be conducted. (*Srbi u evropskoj civilizaciji / Serbs in European Civilization*, 1993)

After nearly two centuries during which the Muslims in ideologically constituted "grey ethnic areas" have suffered ruination, and even after the disolution of Yugoslavia, during which genocide was carried out against them, Ekmečić, who has never made any mention of these crimes over the *longue durée,* nonetheless concludes: "Just as under the Nazi occupation of 1941, in 1992 the Serbs lost not just their state, but the very history through which it had been created" (*A Long Movement of Slaughter and Ploughing*). But in that very history, it was Bosnia's and the Bosnian Muslims' right to history that was denied. Is it possible that this "loss" might actually be a gain for both the Serbs and the Bosnian Muslims that will allow them to find their own place and some peace at last within histories that belong to them and to which they have an unequivocal right?

The twentieth century, too, was replete with this approach to Muslims and everything Muslim. Wherever movements based on the European idea of national emancipation took root, Muslims would, on the basis of this venerable principle of "liberation," be treated as unacceptable, as both internal and external others. The crimes committed against Muslims during the 1912-1914 Balkan wars, so often presented as an attempt to complete the liberation of the lands of the Slavic South from the Turk, differed little from those in earlier centuries (Paul Mojzes, *Balkan Genocides: Holocaust and Ethnic Cleansing in the Twentieth Century*, 2011). These wars of "liberation" preceded the First World War, which saw the disintegration of the Habsburg Empire and the creation of the Kingdom of Serbs, Croats, and Slovenes.

In this new political constellation, Bosnia was simply denied as a historical and political reality, presented as an as-yet unresolved Serb and/or Croat problem – unresolved because of its religious plurality. The Muslim majority was denied the protection of law, while agreement as to the destiny of their country not infrequently assumed that they did not in fact exist. According to the testimony of Ivan Meštrović (the renowned Croatian sculptor), as early as during the First World War, the Serb politician Stojan Protić had proposed: "As soon as our army crosses the Drina, it will give the Turks [that is, the Bosnian Muslims] 24 – perhaps even 48 – hours to return to the faith of their forefathers [which, in Protić's view, was Orthodoxy] and then slay those who refuse, as we did in Serbia in the past" (quoted in Ivo Banac, *The National Question in Yugoslavia: Origins, History, Politics*, 1984).

The approach, whose application to Bosnia Protić announced, was an inheritance of centuries of practice, first in the Habsburg and Venetian West and then in the Eastern Balkan lands. In 1870, in Belgrade, Milivoje Blaznavac, an officer and official in the government of the Principality of Serbia, told Brother Antun Knežević, a Bosnian Franciscan who had gone there to look for support for the idea of a potential national liberation of Bosnia: "As soon as you rise up, you must immediately issue a proclamation to the Turks: they must either convert immediately or pack themselves off where they can, if they don't want to be cut down!" (Antun Knežević, *My Notes From Last Year,* 2001). This same scheme was applied over the centuries to European Jewry. Konstantin P. Pobedonostsev, a late nineteenth century ideologue of Russian nationalism, formulated his "final solution to the Jewish problem" as: "one third conversion, one third emigration, and one third starvation" (quoted in Max J. Dimont, *Jews, God and History*, 2004)

This tried and trusted principle for "dealing with the Muslim question" was also applied during the Second World War. Wherever Serb rebels, loyal to their national heritage, were in control, the destruction of whatever was Muslim, including both the population and its cultural heritage, began. This genocide has been largely ignored in the historiography of the Second World War in Yugoslavia, but in Bosnia, albeit considerably lower, the percentage of the total Muslim population killed was second only to the percentage of the Jews killed (Rusmir Mahmutćehajić, *The Denial of Bosnia*, 2000).

In fact, in the constructions of historiography, this project of destroying the Muslim, which would reach such incomprehensible dimensions, is, like the acts of destruction against Muslims in previous centuries, presented as a heroic act of liberation and associated with modern revolution in all its forms. This mechanism would survive in anti-Muslim ideologies right to the end of the twentieth century, when Sveto Veselinović, a participant in the anti-Bosnian war of 1991 to 1995, would declare: "one third of the Muslims will be killed, a third will become Orthodox, and a third will run away" (Edina Bećirević, *East European Politics & Societies: 24/4*, 2010).

It is possible to discern an uninterrupted flow of murder and persecution of Muslims in the surrounding countries that flooded over into Bosnia itself from the second half of the twentieth century on. These crimes went largely unrecorded and un-described. Their perpetrators continue to be represented in national histories as the dedicated heroes of their peoples. This lack of awareness was sadly evident in the most recent war against Bosnia (1991–1995).

The criminals of that war considered their anti-Muslim programs simply a continuation of their illustrious national histories and expected the support of the major centres of world political power. The extent to which they were correct in their expectations is illustrated by the testimony of Taylor Branch, a close adviser of the former American president, Bill Clinton, who wrote the following with regard to the approach of the major players in the international order to the war against Bosnia:

> Within weeks, the new administration had explored ideas to relax the international embargo on arms shipments to the region, reasoning that the embargo penalized the weakest, most

victimized nation of Bosnia-Herzegovina. Unlike its neighbours in
Serbia and Croatia, the heavily Muslim population of Bosnia was
isolated without access to arms smuggled across the borders. The
Bosnian government wanted the embargo lifted so that people
could defend themselves, thereby opening a chance for military
balance among the antagonists that could lead to a political
settlement.

Clinton said US allies in Europe blocked proposals to adjust or
remove the embargo. They justified their opposition on plausible
humanitarian grounds, arguing that more arms would only fuel
the bloodshed, but privately, said the President, key allies
objected that an independent Bosnia would be "unnatural" as the
only Muslim nation in Europe. He said they favoured the embargo
precisely because it locked in Bosnia's disadvantage. Worse, he
added, they parried numerous alternatives as a danger to the eight
thousand European peacekeepers deployed in Bosnia to safeguard
emergency shipments of food and medical supplies. They
challenged US standing to propose shifts in policy with no
American soldiers at risk. While upholding their peacekeepers as
a badge of commitment, they turned their troops effectively into
a shield for the steady dismemberment of Bosnia by Serb forces.
When I expressed shock at such cynicism, reminiscent of the
blind-eye diplomacy regarding the plight of Europe's Jews during
World War II, President Clinton only shrugged. He said President
François Mitterrand of France had been especially blunt in saying
that Bosnia did not belong, and that British officials also spoke of
a painful but realistic restoration of Christian Europe. Against
Britain and France, he said, German Chancellor Helmut Kohl,
amongst others, had supported moves to reconsider the United
Nations arms embargo, failing in part because Germany did not
hold a seat on the UN Security Council. Clinton sounded as
though he were obliged to start over. He groped amid these
chastening constraints for new leadership options to stop Bosnian
mass sectarian violence. (Taylor Branch, *The Clinton Tapes:Wrestling
History with the President*, 2009)

A series of judgements from the International Criminal Tribunal for the
former Yugoslavia, the International Court of Justice at The Hague and the

domestic courts of the countries of the former Yugoslavia, has proven beyond any reasonable doubt that genocide was committed against the Bosnian Muslims during the period between 1992 and 1995. Such a crime requires four conditions to be met – a criminal elite, a criminal ideology, criminal organisations, and a sufficient number of individuals ready to carry out the crime. This final great crime against the Muslims of Bosnia, committed at the end of the twentieth century, is, however, just one episode in a long-standing tradition, with which not the victims, nor the criminals, nor the key players in the international order have come to terms with, particularly with regard to their responsibility for justice, which is to say for pointing out and bearing witness to the truth.

For, at the end of the twentieth century, before the eyes of the world, that same old schema was applied with a brutal literalness to the Muslims of Bosnia as the internal and external enemies of two European nations, for which read Christian nations (Serbia and Croatia). In the opinion of the elites driving the national programs based on national ideologies, these Muslims remained both internal and external enemies from whom the nations and their territories had to be liberated. So, genocide was yet again committed against this nation, no matter how clean many of those involved kept their hands of direct criminal responsibility. They remained and remain committed to the parameters of their myth, to the impossibility of living peacefully with Muslims, their internal and external enemies, to the myth that justifies their destruction.

This construction of an image of Europe, its peoples, and of Muslims is a major support to the modern political ideologies as they have been assimilated within the ethnic, nationalist, and statist ideologies of our time. Almost any attempt to raise the issue of past or contemporary anti-Muslim feeling and thinking is received as subversive and essentially unacceptable. Even the tribunal and court judgements are denied by some, while the sentencing of criminals is interpreted as conspiratorial anomaly.

In this opposition to establishing Bosnia as a plural society, the Muslim presence is, whether directly or indirectly, singled out as decisive. It is generally passed over in silence that, if these anti-Muslim claims were to be presented openly and accepted generally, no contemporary Western concept of society and its political order could be maintained, except as a type of real-apartheid which would with time be transformed into "a final solution of the Muslim question." Also passed over in silence is the self-evident fact that this position is essentially identical to the position taken by the European Nazis and their sympathisers regarding the Jews before the Holocaust.

During the Second World War, the Yugoslav Communists, in close alliance with the Communist International based in Moscow, joined an antifascist coalition and offered an emancipatory solution to the Yugoslav, and so Bosnian tragedy. The statehood of Bosnia was recognised even during the war, but as that of a country which was "neither Serb, nor Croat, nor Muslim, but Serb and Croatian and Muslim" *(The First Session of the State Anti-fascist Council for the National Liberation of Bosnia and Heerzegovina, 1943)*, and consequently different from all the other states of the Yugoslav federation.

Relying on their formula as a guarantee of a secure future, the Yugoslav Communists prevented any form of deconstruction of national histories or any proper reckoning with war crimes committed against other ethnic groups during the war. While this stored up problems for Serb-Croat relations, both were recognised as legitimate peoples with legitimate national histories. For the Muslims, it was different, however. Their nationality was denied recognition and there was what amounted to a tacit amnesty for most if not all those who had committed crimes against them during the Second World War. Thus, the members of the new party elite, the Communist ideologues, and the state structures they lorded over continued in a more or less tacit way to act in accordance with the accepted national programs of liberation, which continued to rely on anti-Muslimism as an unquestioned ideological category.

For those who had previously committed crimes against Muslims, their new-found loyalty to the Communist order became a secure shield against judicial processing, or even the mere mention of their earlier roles. (For a case of perpetrators of anti-Muslim war crimes in the Bosnian town of Kulen Vakuf during World War II being inducted into the post-war Communist elite, see *East European Politics & Societies: 24/3*, 2010). It was assumed that, under the conditions of Communist totalitarianism in Yugoslavia, the emancipation of the Muslims, just like that of all the other collective participants in state-building, would lead to "liberation" from all the religious and associated baggage whose roots lay in the period before class relations had been resolved, a period whose irrational religious fantasies were an opiate for the people that prevented their class liberation. This thesis had its most harmful and most profound impact on the collective identity of Muslims, as their culture was presented in all the surviving nationalist ideologies and associated emancipatory aspirations and movements as non-

European, backward, foreign, dangerous, and so forth. For them, emancipation meant ceasing to be Muslims, which was a false form of national consciousness, and being absorbed by one of the real nations.

It is no wonder, then, that Yugoslav Communists with Muslim origins would prove their loyalty to the Communist order and their emancipation from those origins by their fervour in persecuting the "backward" Muslim faithful, which was in effect all those who opposed the Communist totalitarianism. These Communists with Muslim roots proved their fervour by destroying their Muslim cultural heritage, which they dismissed as "the ugly and unnecessary remnants of foreign occupation."

Just as the Muslims were defined in the nationalist and so in the Serbian and Croatian ideologies as an absolute break in Christian historical continuity and as lacking any connection with the supposedly ethnic and national unities represented by the Christian nations, every ideological construction of the history of the Balkan peoples tended to separate them off from the totality, while presenting everything associated specifically with them as in some way foreign and indigestible.

Indoctrinated in these ideologies through school and other programs, Muslims began to view themselves as a "people" in the sense that concept has for the European Enlightenment and post-Enlightenment movement. As a result, both consciously and through ignorance, they internalised an anti-Muslim prejudice that was modelled on anti-Jewish prejudice. Once they had accepted this image of themselves as a people and a nation, they came to accept the identification of their origin with the Turkish occupation. In this way, they identified the essence of their own self-witness to plural unity as something inimical.

Two factors played a decisively important role for the Muslims of Bosnia during the twentieth century in rendering concrete this image of themselves as internal and external enemies – pan-Islamism and anti-Jewism. Both these factors brought them into direct conflict with the intellectual heritage of their personal and collective identities and consequently cut them off from the most important values of their Bosnian-ness, namely the intuition and conception of a religiously and ethnically plural society.

The first of these two factors meant that, on the very edge of survival, in absolute existential insecurity, many Bosnian Muslims took refuge in fantasies of belonging to some great homogenous Muslim community to which they then transferred their hopes and expectations. As a result, they were cut off from the reality of the Muslim Commonwealth, that great

Archipelago of difference and existential drama and, consequently, from the reality of their development as subjects within it and their responsibility for it. They have become easy prey to the influence of ideological constructions and to alienation from their real existential circumstances.

Muslims who share this homogenizing worldview see the Arabs, Turks, and Persians as a single Muslim maternal community, while all the internal distinctions, including the collective dramas of the Kurds, the Berbers, the Copts, the Roma, and the Shi'ites, and the countless multitude of other groups, simply cease to exist, as the ideological constructions of a universal nation obscure from view both the world's reality and their own intellectual tradition of luxuriant plurality. And so they have themselves begun to participate in the promotion and legitimation of the anti-Muslim programmes according to which the Muslims are the main external enemy of whatsoever is European and Christian.

Anti-Jewism has spread by capillary motion from the European nationalist ideologies to the Muslim followers of the various forms of European modernist ideology as well. This is certainly the case for the Muslims of Bosnia and has led to a gradual erasure of their immediate historical experience of living together with the Jews of Bosnia, which has been replaced by a fantasy developed under the influence of the worst forms of European anti-Jewism, as interpreted in pseudo-Muslim ideologizing. If that experience of co-existence between Muslim and Jew under the Ottomans should not be idealised as an absolute harmony, there is little evidence of violent anti-Jewish feeling or prejudice in Ottoman-period Bosnia of the sort that would be imported later from both early and climactic forms of Nazism. This was/would later be applied, in an emotional and simplistic way, to the Arab-Israeli conflict.

As a result of this conflict, Arabism has, as a nationalist ideology, been identified with everything Muslim, just as Zionism has been with everything Jewish. This has produced interpretations of scripture that draw on every negative experience in the long history of relations between Muslims and Jews. This construction is also unfortunately representative of the attitudes of many Muslims of Bosnia towards the Jews today. This relationship is structured by an ideological world picture that generates both a distorted image of the Muslim and imposes a grotesque image of the Jew upon that Muslim. Unfortunately, superficial knowledge and hatred based on unresolved fear have meant that many Muslims have internalised both this anti-Muslim image of the Muslim and the anti-Muslim caricature of the Jew.

(Samir Beglerović, Professor at the Faculty of Islamic Sciences of Sarajevo University, has undertaken research into the apocalyptic literature of the Muslims of Bosnia created during and since the last war, from which it appears that anti-Jewism amongst the Muslims of Bosnia has a largely ideological basis and has been imported from the Arab world. According to Beglerović, although some tensions no doubt always existed between Jews and Muslims as separate ethnic and faith communities, virulent anti-Jewish prejudice and persecution do *not* appear to have deeper roots in the culture of the Bosnian Muslims that go back before the Second World War.)

Thanks to their adoption of these forms of anti-Jewism, some of Bosnia's Muslims have thus found themselves internalizing the anti-Muslim image of the anti-Jewish Muslim and so legitimizing the prejudice which considers them not just external but also dangerous internal enemies of the very peoples amongst whom and with whom they live and have lived for the full extent and length of their history. Deconstructing this grotesque is a major precondition for freeing Muslims from this Gordian knot of confusion and trauma.

Such a deconstructive endeavour may be approached in a number of ways – through ideas of the autonomous self and the associated development of political philosophy, sacrosanct human rights, global ethics, etc. It would appear, however, of the greatest importance to put a stop to blind retaliation by Muslims for injustices they have suffered, as the cycle only serves to multiply and deepen their own trauma. Grounds for such a moral responsibility may be sought in the sacred legacy of their tradition.

Whether for Muslims or for others, failure to meet one's responsibilities to justice represents a threat to current and future generations. The Muslims of Bosnia have a responsibility to free themselves from the cycle of retribution, from requiting crime with crime. Instead, they must discover and foster the grounds within the inviolate contents of their own identities for demanding justice for themselves and advocating it for all others. Orientation toward such a goal entails a thorough review of the many elements that constitute their responsibility towards themselves and towards others. In searching for reasons to oppose Muslim anti-Jewism, one should start at the doctrinal core of everything Muslim, namely witness to the unity of God, the apostolate of the Praised, and return to Him.

According to often repeated Muslim traditions, God reveals Himself through three books – the world, humanity, and His discourse in human language. The central revelation is humanity, the being that can fully comprehend the entire revelation and consequently be lower than any beast but more sublime than the angels themselves. These three books form a whole through which flow the signs of God and of our path from Him and back to Him. They allow us an integral anthropo-cosmological vision of the reasons and purpose of all creation. The separation of only some of these signs and their employment in the service of a stunted human vision – whose purpose is to present themselves as independent and self-sufficient – necessarily leads to a darkening-over of the ever-flowing and ever-changing real.

In anti-Jewish and anti-Muslim prejudice, the danger of such separation is evident in the example of modern pseudo-Muslim abuse of the divine revelation to the prophet, the Praised, with regard to the following passage from the Qur'an: "Thou wilt surely find the most hostile of men to the believers are the Jews and associaters" (Qur'an, 5:82 mushriq).

Admittedly, this verse is easy to misunderstand, if taken outside of the context of the Revelation as a whole or interpreted within the context of a pseudo-Muslim reading of that Revelation. With their experience of suffering through the centuries, during the nineteenth and twentieth centuries, many of the Muslims of Bosnia have done just this, thanks to the fantasy of a universal Muslim community, not entirely unconnected with the utopian idea of "the united proletariat of all countries," and set up the Jews as their main enemies. When the Nazis destroyed nearly all the Jews of Bosnia, the descendents of their neighbours from among the Muslims of Bosnia had already lost much feeling for them as their immediate and sacrosanct other, so that the Muslims' self-image as belonging to a plural society became even further obscured. Consequently, instead of deepening their own self-understanding, which is hardly possible in the absence of a responsible relationship towards the Jews, they developed the fantasy of the Jew as enemy, locating it on the killing fields of a distant and obscure conflict between Jews and Arabs, who they identified with all Muslims. Is an alternative understanding possible of this Qur'anic verse and its reference to the Jews as the worst of enemies that maintains the brotherhood of the securers of justice from all the nations and is true to both the spirit and letter of the Recitation?

In the Recitation, God says of the Jews, just as He does of the Christians, Sabaeans, and Magians (i.e. Zoroastrians), who are mentioned as examples from the throng of potential peoples of the Book, that they will be saved so long as they believe in God and the Last Day and the doing of good deeds. He also says that there is a fully realised "just maternal community" amongst the Jewish people as a whole (Qur'an, 5:66). As such a community, they enjoy the same rights and privileges as the other peoples of the Book – prophets and books as supports to the realization of their humanity. This they have throughout the full history of their existence and in the eyes of all peoples. None of this, however, can produce salvation on its own, in the absence of personal responsibility. They are simply means offered to us all as individuals and so available to every nation.

Everyone is called to participate in the establishment of a maternal community or nation of the Just out of the individuals who belong to the nations of the Book, and who are constantly "calling to good, and bidding to honour, and forbidding dishonour" (Qur'an, 3:104). In every generation there are those who respond to this call and in every nation of the Book there is "an upstanding community, that recite God's signs in the watches of the night, bowing themselves, believing in God and in the Last Day, bidding to honour and forbidding dishonour, vying one with the other in good works; those are of the righteous" (Qur'an, 3:113–114).

The "just maternal community" arises from the individual response to God's call for us to become securers of justice. In the example of the Jews Muslims see their own case in an external image. When the Jews are presented as a national group that is *a priori* saved, or chosen, the personal responsibility of each individual Jew is excluded. Rather, one must reject this *a priori* value of the collectivity, accepted regardless of the individual responsibility of Jews or Muslims or any other group for the truth and for affirming the truth through virtue and beauty, because it is, as such, an obstacle to the attainment of full humanity.

The true meaning of the verse about the Jews as enemies is thus in fact precisely a denial of this *a priori* valuation of any collectivity, including the Muslims, in order to affirm our moral responsibility as individuals for our witness to the unity of God, the acceptance of human perfectibility, and our return to Him. Whenever Muslims conceive of themselves as an ethically undifferentiated mass, it is this verse which should remind them that they are their own worst enemies.

This is because it is God who guarantees to them, as cited above, that there is a just maternal community within every people of the Book whose members are the securers of justice, even when that justice is against themselves or their closest kin. Such a community must exist even amongst Muslims. Moreover, that community of Just Muslims cannot be an enemy to the counterpart communities of the Just in each of the other nations of the Book.

Evidence for the alternative view may be adduced only by taking the signs in the Book out of context and subjecting them to the constructions of an unrealized self. An individual that does this enjoys a Pyrrhic victory — instead of submitting to God, he subjects God to himself. This is the form of idolatry, which is the taking of other gods in the place of God and the one sin of humanity that God says cannot be washed away (Qur'an, 4:48, 116). But the Book, which is the world and the self and Book written down in the language of human beings, is the harmony of all the signs in concert.

That this is the case may be seen from another sign regarding the enemies of the faithful, which is to say the faithful as a potential member of one of the imaginal peoples of the Book. In the Recitation, God warns those of us who, as faithful, are linked with Him as the Faithful through our faith: "O believers, among your wives and children there is an enemy to you; so beware of them. But if you pardon, and overlook, and if you forgive, surely God is All-forgiving, Ever-merciful" (Qur'an, 64:14). (This verse should be read as gender inclusive, as in Muhammad Abdel Haleem, *Arabic-English Dictionary of Quranic Usage*, 2008. And this message from the Recitation is entirely in accordance with the words of the Messiah Jesus in the Gospels, Luke, 14:26: "If any man come to me, and hate not his father, and mother, and wife, and children, and brethren, and sisters, yea, and his own soul also, he cannot be my disciple.")

No relationship with or in the world, with other people, or even with the self can have value except in relation to God. They cannot, because that would mean that there is or can be some god other than God and that justice, which is speaking and bearing witness to the truth through virtue, is based upon untruth. When the *muslim* (person of peace), that is the individual who is linked through *islam* (being in peace) with God as *al-Salam* (Peace), denies the possibility of relating to another individual, he in fact denies himself.

This is why Muslim anti-Jewism, whenever it is applied as an ideological category, is actually a denial of what it means to be Muslim, of the Muslim's own Muslimhood, and so is anti-Muslim to its core. Being at peace (*islam*) is the perennial relationship of all of creation with God as the Creator, a relationship which only human beings, as beings of free will, can deny and trample down. By doing so, we cleave to the lie against the truth, to the ugly against the beautiful, and to evil against good. By doing so, we deny and distort our authentic nature.

Once we accept that there are different ways of being on the paths of peace, we find that we need the other and the different, whose possibility of salvation is equally guaranteed by God. We need the other as our constant partner in dialogue, that we may understand and live by the truth that each of us is given only a little knowledge, so that our path towards God is itself growth in knowledge. Even the prophet, the Praised, the mercy to the worlds, the joyful news, and the most beautiful example, prayed for such growth, saying: "O my Lord, increase me in knowledge!" (Qur'an, 20:114)

The vision and experience of the enemy is a standing challenge to each of us in our struggle to realise ourselves in truth, virtue, and beauty. Of this struggle, God says:

> Dispute not with the People of the Book save in the beautiful manner, except for those of them that do wrong; and say, "We believe in what has been sent down to us, and what has been sent down to you; our God and your God is one, and to Him we have surrendered." (Qur'an, 29:46)
>
> Not equal are the beautiful deed and the evil deed. Repel with that which is more beautiful and behold, he between whom and thee there is enmity shall be as if he were a loyal friend. (Qur'an, 41:34)

Editor's Note: for the full footnoting of this essay in Bosnian, please contact the author at International Forum, Sarajevo.

One of Bosnia's most prominent Muslim scholars and authors, Rusmir Mahmutćehajić was born in 1948 in Stolac, Herzegovina. He was educated at the local gymnasium and continued his studies at Sarajevo University, graduating as an electrical engineer in 1973. He served in Sarajevo as Deputy Prime Minister and Energy Minister throughout most of the Bosnian war (1991-95). Now partially blind, he is the author of twenty-four books, including (in English translation) Living Bosnia: Political Essays and Interviews *(Oslobodenje International, 1996),* Bosnia the Good: Tolerance and Tradition *(Central European University Press, 2000),* The Denial of Bosnia *(The Pennsylvania State University Press, 2000),* Sarajevo Essays: Politics, Ideology and Tradition *(State University of New York Press, 2003),* Learning From Bosnia: Approaching Tradition *(Fordham University Press, 2005),* On Love: In the Muslim Tradition *(Fordham University Press, 2007),* Across the River: On the Poetry of Mak Dizdar *(Fordham University Press, 2011),* On the Other: A Muslim View *(Fordham University Press, 2011), and* The Praised and the Virgin *(Brill, 2015). He is President of International Forum Bosnia and continues to live in Sarajevo.*

THAT'S HOW IT WAS:
A REPORT ON WESTERBORK AND BERGEN BELSEN
(1945)

Erich Marx

Ruled by the dregs of mankind.

TRANSLATOR'S NOTE
(German title: *So war es: Ein Bericht über Westerbork und Bergen Belsen*)

This account of his experiences of two Nazi concentration camps was written and typed by Erich Marx soon after his return to Holland in September 1945, only a few months after Liberation. Erich died in 1978 and my father, Erich's nephew, came into possession of all of his papers in 1993, following the death of Erich's wife Carola. The original German manuscript was eventually sent to Yad Vashem in 2001, where it was archived. I was able to obtain a copy, which I have now transcribed and translated for this issue of *Irish Pages*.

Erich Marx, who was born in 1900 in Heidelberg, was a typical secular Jew, part of the large extended Marx family, who owned a thriving cigar factory and had lived in Heidelberg for several generations. Unlike the rest of the family, however, he didn't just work in the family business but was highly educated and, I am told, had a law degree. His wife Carola, née Basnitzki, came from a very wealthy family in Heidelberg and (so the family rumour has it) theirs was not a love match but a marriage of convenience arranged by the parents. He and his wife were unable to have children and moved to Holland in the late 1920s, where Erich had found employment. They lived in a small town, Roermond, near the German border, from which they were taken to Westerbork, a Dutch concentration camp in 1942.

He and his wife had been German citizens until 1939 and after the war they became Dutch citizens, living in Roermond as before. Erich became a very successful businessman: the sole Dutch distributor of Rauch furniture, which was very popular brand of German furniture. He made, I'm told, a large amount of money. He travelled all over Holland and, as he didn't drive, employed a full-time driver.

It seems as though Erich's education, coupled with his fluency in German as well as Dutch, was extremely advantageous during his time in the camps, particularly at Bergen Belsen, where he worked as a clerk. He was able to avoid most of the sadistic roll-calls and harsh manual labour, moving freely around the camp and obtaining food and information for himself and fellow prisoners. He also managed to steal a few vital documents prior to the dissolution of Bergen Belsen, which provided evidence after the war for an unspecified case.

Westerbork, where Erich and his wife were initially interned, was a transit camp in the northeast of Holland. It had been originally set up in 1939 as a refugee camp for German Jews fleeing the Nazis. This was done by the Dutch government and financed by Dutch Jews. Following the Nazi invasion of Holland, the camp was taken over and turned into a deportation camp, as Erich describes in his account. It was very convenient for the Nazis, since the camp was well-established and already contained several thousand German Jews. Dutch Jews (including Anne Frank) were housed there prior to being sent to extermination camps in Poland, along with some Roma.

Bergen Belsen was a concentration camp in Germany itself, in Lower Saxony, near the town of Bergen. It had been a prisoner-of-war camp but parts of it became a concentration camp in 1943. It was later expanded to accommodate prisoners from other camps. Erich's detailed description of the camp underscores the fact that it was not a death camp *at first*, even though so many prisoners died due to starvation, disease and total deprivation.

It was primarily an "exchange camp," where Jewish hostages were held with the idea of exchanging them for German prisoners of war or large sums of money, or because they held foreign passports, dual-statehood papers or "Palestine certificates." I am told that Carola's family had managed to escape from Germany to Switzerland before the war and that Erich and Carola had made every effort to do the same, but had been unsuccessful. It is possible that Erich and Carola ended up in Bergen Belsen rather than Auschwitz due to the possibility of her family paying a ransom for their release.

Erich and Carola were on their way by train to Theresienstadt when Bergen Belsen was liberated in April 1945 by British and Canadian troops. A British Army unit of combat and newsreel cameramen filmed the horrific scenes that awaited them, which mirror and complement Erich's descriptions of the last days of the camp. This footage was edited and partly assembled for a feature-length film by Sidney Bernstein, Stewart

McAllister, Peter Tanner, Colin Wills and Richard Crossman, with assistance from Alfred Hitchcock, in 1945; but the result was not shown until January 2015, 70 years after being shelved for reasons of German Occupation politics, and following a careful reconstruction by the Imperial War Museum of the rushes according to the original script. Interestingly, the title of the film is *German Concentration Camps Factual Survey*, not far off the spirit of Erich's title.

Erich and Carola were on the last transport out of Bergen Belsen, travelling up and down Germany as the Allies advanced, a journey of two weeks which Erich describes as an "endless hunger trek." They were finally liberated by the Russians at Tröbitz, a small town in Eastern Germany, now in Poland.

The account is written in a non-literary, factual, almost "wooden" style of German. One has very little sense of the author even though there are some interjections of anger, dismay and cynicism in between the facts and figures. However, what is most striking is that he never mentions his wife, who was with him throughout, in spite of mentioning other prisoners by name.

In the translation, I have tried to accurately reflect the tone of the piece but have taken the liberty of making a few changes, mainly to ensure consistency. Also, when unable to find an appropriate equivalent in English, I have retained the original German word (i.e., "Kommando").

I find the last line profoundly moving.

Emma Marx

———

Statistical Survey of Westerbork

From the beginning of 1942 until October 1944 100,000 Jews from Holland were "put on transport," as termed by the official language of the deportations. Of these 100,000 unfortunates only about 3,000 were sent to Bergen Belsen.

Of the 5,000 or so Jews who were sent to Theresienstadt, the majority went from there to the gas chambers of Auschwitz. Well over 90,000 Jews went directly to the death camps in the East. In total, over 100,000 Jews were sent on from Westerbork. Without taking the "transit camp" Westerbork into account, several "Transports" of mentally ill and sick Jews were sent to their deaths in Germany in December 1942 and further, in the Autumn of 1943, the remainder of the Jews in (concentration camp) Vught were deported to the East.

Only approximately 800 Jews remained in Westerbork at liberation, among them about 100 people, who were keeping the camp going, the rest were Jewish "convicts," who had been arrested in the final months before liberation and who it was no longer possible to deport due to the advance of the Allied troops.

Bergen Belsen

About 3,000 Jews from Holland were sent to the "residential" camp of Bergen Belsen and of those about 1,000 died of the deprivations there.

About 600 people were sent from Bergen Belsen to other (better) camps like Biverach or "exchanged" (Palestine, Philipville).

The rest, about 1,400 Jews, survived and returned to Holland after Liberation.

Balance

In 1940 the Jewish population of Holland was approximately 120,000. Of those, only about 20,000 survived the Nazi Terror:

Approximately 15,000 "hidden" Jews
Approximately 1,400 Jews from Bergen Belsen
Approximately 600 Jews from Theresienstadt
Approximately 800 Jews from Westerbork
Approximately 1,000 from Auschwitz and other camps in the East

Also, a few hundred Jews from Holland went to Palestine and stayed there.

Over 100,000 Jews from Holland alone were murdered by the Nazis.

Camp Westerbork

Westerbork was originally a camp for Jews who had escaped from Germany and had hoped to find refuge in Holland. The original camp had some farm buildings as well as a number of shacks, which were designed as small houses and had small front gardens. After the German occupation of Holland, the character of these residential shacks changed significantly and formed part of the new "Reception" and "Transit" camp. In order to accommodate this, the Germans built a large number of new shacks, more than 25.

These so called "large barracks" were intended to accommodate huge masses of people, up to 1,000 per barrack. The design of each one was the same: at each end there were washrooms with toilets, in the middle there was a room, which was the hall and kitchen. On either side of the "kitchen" there were large dormitories, where one side was intended for men and the other side for women. In general, they were separated but in some cases men and women were put up together.

We slept in two or three level iron bunks, which had straw mattresses. During "quiet" times there were enough tables and benches set up in the room but when large Transports arrived, these had to be moved out. At that point, the dormitories were like warehouses filled to the brim with miserable people.

It was virtually impossible to keep the overfilled barracks clean. Also, the barracks were very damp and this was a huge problem. All of our clothes, shoes, food, etc., was ruined by the mould. Thanks to a strict regime of checks and quarantine we didn't suffer too much from vermin. The washrooms were large and sufficient, so that we were able to keep ourselves clean.

Also, Westerbork camp had a bathhouse with approximately 40 showers that we were allowed to use regularly. This bathhouse was one of the very few camp "comforts."

We also had spacious medical barracks, with trained doctors and staff at our disposal, so that medical care was provided.

If it hadn't been for our loss of freedom, the ongoing horrors and our fears for the future, our stay in the camp would have been bearable, especially in comparison to so many other camps.

Our official food rations consisted of a stew at lunchtime and a dark "coffee" in the morning and the evening. We also received a 300g piece of bread, 10g margarine and some jam and cheese every day. Anyone trying to live on this alone would have certainly slowly died of starvation. However, our special circumstances brought relief: first of all, we were able to receive food parcels and these were delivered to the camp in large numbers, from friends as well as strangers, both legally and illegally. Also, it was still possible to buy or "organise" supplementary food. There was even a canteen in the camp and later there was "camp money." Also, there was a food store, which received donations from outside the camp, where one could go for extra food. In general, one could say that in Westerbork, although the food was very basic and there wasn't much food, we didn't starve.

The camp was guarded by the Dutch *Marechaussee* (Royal Military Constabulary), and order inside the camp was organised by the "Jewish Administration." We rarely saw the SS and the "green police" (*Ordnungspolizei*, the Nazi police force with a green uniform) accompanied the Transports.

On average, there were always between 6,000 to 8,000 people in the camp, the highest number was 15,000. Due to the regular Transports, it was a constant coming and going.

On arrival at the camp, each person was registered and received a camp identity card. Luggage was seized and inspected by the SS and these gentlemen helped themselves to whatever they wanted. One was escorted to one of the large barracks and, as it was impossible to change barracks, everyone knew where you were. The Transport lists were compiled on the orders of the SS by means of a card file. The fact that this was done by Jews under SS pressure is one of the most tragic stories of Westerbork. The night before a Transport, the lists were delivered to the barracks and read out. Those were the worst times.

The Transports, each inmate's worst nightmare, were carried out with German efficiency. At first (1948), it was only about 500 to 800 people a week that had to face the journey into misery, later the number of unlucky people was increased to 2,000 or 3,000 per Transport per week. At the beginning, it was still sometimes possible to avoid the Transport in one way or another – the trains would leave, even if there were less people than had been ordered – but later, everyone on the Transport list would be on the train. There was also a "reserve" list in some cases, to ensure the correct number of people boarded the train.

Because we at Westerbork didn't know what our fate was in the East, but had a sense that something terrible awaited us there, each person tried to stay at Westerbork as long as possible. In spite of the hopeless circumstances, we were still on Dutch ground and could try to get used to life in the camp. In spite of their despair, those being deported to the East had an incredible attitude. They boarded the inhuman goods trains proudly and defiantly and the young ones even had the strength to sing.

For a very long time (due to the fact that it was a transit camp), our main occupation in the camp was limited to its upkeep and maintenance. Later, we were involved in industrial work, when the inmates did more of pretending to work. This industrial work involved, among other activities, taking apart cables that had been looted by the German occupiers in

Holland. This was done in order to deliver raw materials to the war effort. So old batteries were dismantled, silk backing paper was removed from old fabrics. There were also workshops in the camp: a cobbler, a tailor, carpentry, blacksmith, etc., so that all sorts of work could be done by the inmates.

At first, the SS commanders arranged for Jewish performers to put on plays, cabarets and musical evenings for them. We prisoners kept away from these "official" evenings, we had our own improvised presentations in the barracks.

To complete the picture, it must be mentioned that the SS commander even allowed a "camp warehouse" to be set up, where one could buy many things that were no longer available "outside" at a normal price. We were advised to buy these items and to take them with us to the East. On arrival in the East, though we weren't aware of this, all of these things were confiscated. In order to supply these Transports with goods, Jews were sent on shopping trips out of the camp. Thereby many a kind and helpful Dutch citizen unwittingly supplied these desirable goods to the Germans via Westerbork.

All of us who didn't have special "reserve" papers or who weren't involved in the running of the camp were deported to Auschwitz or other camps in the East (Poland).

Those who had been decorated soldiers in the war, as well as a number of Jews who were to be given "preferential treatment," were sent to Theresienstadt. In this group there were a number of artists, whose performances the SS commander had attended, as well as a small number of people, who had been chosen by the German authorities in Holland. Those Jews deported to Theresienstadt were usually bitterly disappointed: with very few exceptions, sooner or later they were all sent to the gas chambers of Auschwitz.

The so called "Exchange Camp" of Bergen Belsen was the eventual destination of those of us who had "exchange papers." These included Palestine certificates, South American and other foreign passports, and "dual statehood" papers (i.e., English-Dutch or American-Dutch). In addition, there were a number of Jews who were sent to Bergen Belsen because of their personal or commercial links to foreign countries, so that the Germans regarded them as useful "exchange" collateral. The "Diamond Group" was one of these groups of Jews. And finally, there were those of us whose racial origins were still being investigated, the so-called "Kallmeyer Jews."

During our free time, we were permitted to move around the camp freely. The camp was surrounded by a deep and wide ditch, which was filled with water. There was a high fence around it and behind the fence the guards patrolled the area. High observation towers and searchlights completed our prison.

The so-called "convict" prisoners ("*S-Fälle*") were treated much more harshly. These were primarily Jews, who had been captured while in hiding and they were housed in special barracks and were under heavy guard. We were forbidden to have any contact with them and their life in the barracks was much more restrictive. They laboured from morning till night, were badly abused and, apart from a very small number, they were all deported to the East.

On Transport to Bergen Belsen

In the middle of March 1944 I was put on Transport to Bergen Belsen, part of a group of 300 people. We had no idea of what awaited us there. There was the idea that we might be exchanged once we were there. Of those Jews who had gone ahead of us – about 2,000 – there had been no news. The stories that we heard unofficially were of course encouraging. But didn't we also know that in the East one "only" worked? Could one believe that "in spite of" Bergen Belsen being run by the SS, that it was a good camp, that one didn't have to labour, that one would live in stone houses, that the camp was healthy and in the countryside and most importantly: one would soon be exchanged.

Because we were not put into goods trains, like the Transports to the East, but were put into rundown but actual passenger trains, because the doors were not sealed and locked like in the Transports, we were cautiously optimistic, especially with the hope of freedom in the near future.

We were put in three carriages (escorted by about 20 men from the green police) which were coupled to various passenger and goods trains. The journey took a good two days. The first night we stopped at the goods station Löhne, the other night in Lehrte.

We received about 400g bread each for the journey, nothing else. There was plenty of food on board for us, but this was confiscated by the guards. We were extremely thirsty on the journey as there was virtually no water. The compartments were overcrowded, there was no chance of sleep, we were too agitated. We all had the very strong impression that the journey proceeded without any obstacles and none of the tracks were damaged. Apart from at Osnabrück and Hannover, there were very few signs of bomb damage. We encountered many other goods trains and passenger trains on the way and all the stations were, as far as we were concerned, far too busy with people. We had imagined a far worse scenario after four years of war. And it was a huge disappointment for us.

Exhausted, we arrived at Bergen station at noon on the third day. What we saw on our arrival filled us with horror: a number of SS men armed with bayoneted guns and a huge number of dogs were waiting for us. No wonder we feared the worst, as they shouted orders at us.

The trains were emptied quickly and with the exception of the smallest children and the sick, who were transported to the camp on carts, everyone else had to march to the camp, which was about 10km away, escorted by the SS and their bloodhounds. We were terrified as the SS screamed and cursed at the weakest of us, who could only manage the long journey with the greatest of effort.

And so we arrived at the camp.

Camp Bergen Belsen

The camp consisted of an enormous complex of buildings, which we were able to see throughout our 10km-long march. It was actually a military parade ground and, to a large extent, parts of it were used for the training of troops. Other parts were used to accommodate prisoners of war, mainly Russians.

The troops were put up in custom-made barracks and the prisoners-of-war were put up in partly old stone and partly wooden barracks. The remaining part of the camp was the concentration camp, where we were.

The first part of the camp that we saw, which is where we were admitted, and which was used to accommodate the SS, consisted of small, apparently very clean wooden barracks, with bedrooms and living rooms. One more gate and we arrived at the "Filth Prison Camp."

A triple barbed wire fence and high watchtowers surrounded the camp. On one side the camp bordered on woodland and the Camp Main Street was on the other side. Alongside the camp there were several other camps. At first, we couldn't see the full extent of the camp. On the Main Street side of the camp there were industrial barracks, kitchens and storerooms.

Initially, our group was put into quarantine, which consisted of two long barracks. These were narrow and cramped, and were stuffed with wooden bunk beds, which had straw mattresses. At that time it was still reasonably clean and the camp wasn't overcrowded. There were probably no more than 3,000 people in the various buildings. It was therefore relatively easy to keep the camp clean.

We only stayed in quarantine for a short time, as we needed to make way for a newly arrived Transport of camp convicts. However, we remained in the same barracks, stone barracks that had been used for quarantine as our group contained a few cases of polio and diphtheria. At that time, as can be seen by this, sanitary regulations were still in place.

So we were strictly separated from the rest of the camp for a month. For us, this was a fortunate turn of events, as we were spared abuse during this time. All we had to do was keep the accommodation clean. Although we were terrified to see and hear what went on in the rest of the camp. What still awaited us.

We all still had a small store of provisions, which we were able to take with us from Westerbork so at this time we did not go hungry. The camp rations then consisted of one litre soup at noon, cooked swede with potatoes and at that time some fat, day in day out the same food, plus "coffee" in the morning and the evening, which was an indefinable drink without milk or sugar. Three days a week there was at that time a thin pearl barley soup or something similar. And then we got a piece of bread of about 300g and twice a week some margarine and jam.

This was – for Bergen Belsen – paradise.

In the middle of April 1944 our quarantine period ended and we joined our fellow sufferers in Bergen Belsen. Along with many other terrible things this meant: work duties.

The Main Camp

The so-called "Main Camp" that we found ourselves in now consisted of three parts: the men's camp, the women's camp and the "hospital" camp. In total we were – as I said – about 3,000 people, inside 18 barracks, plus a large number of stone barracks, in which up to 800 people could be accommodated.

In contrast: at the end of our stay in Bergen Belsen there were only four barracks for the same number of people. Having had six large washrooms at the beginning, later there were only two, one of these was in the hospital area. So as was the case throughout, the screw was constantly slowly turning towards the unbearable.

Ever since the Nazis came to power, there had been a constant decline into utter misery and even greater suffering. If we think about the past today and what we went through, we cannot understand how a human being can be capable of surviving this depth of misery.

And this is bearing in mind that our group were the "fortunate" ones. We stayed together with our families, we wore our own clothes (even though they were rags) and not prison uniform. We even received post and parcels from time to time and were occasionally allowed to send a postcard (though scripted) to the "outside." But most of all: we were not gassed like the many, many other millions of our peers. Even in our worst moments we still had the hope that we would be "exchanged" and therefore be free.

We did actually witness a few very small exchange groups leave the camp and their joy that they had won this fantastic lottery, and this increased our sense of hope.

And then the time came when the invasion started and we began to wait for the liberators...

Daily Life in Our Camp

Whether it was winter or summer, we had to get up at 5 am. At 6 am – if we were lucky – after enjoying a black "coffee" – all able men and women (men aged 15-65 and women aged 15-60) went to "Labour Kommandos." At 6:30 am they began their march to work. At the end of this, at about 7:30 am, the "Sick Roll Call," which is described in a later section, began.

In the early days, the Labour Kommandos would return to the camp for lunch at 11:15, so that they could go back to work at about 12:30, but later they stayed at work over lunch and didn't return to camp until about 6:30.

With the exception of Sundays, when one "only" worked in the morning, the working day was 11 hours long. However, the fact that the Labour Kommandos shuffled back to camp at lunchtime on Sunday didn't mean that the rest of the day was free. The SS bruisers regularly found reasons to deprive us of this small amount of free time, as they would arrange punishment exercises, punishment roll calls or "general" roll calls on a Sunday afternoon, which would then last late into the evening.

Those not assigned to work had to attend a "Head Count Roll Call" at 9 am. Apart from the Labour Kommandos and those who were "sanctioned" sick, everyone in the camp had to attend this roll call. This roll call, held outdoors in all weathers, normally finished at about 11 am. In all cases, it went on until everything was "correct," which meant that the SS guards made constant deliberate or accidental mistakes in their counting, so that it often took many more hours, until we were allowed back into the barracks. A particular speciality was "punishment roll calls," where we had to stand all day, often at night too. These roll calls were a terrible torture for the many children, women and the weak. Countless numbers became ill and died from them.

Once the roll call was over, the prisoners were generally left in peace and to their own devices.

In order to imagine the scale of the roll call: of approximately 4,000 inmates in our camp, about 1,300 men and women were in Labour Kommandos. Then another 500 or so people were working inside the camp. There were also about 800 small children in the camp, so that about 1,400 adults were not at work. In the "hospital" area there were about 500 people so that on average, 2,000 people had to endure the outdoor roll call.

And what was in force for our group was far worse for the other groups in the camp.

The age range of our group was very unfortunate, few young people, many old people. This situation would result in many sacrifices for us. The more we succumbed to illness and scourges, the less labourers we had. This sad picture is illustrated by an inventory that I still have, which portrays those fit for work and those unfit for work on 20 January 1945:

Roll Call:

20 January 1945	Men	Women	Children	Total
Sick Barracks	158	78	15	249
Invalids' Barracks	35	50		85
Other Invalids	85	150		235
Elderly Barracks	120	128		248
Medical Register	29	1		30
Mobile Sick	277	403	151	831
Pregnant Women		12		12
Mothers with Children Under 3			552	552
Diamond Group Asscher	10	14		24
Total	714	902	718	2,334

Note: 2,334 not fit for work out of a total of barely 3,000 in our group at that time.

(Editors' Note: The addition is incorrect in the original.)

In March 1945 exhaustion and illness had developed to such a degree that there were barely 100 healthy men who were fit for work in our camp.

Camp Life

As mentioned before, once we were out of quarantine, we were at the "Main" camp, which consisted of three separate parts.

The Sick camp with the Infectious barracks, a total of five blocks, was separated from the rest of the camp by barbed wire. On particular days and times, we were allowed to visit the sick. The nurses as well as the doctors were from our group and they provided superhuman care under the circumstances. The lack of medicine often made it impossible to provide any help.

In another part of the camp, also surrounded by a barbed wire fence, was the Women's camp. And finally, we men were housed in the Men's camp.

At the end of the Head Count Roll Call, up to 8 pm, men and women were allowed to visit each other. Those who were working were allowed to visit at lunchtime, if the short break allowed it, and in the evenings after work they could be with their wives and children. But in this short time one also had to wash oneself, put one's things in order and also perform other necessary things. At 9 pm we had to be in our "beds," in summer and in winter.

So the "free" time we had was not a relaxing or quiet time, we were constantly under pressure. But we weren't supposed to rest.

Due to the constant stream of prisoners we became more and more tightly squeezed together. In the summer of 1944 the fence between the Men's and Women's camp came down, because the barracks were needed for other prisoners and eventually our group of 3,000, almost all sick, were packed together into the remaining four barracks.

The wooden, three-level beds were very close together. In each of these cribs, which were about 80cm wide and 180cm long, two of us had to sleep top to tail. One infecting the other.

Life in the barracks had become unbearable for all of us, we were all overanxious and oversensitive. Whoever was engaged in a relatively bearable Kommando was happy to at least escape this misery during the day. Lack of activity was our worst punishment.

So it was perceived as a dreadful measure, when at the beginning of 1945 all of our Labour Kommandos (apart from about 50 men) were dissolved and taken over by women and men from the concentration camp. It therefore became impossible for us to "organise" any food rations to supplement the totally inadequate camp diet. The death toll and misery rose day by day. If Liberation had not come, none of us would have survived another summer. Also, without labour we had to get up at 5 am as before. If we didn't voluntarily crawl out of our cribs, then the SS beat us. And so followed another day of hunger and doing nothing.

Up to the end of 1944 we had a Jewish Camp Leadership. It was responsible for keeping order in the camp, as opposed to the SS. These fellow prisoners, who were guided by the Camp Elders, worked from morning till night to lighten our load and to offer whatever help they possibly could and for this they deserve the highest praise. In the atmosphere of high anxiety that affected us all, they constantly had to deal with difficult questions. We cannot thank them enough for what they sacrificed for us.

In this area the inconsiderate camp commander also interfered: at the end of December 1944, after driving away our own leaders, we were given a new camp elder from the concentration camp, who was a professional criminal, Fritz Hanke, who was to rule over us from then on with the help of his *Kapos*. How those "foremen," *Kapos*, beat us. It is unbelievable that convicts would degrade themselves and abuse other prisoners in this way, becoming willing tools of the sadistic SS.

The Composition of the Camp

Apart from the Transports that arrived from Westerbork, about 3,000 people from Holland, there were a variety of other groups in our camp.

First of all, there were the Greeks, the oldest prisoners, about 80 in number, the only remaining Jews deported from Greece. All the others were gassed in Auschwitz. Then Italians, who were shlepped from North Africa to Bergen Belsen, about 300 people, including many children. Further, a few hundred French women, who were the wives of French Jewish prisoners of war, who were also the exception as they were sent to Bergen Belsen and not Auschwitz. Finally a larger group of Yugoslavians and Albanians, about 500 men, women and children. There were also a few Belgians among us and even one family from Berlin.

The North African group was lucky; they were exchanged relatively quickly. They were all families with English or American papers. But how they and their many children froze during their stay at Bergen Belsen. But how they sabotaged all of the SS rules. They weren't frightened by the punishments and in order to avoid working they always had many new tricks.

Our group of about 4,000 people was only a small part of the prison population of Bergen Belsen. Apart from our "Main Camp," there was also a camp called "Schneebaum," the name of its camp elder, which was set up in the spring of 1944. It housed about 600 Jews from Poland, most of them had English or American papers, some also had Palestine Exchange certificates.

And in March 1944 the first Transports from German concentration camps began to arrive, with prisoners requiring "convalescence," who were all non-Jews, mainly from the work camps of Dora, Neuengamme, etc. The mortality rate of this group was terrible from the start. Every day 10 or 15 or more of these poor inmates died. Every month the barracks vacated by death were refilled with more "convalescent" wrecks. The term "convalescent prisoner" was the official description that had to be used in communication with the SS and the authorities in Berlin. Bergen Belsen therefore officially became a "convalescent" camp.

For a long time the capacity of the camp was about 6,000 prisoners. Among the prisoners all the European states were represented. Many Russians and Poles, but also many Germans and *Volksdeutsche* (ethnic Germans). Alongside the political prisoners there were – primarily among the German prisoners – many professional criminals.

In the summer of 1944 and then from the autumn of 1944 onwards more and more masses of prisoners came to Bergen Belsen. Now there were also Jews among these concentration camp prisoners and soon more came from the various work camps. From Hungary no less than 6,000 Jews arrived, of which a group of about 1,000 were exchanged and sent to neutral countries abroad. The remaining Hungarians were kept in a separate part of the camp. And finally there was a small group of *Mischlinge,* 100 Slovaks who were the issue of mixed marriages, who were brought to the camp.

At the end of 1944 the stream into Bergen Belsen was so heavy that in the Men's camp alone, there were over 20,000 people crammed in together. And in the month of March 1945 nearly 15,000 – *fifteen thousand* – of the total of about 27,000 male prisoners died of exhaustion.

The first female prisoners came to Bergen Belsen from the East in August 1944. Their numbers kept on increasing. By March 1945 there were more than 30,000 women from concentration camps in Bergen

Belsen. It was notable that the mortality rate of the female prisoners was lower than that of the male prisoners. Still, in the month of March 1945, over 2,000 of these women died.

In order to put up these outrageous masses of unfortunate prisoners, in the summer of 1944 25 old barracks were brought to Bergen Belsen from a dissolved concentration camp (Stutthof) in the East and set up. In addition, a "tent" camp was set up. In the October storms a number of these tents collapsed and many women were killed or severely injured in the wreckage. After this disaster, which can be attributed to the thoughtlessness of the camp leadership, the tent camp was declared "uninhabitable" and the poor prisoners were stuffed into the overcrowded barracks. In the middle of January 1945, part of the camp that had been previously occupied by Russian prisoners of war became free and was taken over by the *Wehrmacht* (army) and SS. But even this measure didn't make any difference to the lack of space. In one barracks, which would normally barely accommodate 100 people, up to 1,000 people were crammed together, in order to perish miserably.

Whereas in March 1945 there were, on average, no less than 600 – a horrifying number – of daily deaths, in the month of April and up until Liberation this terrible number increased. Bergen Belsen had become a death camp.

There were thousands and tens of thousands of corpses piled up, it being impossible to bury or burn the bodies. Words cannot describe the environment in which we had to live. Our days were numbered and if the liberators hadn't come, the last prisoners would have all starved to death within a few days.

Many thousands died of their suffering after liberation. The most wretched ones could not be saved.

Due to my work as a clerk, I had an insight into this terrible situation. Whatever I could do in my weakened state, it was never enough, what was the point of stealing 30 or 50 litres of soup from the kitchen and smuggling it into the camp. Not a drop of comfort, and yet it saved one or two from starvation. I saw all incoming and outgoing Transports, I had to "log" the daily death lists and to put together the "statistics" for Berlin. I could move between the different parts of the camp and keep family members in touch with each other, as well as being able to pocket some food here and there, in so far as there was any food to be found. The fact that these activities were strictly forbidden and that I would have been severely punished for them goes without saying. We all tried our hardest to deceive the SS guards. How I managed to do this for weeks and months seems like a miracle to me even now.

The horrific conditions of the concentration camp cannot be described. And if I did try to describe them, one wouldn't believe they were true. "German Culture." For certain all prisoners were starved. The pathetic lunchtime soup – ¾ litre swede water – was distributed to the camp at the most impossible times of day: sometimes at 6 am, sometimes at 7pm. And then the little piece of bread – dry of course – and in the last weeks before liberation there was no bread at all. Who could survive this.

And then the vermin: fleas and bugs didn't bother us anymore, they were the "friendly" pets. But the lice … how our bodies must have looked.

Stealing food was punishable by death. If a starving prisoner desperately took one swede from the pile in the kitchen, he risked his life. The guards on the street or on the towers had no mercy. Because Kommandant Kramer had ordered: whoever is found on the High Street without permission is to be shot. So some of us unfortunates crawled under the fence, ran to the pile of swedes, if they were spotted, they would be shot down. This is how, every day, many starving people were "killed trying to escape," as was "officially" reported. How many of these unlucky ones did I see myself, lying shot on the ground.

And another image haunts me: the prisoners who died in the barracks were dragged, naked, with a rope around their feet, across the ground to the huge pile of dead bodies. One after the other in endless succession. It couldn't be any more inhumane.

If the fate of our group was unbearable, vegetating in misery and filth, the fate of the concentration camp prisoners was a thousand times worse. If 300 people in our group died in the last month (March 1945), which was about 12% of the camp population, in the concentration camp about 15,000 men, about 60%, were murdered through starvation in March 1945. And with regard to these figures, that he was very familiar with, Kramer dared to say, when confronted: I am not guilty.

If our roll calls were torture, the concentration camp prisoners' were far worse. Their roll call, starting at 5 am in snow, wind and cold, was never ending. Whoever couldn't stand up, fell down and stayed lying in the shit. Many died every day in this way during the roll call.

The short path from our barracks to the High Street passed the blocks of the concentration camp. There were dead bodies piled up in front of and in between the barracks, naked and partly decomposed. And in between, catatonic, without the will to live, like caged animals, the "living." The fact that they were reduced to "cannibalism" by these terrible conditions, that is, they ripped flesh from dead prisoners and ate it, who could be surprised? The lunatics tore off liver and other parts and ate them raw. Of course there was "honest outrage" from the vehicles of civilisation: if they caught some poor person, he paid for it with his life.

How could "human beings" and that was what the gentlemen of the SS claimed to be, watch these horrors.

As I mentioned earlier, the crematorium hadn't been able to deal with the masses of dead for a long time. That's why the corpses were piled up outside and burned in a wooden pyre. There was a *Stampfkommando* (literally, a stomping Kommando), that was its official name, which consisted of 20 men whose job it was to ensure that the burnt remains were reduced to bones. But even with this method, it was impossible to keep up with the quantities of dead. Many thousands of dead remained in piles in the camps.

It is therefore not surprising, that the American troops, who arrived on the 12 April 1945 to liberate the camp, couldn't not grasp the terrible situation and that there was an international outcry of indignation. The conditions in Bergen Belsen and the other German concentration camps gave the world a fright. That it was possible to create these death colonies in such a way and on such a scale, until then, one did not want to believe it and did not want to conceive of it. May the world ensure that such human torture never and never happens again. That would be the only thing that could be done to redress what happened. The millions of innocent murder victims, they cannot be brought back to life. And the many thousands who survived the hell of the German concentration camps, they will be marked for life with the stamp of suffering.

Hygiene Conditions of the Camp

As I have explained above, at the beginning of our stay there were sufficient washing and toilet facilities at our disposal, which was a situation that eventually changed with the ever-increasing number of prisoners and became unbearable. In the early days, before the huge Transports from the other camps arrived, we were also permitted to wash in a special bathroom once a week. We showered there, about four men under each shower, an unusual treat for us. Of course even bathing was done under the strict supervision of the SS. For us men, this wasn't anything unusual. But that these "gentlemen" also had to watch while the women showered, was very embarrassing for the women. What did I say? "German culture."

While we could keep clean by washing and bathing, while the barracks were not unbearably overcrowded, we could avoid vermin and epidemics. At that time the state of health of the camp was normal, even though we became more and more emaciated due to the starvation diet. As soon as the washrooms were withdrawn and we were no longer able to wash, at that moment we also had to sleep two to a bed, it was then that people began to die en masse.

One cannot imagine the hygienic conditions during the winter of 1944/45. The toilets in the barracks were unusable, frozen and bursting. In the only washroom we had left, the taps were frozen or the room was flooded with water from the burst pipes. There was excrement and urine. A stink – unbearable. We tried but there was no chance of keeping oneself clean and therefore healthy.

Conditions in the concentration camp were even more outrageous, at least we tried to keep some sort of order with the pathetic resources we had left. Over there, people didn't care anymore. And on top of all the terrible conditions, it must be said that almost everyone in the camp suffered from severe diarrhoea, which was the consequence of the swede diet. One must bear in mind that the watery diet forced everyone to step out every couple of hours or more frequently and then one can imagine the "nightlife" in the overcrowded barracks. Who could rest and sleep like this.

As a result of the nightly air strikes, we were strictly forbidden to put any lights on in the barracks, from dusk till the next morning, not even a pocket torch. The smallest infringement of this rule was punished with severe beatings.

All of these memories are like a nightmare. And if one had to bear all of this on one's own, it would have been impossible. How a human being can cope with suffering when with others.

The barracks housing the sick and the invalids could only accommodate a fraction of the sick. Death records were broken every day. Doctors and nurses gave whatever help they could, but it was of no use without medicine. The drugs supplied by the SS pharmacy were totally insufficient and the drugs sent to the camp by the Red Cross were stolen by the SS bruisers and used for themselves. And thousands of these infected and deathly-ill prisoners were put on transports just days before Liberation. Some were sent to labour and others to the gas chambers.

There is a frightening illustration of how the SS abused the sick from the very beginning: the Sick roll call. The Sick roll call was the terrifying legacy of *Usha* (abbreviation of *Unterscharführer*, a paramilitary rank of the Nazi party) Fritz Rauh, the leader of the "Labour Service." Isn't it ironic, that the worst torturer of human beings had to have the name "Rauh" (rough or crude). This Rauh was the murderer of countless prisoners. For example, at the 6 am morning roll call, all those who were unfit for work due to illness had to turn up and report to him. Those who had a temperature of less than 39° were forbidden to turn up at the Sick roll call and had to go to work. Those who had a temperature higher than 39° were allowed to report themselves as sick. And these poor people were the daily sacrifices. They were forced to stand up – in all weathers – for this roll call at 6 am. In the summer and the winter. Their names were entered into the "Sick Register" and then they had to wait: wait until all the Labour Kommandos had shuffled off, to wait until "Mr" Rauh had "time." Waiting and standing. For one or two hours. Then their names were called from the "Sick Register," in which Rauh had written malicious comments, and then the patient had to go for an examination by the SS medical orderly. Woe betide him, if his temperature didn't tally.

Countless prisoners became seriously ill as a result of these sick roll calls: premeditated murder. But it was strictly forbidden to register as sick during the day.

News Service

In spite of all of the many rules and restrictions we were not unaware of the events of the war. We thirsted for news, which would give us hope. I myself managed to bring daily news into our camp for many months. I managed to listen to the radio that was in the guards' room, primarily the army news, which was transmitted at dictation speed. Moreover, I managed to secrete a newspaper from the SS guards almost every day, which would be lying around somewhere. Finally, I also managed to sneak into the SS toilets, where I could ferret away a newspaper from time to time.

And then there were other reports from the Labour Kommandos who were responsible for cleaning the SS barracks and who didn't miss any opportunity to get hold of genuine news reports. Those Kommandos who worked at the train station also brought many valuable news reports.

Of course, no one in the camp must ever know who the bearer of news was. The punishment would have been death. So I let my fellow inmates tell me the latest news, which I had just smuggled into the camp, and to which I listened with great interest. And they were always amazed at how badly informed I was.

And still there were wild rumours which circulated: the advance of the Allied troops seemed far too slow to us. The fact that we were regularly made aware of the developments of the war was a source of great moral support for us. This information gave us renewed hope and strength.

Activity

The prisoners who were fit for work were either put to work doing things that were to do with the management of the camp or so-called "war-related" activities.

As I have already explained, the working day in a Kommando was 11 hours long. In general, it was more "occupying one's time" rather than serious work. There was, however, a range of very heavy duties. The "large" Kommandos, in which many hundreds were employed, were in essence devised to be a means of inflicting sadistic torture. What other conclusion could one draw from, for example, a large Kommando whose sole task was to move sand from one area to another and then back?

The Kommandos that were connected to the management of the camp were of course the most desirable. One could organise various things for the stomach. So it came about that the most sought after Kommandos were often the most strenuous ones, for example, working in the kitchen, which was very tiring, or the filthy and heavy duty Coal Kommando, that served the kitchen and provided "extra" food. And whoever got to work in the "grocery store," the grocery distribution centre, had won the biggest prize in the lottery of "extras."

In total there were no less than 80 different Labour Kommandos. The physically most demanding ones were the Road Building, Forest, Transport and Train Station Kommandos. And it was those that got the worst beatings from the SS. Other Kommandos that were purely for bullying, were the Barrack Construction and *Holzhof* (wood yard) Kommandos. How those working here – mainly the elderly and weak – were abused and beaten. The SS guards who supervised the work were always armed with sticks and bats.

The beatings were without reason, purely voluntary and the keen workers got even more angry beatings than those of us who kept out of sight. The weaker one was, the more one was abused. And the beating of prisoners was actually "officially" forbidden.

Worst of all was the *Stubenkommando*, those who had to dig up the remains of trees in the forest and remove them. Not a day went by without casualties and we were always especially fearful when we saw this Kommando returning. How many young people were beaten here.

When I think back to these Kommandos and all of the tortures that were involved, I must just briefly talk about the so-called "large" Kommandos. There was firstly the Shoe Kommando, in which many hundreds of men and women were occupied with dismantling. There were huge quantities of old footwear and old clothes that had been collected by the Hitler Youth in Germany and these old materials were sorted and dismantled in the camp. As it wasn't possible to move all of these materials out by train, they were simply piled into a huge mountain in the camp and everything was just left there – until Liberation. A magnificent result for all of the collections that had been driven by so much propaganda. There was one advantage of this though: we prisoners could at least organise repair materials for ourselves.

Hundreds of men and women sat in their Kommandos for 11 hours a day, one would work as little as possible, so as not to further the Germans' interests. The way it was in these large Kommandos, the similar ones, the Spinning, Braiding and Weaving Kommandos were just the same.

Naturally, all labour results and outcomes were bureaucratically logged. The camp was reimbursed for its "industrial outcomes" by Berlin. And to save face I only submitted a fraction of the actual occupations in my reports to the *Reichswirtschaftsversorgungshauptamt* (head office of industrial affairs of the realm). The real daily average result of an 11-hour day per person was never more than four Pfennig. This is clearly the result of our sabotage, which occured in spite of all the abuse from the SS guards. The officially stated outcomes were put down as a daily rate of four Reichsmarks and this amount was actually implemented by the top authorities. I myself always took particular pleasure in writing out these "calculations" in my job as assistant clerk to the head of Labour activities.

In the "Spinning" Kommandos mentioned above, silk worm cocoons were taken apart and the Weaving and Braiding ones were for making straps out of waste materials. But as I have already mentioned, it went no further than separating and putting together and the results staying lying in the camp and were ruined by the weather. And these pointless jobs were kept going until the end.

In these Kommandos the SS also came up with all sorts of abuses. There was a lot of beating and kicking. One particular sadistic rule was the "toilet rota," which forbade anyone to use the toilet before 9 am. And from 9 am onwards, small groups were permitted to go at half-hour intervals. With our watery diet, this caused us indescribable torment and suffering.

Punishments

When describing the punishments we were subjected to, I am talking about the official rules that were in place and carried out on the order of the head of the camp. I am omitting the daily torture by the individual SS men.

It was especially common to punish us who were starving with the withdrawal of food. These punishments were generally collective, and even children and the sick were not exempt. Withdrawal of bread or soup for days was the equivalent of murder.

Though only some groups of people were punished with the withdrawal of food, they had to stand at the fence during mealtimes and in the evening, "as punishment." This was to ensure other prisoners didn't give them any food.

The next level of punishment was "bunker." The bunkers were small stone cells, with a stone floor, no light and no windows, they had a wooden stand without a straw mattress. Depending on the punishment, the prisoner was permitted one blanket, or nothing. The diet was water and a piece of dry bread – 300g per day – and a bowl of soup every fourth day. The prisoners remained in the cells continuously and some bunker punishments lasted a month or more. And for nothing. Very few survived these punishments.

There were also punishment beatings, 25 strokes with a wooden stick on the behind. The one being punished even had to count the strokes themselves. These strokes were delivered with such rage that the sticks broke.

And then there was another form of punishment for our "exchange" group, to be sent to a concentration camp, i.e., the loss of our "exchange privileges," as it was officially called, in reality it was a death sentence.

This is how, as a result of the "theft" of a crate of potatoes, two friends (Pick and Mayer) were sent away from our camp in the summer of 1944 to into concentration camp Neuengamme. And the wives and children of these men, even though totally innocent, were sent to Auschwitz. Obviously, we never heard from these poor unfortunates again.

As a result of "theft" from the camp kitchen a woman (Spijer) was deported to Auschwitz as punishment. Even though this woman was acting under extreme duress, to try and get something for her seriously ill husband. Mercy? An unknown word for our jailers.

Two boys from our group, barely 18 years old, were put to work in the crematorium. These two boys were not allowed to have any contact with us from then on. We were not to find out what was going on in the crematorium. So they were put up in a small hut outside of our camp. And they stayed in this hut, even after a large group of convicts took over their work. They were not allowed to leave the hut and worked there as overseers until one day in December 1944 the order came that these two witnesses of German inhumanity were to be transferred to Neuengamme. Their death ensured their silence.

The Fate of the Diamond People

The Diamond group among us exchange prisoners had a particularly tragic fate. It was especially tragic, because for a long time they had preferential treatment due to various promises that had been made by the German authorities. This group was mainly composed of diamond workers from Amsterdam, that is to say, professionals, and there were very few like them in the world. For a long time, they were released from any sort of labour in the camp, and the plan was, to put them to work as specialists in the diamond industry in Offenbach. For this reason, their delicate hands had to be protected.

At the end of November 1944 these men – 121 of them – were sent to the concentration camp Oranienburg and gassed there. A small number avoided this fate and were sent to work camps, they later returned to Bergen Belsen, skeletons condemned to death. The 104 wives and children of these poor people were put in the concentration camp part of Bergen Belsen and a few days later, they were put on Transport to Auschwitz. I only know of one person – Willi Bär – who managed to survive to the end of the war and who returned to Holland. The only people spared this fate were the 24 members of the Asscher family, who were in the original Diamond group.

A White Raven

Up to this point I have talked about so many terrible and almost unimaginable things so that I now want to report the only exception to the rule that I know about.

The one exception among the SS men, who were all trying to outdo each other with horrible abuses, was the head of the "grocery store," Uscha

Müller. Hundreds of prisoners owe their lives to him. Unbeknownst to the camp authorities, he cheered us up by tasking two women, day in and day out, with the production of sandwiches for the prisoners who were able to come into the store for some reason. He was also the one who managed to provide large quantities of food to the camp elders, who could then distribute these to the neediest. Naturally he couldn't alter the fate of the masses.

Müller himself died of typhoid before liberation. He is for certain the only person we remember without feeling hate, as he was the only human being among the savages.

The Burial

When dealing with the dead, there was a marked difference (for that mentality) in the way the SS behaved. The dead from the concentration camp were all piled up (naked) and then thrown into carts, which were then pushed to the crematorium by prisoners. There the corpses were thrown into heaps and later burned.

The dead in our camp were placed on benches in a specially reserved area of our washroom. Every morning the prisoner in charge of driving the cart arrived to ask how many dead there were. Then he came back with his cart and brought the required number of crates. The dead were rolled into their blankets and put into these crates. As there was a limited number of crates available, later on the dead had to share a crate between two.

Then our dead were transported through the camp to the crematorium and we were allowed to accompany the cart up to the border of our camp. Once they arrived at the crematorium, the "special treatment" was at an end. The crates were tipped over and the bodies spilled out onto an enormous heap. The empty crates then returned to the camp the next day for the same purpose. However, the blankets were disinfected and returned to the camp.

Religious Services

Whereas we were permitted to have religious services at Westerbork, where we were given specially allocated space for this, in Bergen Belsen it was strictly forbidden. The rabbis who came to the camp with us, were persecuted in a particularly hateful way by the SS. They had to do the worst jobs – i.e., to clean the latrines, etc. The efforts made by the Jewish camp elders to employ them as teachers and educators or other social activities were in vain.

None of these carers of the soul survived Bergen Belsen.

Air Strikes

Day and night we saw and heard thousands of English and American planes fly over our camp on their way to the largest cities of central Germany and Berlin. But the only serious attack on our camp came at Whitsun 1944. Unexpectedly, about a dozen "mosquitoes" swooped over the barracks and fired at them at low flight. One industrial barracks was set on fire and some of our camp inmates were killed and wounded. The planes circled the camp several times and fired on each circuit. While we had very few casualties, the concentration camp had many. Their prisoners were standing at roll call and they must have come to the attention of the pilots, who were under the impression that these were military people. The prisoners were mown down by the gunfire.

In early 1945 there were more attacks, mainly at night, but these were only on the buildings occupied by the SS. They became more and more nervous; they were only heroes with regard to the powerless. And they were absolutely terrified of the English and American planes.

Camp Guards

The camp was guarded by a company of SS *Totenkopf* ("death's head") soldiers. At first this consisted of 120 men, later 300 men. There were also about 33 SS female supervisors and a so-called staff command of about 50 SS men in the camp. There were a large number of specially trained dogs to support the guards.

Supervision was done from the watchtowers that circled the camp. The towers were equipped with machine guns and at night the floodlights lit up the camp. There were also guards posted on the High Street and along the barracks at night. We normally didn't come into contact with the guards in the Street or on the towers. Of course we avoided anything that would put us in the line of fire. Even so, prisoners were shot from the towers. I remember in April 1944, when one of our group was shot on the way to the toilet.

The labour Kommandos always had extra guards, who were mainly responsible for maltreatment. There was a whole group of such escorts, who one could not fear enough. And then the SS head of the Kommando.

I have strong memories of, among others, the devil in human form, "red" Müller, who has innumerable prisoners on his conscience, and of the terrible beaters Wernicke and Hamer, of the sadist Herzog from the Shoe Kommando, Fritz Gaus and Heinz Reddehaase, of Chris the violent head of the kitchen, and last but not least Lübben the devourer of Jews and Trenkle, the head of the "dirt camp," always drunk and always ready for abuse and I mustn't forget the inhuman head of Labour Fritz Rauh. And then the monster Kramer, the head of the camp, who permitted and encouraged all of these terrible things. These few names personify the "hell of Bergen Belsen."

We were ruled by the dregs of mankind.

Outgoing Transports

A whole series of "supplementary labour" Transports left our camp, destined for other camps. In particular, in the last months of 1945 huge masses of people were needed for various types of labour. These Transports were assembled and "executed" without any consideration of the physical condition of the prisoners. Even though it was clear to everyone that these human wrecks were not fit for any type of work.

I remember one Transport of 2,000 prisoners, who were sent to work in Pöhlitz near Stettin as late as March 1945. This Transport was to be examined by the notorious camp doctor Klein, to assess their fitness for work. The speed and thoroughness of his examination had the following result:

On the way to Belsen station 20 "fit" men died and on arrival at Pöhlitz, the commander there refused to take charge of the Transport, because none of the men were fit for work. So the Transport was sent back to Bergen Belsen, on the same train. And the result: more than 600 dead had to be removed from the wagons on arrival at Bergen Belsen.

Mass murder.

The Destruction of the Camp Management Documents

As the Allied troops approached, our situation became more and more hopeless. Preparations were made to kill us off, the surviving witnesses to the terror. It was of course the plan, to destroy everything and everyone who could bear witness to the Nazi horror. So in order to prepare for "liquidation," on Saturday the 7th of April, the order was given to firstly burn all written papers, card files and documents. All paperwork was piled up and brought to the bonfire and destroyed. All evidence was burned so that no one could determine who was killed in the camp. So tens of thousands of relatives would never be able to find out for certain, when and where their loved ones were murdered.

Together with my colleague, I had to take all of the files from the Labour office to the crematorium. I managed to steal two documents and secrete them on my person, they were signed by the head of the camp Kramer and testified to the numbers of people present in the camp in the month of March 1945 and the number of deaths. I stuffed them both into my mattress and managed to take them back to Holland with me. To my knowledge, they are the only official documents that were not destroyed.

As I write this, they are in the file of the prosecutor in Lüneburg, silent witness to the thousands that were murdered. This is the overview of the numbers of male prisoners in Bergen Belsen on 31 March 1945: of the total 21,688 men imprisoned, no less than 8335 died in the two-week period 15-31 March 145. Note: signed by "Head of Camp Kramer." And of the 32,204 female prisoners in the camp at the same time, the other rescued document shows that 1,223 women died of exhaustion.

And Kramer, when confronted with these numbers, dared to say, not guilty.

Our Group Is Put on Transport

A few days before the liberation of the camp by the Allied troops, on Saturday 7 April 1945, the order came, that all "exchange prisoners" were to be put on Transport to Theresienstadt. We had prepared ourselves for many things, but hadn't prepared for onward Transport, which meant certain death. One can't imagine our anxiety and upset. Today we know that the satanic plan was indeed to take us all to the gas chambers. We left Bergen Belsen on three Transports containing about 2500 people. I myself was on the last Transport on Sunday 8 April.

On Transport to Theresienstadt

Without exception, we were all so weak that we were not in a fit state to walk back to Bergen station. Lorries took us to the trains. Only a few very severely ill people were left in Bergen Belsen.

Our train consisted of 50 goods wagons, horrifically filthy and lousy, they had brought the last Transport of prisoners to the camp the day before and we had no opportunity to clean the wagons. Our escorts were about 30 old navy soldiers and no SS, apart from one man who was the leader. At first we had no idea where we were actually going. First we went to Standal via Soltau and then back to Lüneburg and from there over the Elbe to Lauenburg. The advancing Americans were always nearby. In Soltau the train station was bombed right after we left. We went on to Wittenberg and from there to Berlin and then southwards. We went back and forth like this for 14 days, until our mad journey ended not far from Dresden.

Our train was constantly under attack by air strikes, but luckily there were not many casualties. Those hours and days were full of fear. We had a very limited supply of food with us: per head 1200g bread, a piece of sausage and a bit of margarine. Nothing else. Not even enough for two days. So this journey with all of its terrors became an endless hunger trek. What use was it, if one could rustle up a few potatoes or a bit of bread from time to time, with the help of the escorts. Every day the despair of us 2,500 sick and worn out people increased. The memory of this journey is one of the worst of the years of captivity. More and more of our dead had to be buried when the trains stopped.

We had given up all hope when, early in the morning on 23 April 1945 we were liberated by Russian troops near Trobitz, a little village in Lower Lusatia. Our joy and happiness cannot be described. The Russians looked after us as well as they could, they quickly organised hospitals for us and gave us as much help as possible. There was only one thing we couldn't do which was strictly forbidden to us: we couldn't have any contact with the "West," the English and Americans who were posted only a few kilometres away. And it was only after huge efforts and more or less a coincidence that we were discovered by the "West" and after longwinded negotiations between the Russians and the English we were transported out of the East.

In the middle of May, I also succumbed to the treacherous typhus, which caused me to be bedridden until now. The horrors and deprivations I had suffered left my body so weak, that it was only thanks to the most consistent care that I recovered.

On 23 June 1945 a French ambulance brought me to Leipzig and after three-days' stay in a hospital there I finally returned to Dutch ground via American ambulance.

I was severely ill but I was free. As a free man I was full of hope for the future.

Roermond, September / October 1945

Translated, from the German, by Emma Marx.

Emma Marx was born in 1964 and grew up in Germany, Holland, the United States and England. She attended Wadham College, Oxford, where she took a degree in Modern Languages. She still lives in Britain, where she continues to practice psychotherapy. Her first essay was published in "Sexuality" (Irish Pages: *Vol 6, No 2*).

A TRIAL
(1946)

Hubert Butler

Witness to the past – and the future.

The trial of General Kvaternik and five other Quisling ministers of Croatia and of Siegfried Kasche, German ambassador to the Independent State, which has just concluded in Zagreb was of the highest importance, yet, as it happened at the same time as the Zagreb fair, it excited relatively little interest.

Croatia was for a long time the most satisfactory of the Nazi puppet states. It had a ready-made Quisling government which had only to be recalled from abroad and that government had a small and noisy following at home. The Ustashi were able to organize a constant and almost convincing parade of enthusiasm for the "liberator" and yet they could never become formidable enough to interfere with his plans. Kasche, as German ambassador, had the delicate task of exploiting the Croatian people through their government for German ends. There is evidence that he did it rather well, and in the dock he gave an appearance of resourcefulness and conviction, which was not shown by the other defendants. The trial was conducted on lines that seemed to touch the destiny of the prisoners at a tangent only because it was the manifest purpose of the judges not to prove the guilt of the defendants, which was obvious, but to show that they had the collaboration of the Peasant Party and its leader, Dr. Machek. The Peasant Party is the most serious rival to communism in Croatia, and its leaders, like the leaders of so many other parties in Europe, appear to have behaved in a feeble, subservient way towards the Nazis, before and after the German invasion. So complete was the preoccupation of the court with Dr. Machek, that often the Croatian defendants seem to have persuaded themselves that if they, too, made eager little sallies at Dr. Machek, their own vile crimes might be forgotten. They seldom rejected any of the invitations to vilify Dr. Machek that came to them from the bench. Not so Siegfried Kasche – this horrible man grew in stature as the trial proceeded. No doubt he knew that he would not save his life by being obliging. He refused to be distracted from his purpose. His defence was that all he had done was in loyalty to the German people and its leaders. The internal affairs of the Croat people, except in so far as they affected Germany, had been no concern of his. He had not had any intrigues with any of the Croat politicians mentioned. He had sufficient control to keep the sneer out of his voice.

The three judges and Blazhevich, the public prosecutor, did not bully or rant, they were always courteous to the prisoners. The president, Ivan Poldrugatch, was a strikingly handsome man with a bronze face and snow-white hair. One of his colleagues was chubby and alert, the other was sleek, relaxed, watchful. Blazhevich had dark untidy hair and a loose unprofessional build. He sprawled across the desk to ask his questions, as if his curiosity could no longer be repressed. Whenever Machek was mentioned they all became tense as fox-terriers, their eyes brightened, they sniffed the air. But they were on the wrong scent. Machek's offences were of a very ordinary kind; Kasche, dead or alive, was important. Fascism is not extinct in a country in which a callous and cynical bully is allowed to appear so aloof and distinguished. He was like an unamused spectator at a squalid family brawl. He had a nearly bald head, bushy eyebrows and an important, ambassadorial presence. He thrust out his replies with great lucidity and emphasis, rising out of his chair slightly and then relaxing again with clasped hands. "Das habe ich nicht getan!" "Das ist nicht der fall!" "Das ist eine gemeine Lüge!" He seemed to be a man who would lie for political but not for personal reasons. Many of his sharp denials and belligerent retorts had a ring of sincerity.

The prosecution devoted too much time to proving that Kasche took large bribes for remitting death sentences. Very likely he did, but venality is a touchingly human frailty in one who had planned the deportation of half a million Slovenes and Serbs, who had sponsored the introduction of the anti-Semite laws and had been the interpreter to the Croats of the Nazi policy of hatred and extermination. His power and his wickedness derived from his fanaticism, not from his greed for money, which was incidental. It was only by a ruthless exposure of fanaticism that Kasche could be made to appear small. The communist court was not prepared for that.

I kept thinking what a priceless psychological document the report of the trial would be for posterity, for though they had collaborated closely each had succumbed to a different temptation. Navratil for example, the air-minister, was the nicely-tailored military journalist, who had been fascinated by the technical achievements of the Nazis. He was a success snob and with his wet face, wet hair and soft ingratiating tones seemed the only one of the seven to have completely capsized. Kulenovich, an old and foxy Moslem, and Alaibegovich, his compatriot, a puffy, sad-eyed dandy, had been flattered into thinking they could protect Moslem interests better by taking part than by holding back. Koshak was a self-satisfied business man, who as a student at Frankfurt had learnt to disguise his shallow egotism with Nazi theory. Perchevich and Kvaternik were elderly men, whose sympathies were with the vanished Austro-Hungarian military caste. They liked uniforms and parades and compliments and for a few years they tried to call back to life the Zagreb of the Habsburgs. Almost all of them raised the cry that they were simple straightforward experts, who just did their job and let other people get on with theirs. The massacres? The brutality? Oh yes, they had heard something about that but that had nothing to do with their department. After this plea had been made several times it became clear that there are few accomplices of evil so formidable as the expert, who minds his own business.

Sometimes the speakers were not easy to follow but I reminded myself that they would be reported in the papers. In this I was over-optimistic. The reporting was pitiful in its inaccuracy. The answers of the defendants were interlarded with the fatuous comments of the reporters. I do not impute malice but laziness and perhaps the desire to give pleasure to authority by anticipating its verdict. Kasche, in his defence, exposed his arrogant but not unsubtle soul with clarity, yet the reporters paraphrased and blurred his well-turned phrases as if they were frightened of them. They explain that they were uttered with "typical Nazi cynicism," or with "characteristic insolence," or "conscious of his own guilt." Sometimes these interpolations are worse than silly. When Blazhevich asked Kasche if he knew his nickname, the "Trinkgeld Diplomate," and said that even Stepinac had in his trial referred to this weakness, Kasche, it is reported "fidgeted uneasily in his chair and was silent." He did nothing of the kind. In resonant tones he demanded the evidence of Stepinac's advocate. On another occasion Kasche asserted that in all his dealings with the Croat government his principal object had been the successful prosecution of the war against England, and he made the curious statement that at the beginning of the war the British Consulate in Zagreb had been filled with explosives. This remark and the references to England were neither translated by the interpreter nor reported in the Press.

When Blazhevitch asked Kasche what had happened to the property of the Slovenes whom the Germans deported, Kasche replied without a moment's hesitation, "The Slovenes were treated in the same way as the Germans, who since then have been moved from Slovenia," but you will not find this reply in the daily papers. Once, Kasche was caught off his guard. He had been insisting on how the Germans had respected the independence of the Croatian state and Blazhevich asked him "How long would the independence have lasted if the Ustashi had shot twelve Nazis in Jelachich Square? What would you have done?" "I should have lodged a protest," said Kasche with snuffy dignity and the court roared with laughter. Yet for some reason this, the only question by which the ambassador was discomforted, was not recorded.

Obviously in Yugoslavia, a new philosophy of justice quite different from ours is shaping. Each trial seems more closely related to immediate needs than to ultimate principles. It is possible that when the need for stability becomes less urgent this tendency will be reversed. In the meantime, it must be admitted, the guilt of the accused has usually been so obvious that justice has not suffered conspicuously by the preoccupations of the judges.

Yet there is no hint that the patient diagnosis of a criminal defect might have a bearing on its cure and that treason is a trouble with which a Southern Slav government in the future, as in the past, is likely to be afflicted. There is no recognition of the fact that by the Nazis a vicious circle of hate and extermination had been established from which each nation will have to find its own way of release or perish. Yet such considerations would not have been half as irrelevant as those which actually occupied the minds of the judges. The judges were no longer interested by the seven prisoners, who had been caught. They were after Machek, who was free. If there was a young Kasche in the audience I think he would have taken heart and said to himself: "The next time we may succeed, for the Croats do not hate us half as much as they hate each other."

All seven prisoners were condemned to death. It was a just sentence and the trial, in so far as it concerned them, was fair enough.

This unpublished and uncollected 1947 essay appears simultaneously in Balkan Essays, *by Hubert Butler (The Irish Pages Press, 2016). It is one of the first post-war accounts of a war crimes trial – possibly, the first – written by a writer of major literary quality. Hannah Arendt's celebrated account,* Eichmann in Jerusalem *(Viking Press, 1963), was published 16 years later.*

The Quisling "Independent State of Croatia" (1941-1945) was established by the Croat Separatist Leader Pavelić under the patronage of Nazi Germany and Fascist Italy, after the Axis invasion of royal Yugoslavia. This fascist, ultranationalist and genocidal regime murdered at least 300,00 Serbs, Jews, Roma and anti-fascist or dissident Croats in what is now mainly Croatia and Bosnia. Many of its leaders and collaborators were tried by Tito's Communist Yugoslavia in the late 1940s.

Hubert Butler (1900-1991) was twentieth-century Ireland's most distinguished essayist. He was the author of five collections of essays published by The Lilliput Press in Dublin: Escape from the Anthill *(1985),* The Children of Drancy *(1988),* Grandmother and Wolfe Tone *(1990),* In the Land of Nod *(1996) and* The Appleman and the Poet *(2014). Two new selected editions of his work,* The Eggman and the Fairies: Irish Essays *and* The Invader Wore Slippers: European Essays, *both edited by John Banville, were published by Notting Hill Editions in England in 2012. A sixth volume of his essays,* Balkan Essays, *bringing together a half-century of writing on the region, was published by The Irish Pages Press in September 2016.*

SYRIA: APEX OF THE ARC OF INSTABILITY

John McHugo

Time to learn the history.

The Arc of Instability

Syria now sits at the centre of an arc of instability almost identical to what, in happier times, we knew as the Fertile Crescent. This arc begins on the shore of the Persian Gulf and then travels up the Tigris and Euphrates towards their headwaters in the predominantly Kurdish parts of Turkey. It then turns west along the ancient trade route to the Stalingrad that is today's Aleppo, then on to the Mediterranean before continuing southwards to war-torn Damascus and Lebanon, Israel, Israel's Occupied Palestinian Territories (the OPT), and Jordan. In some parts of this arc – basically the whole of Syria and Iraq north and west of Baghdad – war prevails; in others – southern Iraq, Lebanon, Jordan, Israel and the OPT – the question might almost be when, not if, things will become grimmer.

It is easy to point fingers of blame when asking why this area is in such a state. Allocating blame may indeed be inevitable, since we need to establish the historical facts that have made it the most unstable part of the entire world. But the history of this area is also a front line in certain cultural wars that disfigure objective public discussion of important issues. It is impossible to examine the history of Syria without weighing in the balance matters such as the after-effects of British and French policy during the colonial era, the rights and wrongs of the creation and expansion of the state of Israel, and the aims of American and Russian policy both during the Cold War and now. Two incompatible paranoid narratives are all too often given the oxygen of publicity in Western countries. One is that "the Arabs" or, latterly, "the Muslims" blame the West for everything that has ever gone wrong in their lands; the other is that Arabs (or Muslims) were doomed to mess everything up because of a defect peculiar to their societies.

Some people are tempted to look back with rose-tinted spectacles at the multi-faith and multi-lingual Ottoman Empire that ruled all these countries until the end of the First World War. Under its ancient *millet* system, religion had been the prime marker of identity for the empire's people. This enabled its various religious groups to rub along together while each having their own, particular relationship with the Sultan-Caliph's government. The nineteenth-century Ottoman *tanzimat* reformers attempted to transform the empire into a secular state in which there would be a common citizenship, an elected parliament and full equality before the law. But the project of a liberal, multi-ethnic empire proved to be a mirage, as loyalty to the Sultan-Caliph melted under the impact of nationalism. By 1914, the empire was run by a junta of Young Turk nationalists who saw one of their tasks as the turkification of the empire's Arabic speakers.

Before the First World War it is doubtful how far Arab nationalist consciousness had spread among ordinary people in the Arabic-speaking parts of the Ottoman Empire, especially among the overwhelmingly illiterate majority who would have identified themselves everywhere by their locality, their tribe (if they had one) and their religion (which they all had). Yet nationalist consciousness was beginning to make an impact. In *Bilad al-Sham*, or historic Greater Syria which stretched from the Sinai peninsula to the Taurus mountains, the arrival of modern education for a privileged few led to a growing pride in the Arabic language and culture. Despite tensions between the Muslim majority and the large Christian minority (perhaps 20% or more of the population), this pride was shared by both communities and by heterodox Muslims such as Druze and Alawis. Many Christians – especially Orthodox – conceived of an Arab nation in which they would participate as equals alongside their Muslim brothers. It seems there were also some Jews among these dreamers. Sulayman Anbar, a member of Baghdad's huge Jewish community, was one of two representatives from the city's Arab nationalists at a pan-Arab conference in France in 1913.

The Foundations of Modern Syria

Yet after the Ottomans joined the German side in the First World War, hangings of suspected nationalists in Damascus and Beirut in 1915 provided fuel to an Arab uprising which began the following year in the Hejaz under the nominal leadership of the Sharif Hussain, the guardian of the Holy Places of Mecca and Medina and a descendant of the Prophet Muhammad. Most fighters in the revolt were fickle Bedouin tribesmen, but it also managed to raise a small regular force and attracted a number of talented Arab officers in the Ottoman army who were natives of Greater Syria or Iraq. At the end of the war, an Arab state was proclaimed in Damascus as a constitutional monarchy under Prince Faisal, the son of the Sharif Hussain. His provisional Arab government was heavily reliant on British support but was in loose control of inland Greater Syria east of the coastal mountains and the Jordan. Britain was in full occupation of the land west of the Jordan. To the north, France quickly took control of the littoral, evicting where necessary the local administrations which nationalists were attempting to establish.

There is no space here to discuss the three competing promises Britain made in respect of parts of Greater Syria to the Sharif Hussain, the French, and the Zionist movement. The Ottoman Arabic-speaking lands were partitioned into Mandates by Britain and France, the two nations chosen by the League of Nations to steer the peoples of the mandated territories to independence. The terms of the Mandates, when read with Article 22 of the League of Nations Covenant, made it clear that this duty constituted "a sacred trust of civilisation." Thus it was that Syria, in the form of the country that today is in such dire chaos, became a distinct political unit for the first time. It is also how it gained (most of) its borders. The southern parts of Greater Syria were placed under the British Mandate of Palestine and would be forced to go their separate way. The Arabic dialects of Syria, Lebanon and Palestine overlap and intermingle, and it is arguably only the burden of subsequent history that has forced the inhabitants of these three areas to become distinct peoples.

John Grainger in his *The Battle For Syria* (2013), which examines the military history of the campaigns there in the First World War, concludes that "it does seem that the best chance of a normal peaceful life and development for Syria lay in its establishment as a united constitutional monarchy under King Faisal from 1918 onwards." There can be little doubt that he is right in this. The form of Arab nationalism Faisal and the nationalist intellectuals known as *al-mutanawwirun*, or "the enlightened ones," were spreading was tolerant, inclusive and authentic. Consider words taken from a speech Faisal gave in the multi-cultural city of Aleppo on the day the First World War ended.

> The Arabs were Arabs before Moses, and Jesus and Muhammad. All religions demand that [their adherents] follow what is right and enjoin brotherhood on earth. And anyone who sows discord between Muslim, Christian and Jew is not an Arab.

He also recognised the diversity of the Arab world. He attacked the imposition of an artificial unity from above, as well as the partition he knew the great powers were contemplating. The only serious attempt to assess the wishes of the people of Greater Syria was carried out by the King-Crane Commission in the summer of 1919. It found widespread support for Faisal's constitutional monarchy over the whole of Greater Syria south of what is now the Turkish border. There were just two exceptions: the Maronites of Mount Lebanon and the small groups of Zionist colonists in Palestine (well under ten per cent of the population). Yet Britain and France were unmoved, and prevented publication of the report until it was too late for it to be taken into consideration.

Dismantling Faisal's tentative kingdom proved to be simplicity itself. Forced by Britain and France into compromises, and opposing resistance he knew to be futile, his support ebbed away. He would come to be reviled as a traitor, although it will be interesting to see to what extent the recent biography of him by Ali Allawi restores his reputation.

Most of the boundaries of the entities that became Syria and Lebanon were agreed by Britain and France, except for the northern boundary of Syria which was negotiated between France and Ataturk's new Turkish Republic. The area's inhabitants had no say. There were many illogicalities in the new political unit. Most glaringly, perhaps, the two great cities of the new Syria, Damascus and Aleppo, were shorn of large parts of their natural hinterlands. Half of Aleppo province remained in Turkey, while Damascus was now cut off from Jerusalem, Haifa and Jordan which suddenly all lay in the British Mandate of Palestine. Haifa had been one of Damascus's principal ports; the other was Beirut which France would include in its new Lebanon which would become independent separately from Syria at the end of the Second World War. Aleppo's links with Damascus were weak. Its connections with Gaziantep in Turkey and Mosul and possibly even Baghdad in Iraq were stronger. Customs posts were erected along the new frontiers, stifling trade and free movement.

Although the French had disposed of Faisal almost effortlessly, they found they had to use their army to establish control of Syria. First they had to subdue the Alawis of the Nusayri Mountains in the northwest of the country and put down a rebellion around Aleppo. But these campaigns were only a foretaste of the great revolt of 1925 which began among the Druze of the remote Hawran area southeast of Damascus. The Druze were known to be fierce warriors, but the French underestimated them. Some local Muslims and Christians joined the revolt, and then it spread more widely: to the Ghouta, which is the fertile area of countryside around Damascus, the conservative Sunni Muslim city of Hama, the city of Damascus itself, and the Shi'ite areas of South Lebanon.

It took two years of state terror for France to re-establish control. Damascus, Hama and many towns and villages were crushed into submission by indiscriminate shelling and air bombardment, aided by massacres committed by a hastily recruited militia of Armenian refugees. But a massive reinforcement of the French garrison was required before it could retake the areas which slipped out of its control. The French had planned to split Syria into mini-states, some of which would be established for locally predominant religious minorities. Yet the rebellion of 1925, which had begun as a grassroots movement, united people from different areas of the country and different religions behind a mixture of local grievances and an instinctive feeling that the Mandate had no legitimacy. A genuine Syrian nationalism now indisputably existed. It was Arab and secular, not sectarian.

Threats to Syria's Secular Nature

Syria's interfaith character had already been demonstrated by the approach adopted by Faisal and the nationalist leadership in 1918-20. Yet on the horizon there were already three clouds which threatened to rain on Syria's emerging secularism.

The first was the privileging of Jews in the Balfour Declaration which was incorporated into Britain's Palestine Mandate and affected all the territory between the Jordan and the Mediterranean. Zionist emissaries sought to drive a sectarian wedge between Syrian Jews and other Arabic speakers by urging them to back the project for mass Jewish settlement in Palestine – something that threatened the future of all non-Jewish Palestinians, and was seen as an outrage by all other Syrians. This split only deepened over time. When the UN General Assembly resolved to partition Palestine in 1947 vicious anti-Jewish riots took place in Syria. Laws restricting the lives and activities of Jewish Syrians and sequestrating their property soon followed. By the end of the twentieth century, virtually the entire Jewish community (once 30,000 strong) had been forced into emigration.

The second cloud was the way the French privileged Maronites and other Christians over Muslims. In 1860, there had been open war on Mount Lebanon between Maronite Christians and Druze, which led to massacres of Christians in parts of Damascus. The Maronites, a cohesive, peasant community with their own autocephalous church in union with Rome, dreamed of expanding the mountain fastnesses where they predominated into a viable and independent state under French protection. Within a month of the start of its Mandate, France arbitrarily added large areas to the Maronite heartland to create what is now the sovereign state of Lebanon: Beirut, Tripoli, Tyre and Sidon with their rural hinterlands, and Ba'lbek which came with the Baqa'a Valley. Almost half the population of the expanded Lebanon were Muslim – Sunnis, Shi'is and Druze – who were bitterly opposed to their inclusion in a new structure deliberately established in order to favour the Maronites.

Despite this, Christians retained their place in the newly created Syria. Major figures in the nationalist movement such as Faris al-Khury, the constitutional expert who at various times was prime minister and speaker of parliament, were Christian. It would be the frustration of Arab nationalism and the rise of Political Islam in the final decades of the twentieth century that would put Syrian Christians in a truly exposed position.

The third cloud was linked to the role pride in Islam played in Arab identity – a pride that was shared by many Arabs who were not Muslim. Thus, Yusuf al-Issa, a Christian journalist, issued a call in 1923 that the birthday of the Prophet Muhammad, the popular folk festival of *Moulid al-Nabi*, should be made a national holiday to unite all Syrians. But if Christians or Jews became perceived as collaborators with the Mandate authorities in what had become Syria and Palestine, there was inevitably a risk that some Muslims would see either or both of these communities as traitors, tainted with complicity in the agendas of the mandatory powers.

After the great Syrian rebellion had been finally crushed in 1927, France found itself forced to collaborate with nationalist politicians. It established parliamentary republics for Syria and Lebanon while retaining control of security and keeping an effective veto against anything that threatened its position as the mandatory. The parliaments of both embryonic states were dominated by the notable classes – the wealthy, elite families with large landed estates who had run Syria under the Ottomans. France's control seeped away because of her enfeeblement during World II, but her presence ended in a fit of pique. In May 1945, French artillery shelled Damascus for a second time, as officials went into denial about the end of their attempt at empire in the Levant.

Independence and The Ba'th Party

When the last French troops departed in 1946, they left a newly independent state that was in an impossible position. The countryside was still inhabited by an illiterate peasantry living in squalor and who were often permanently in hock to their landlords, while illiterate young men without work flocked to the towns. Although the shared experience of the Mandate had created a sense of Syrian-ness almost by default, the country was first and foremost proudly Arab (save for the Kurds and some smaller non-Arabic speaking minorities) and the divisions imposed by the Mandates were deeply resented. Shorn now of Lebanon, as well as Antakya (which France had transferred to Turkey for its own purposes in 1939 in breach of the terms of the Mandate), it did not have its own ocean-going port or even a direct railway linking Damascus with Aleppo and the north of the country. Average per capita income had probably not increased at all during the period of French rule.

Shukri al-Quwatli, Syria's first president, also had to glance nervously at all directions of the compass. Such armed forces as his government inherited from the French had been recruited disproportionately from religious and ethnic minorities: their sole purpose had been to uphold the French Mandate against the threat of Arab nationalism. But now that that it was truly independent, Syria was surrounded by external threats. To the south, King Abdullah I of Jordan openly called for Syria to be added to his kingdom; to the east, the Iraqi government conspired with wealthy politicians in Aleppo to join Syria to Iraq; to the north, Turkey was a brooding military giant that had already gobbled up one Syrian province and might cast covetous eyes on more territory. And Palestine was about to dissolve into inter-ethnic conflict between Jews and Arabs in which hundreds of thousands of fellow Arabs from *Bilad al-Sham* would be driven from their homes, and Syria would find itself powerless to offer them any real support.

The big ideas that dominated public discussion in the Arab world over the decades following Syria's independence were Arab freedom and unity, and the quest to build a modern society. Linked to these were practical issues which preoccupied Syrian rulers: how to dodge the sticks and win the carrots which were presented to them by the rivals in the Cold War, how to help other Arab countries become independent, and how to achieve justice for their Palestinian kin. Although there was now a Syrian branch of the

Muslim Brotherhood which supported candidates in elections (and socially conservative Muslim attitudes were shared by most politicians from the notable class), it is a striking feature of this period how unimportant questions of religion generally seem to have been in Syrian politics.

Syria's parliamentary republic was fragile. There were three military coups in 1949, another in 1954 (which restored parliamentary rule), an ill-thought-through union with the Egypt of Nasser in 1958, another coup which dissolved that union in 1961and restored parliamentary democracy for the last time, and then a period of chaos which began with another coup in 1963 and lasted until 1970. During those last seven years there were several attempted coups and purges, while Israel took advantage of Syria's weakness and the chaos in its armed forces to seize the Golan Heights during the Six Day War in 1967. Israel's attack came during the last two days of the conflict in breach of a UN ceasefire which Syria had accepted.

Although private enterprise flourished in Syria in the years after independence, there was also an impatience to modernise the country felt by many young people who had been the first generation in their families to receive a modern education. During the Mandate, intellectuals had already begun contemplating this task. Two teachers, Michel Aflaq, an Orthodox Christian and Salah al-din Beitar, a Sunni Muslim, had founded the Ba'th ("Renaissance") Party in Damascus during the Second World War. Aflaq was the movement's thinker, and he formulated a top-down nationalist ideology which was enthusiastically spread by the party's many devoted cadres. The Arabs were a single people who were entitled to sovereignty over their homeland and natural resources. No part of that people could go its separate way. Sectarian and local divides were to be swept aside so that a united Arab state could be created. Unity, freedom and socialism were Ba'thism's objectives, and the three formed an interlocking, inter-permeating trio like a shamrock. Freedom meant, above all else, freedom from foreign domination. Yet the united Arab state that was to be created – by force of arms if necessary – was intended to be democratic and have the rule of law, full rights for women and freedom of artistic expression.

The fact that Ba'thism was conceived and born in Damascus testifies to the depth of resentment against the partition of Greater Syria and the yearning for Arab unity at that time. The Ba'thists were interested in social reform, while generally speaking the notable politicians were not. Although the Ba'th Party became one of the most powerful forces in parliament, it never came close to winning a majority, and regarded Syria's parliamentary republic as essentially a cosy system used by the elite to retain power and share its benefits. But the notables had a weakness. Unlike many European aristocracies, they had looked askance at grooming their sons for a military career. The result was that bright young officers from peasant and petty bourgeois backgrounds forged ahead in the armed forces which now had to be built up because of the threat from Israel, to say nothing of that from other neighbouring states.

Throughout the 1950s, Egypt and Iraq battled for leadership of the Arab world. Both countries (as well as Saudi Arabia) used bribery and other nefarious means to try to gain control of Syria. The Arab-Israeli conflict and the anti-colonial struggle also placed Syria in the front line of the Cold War. The western powers refused to arm Syria so as to give it military parity with Israel. Finally, after the Suez Crisis of 1956, this pushed Syria into the arms of an eager Soviet Union which supplied at least some of the weapons it so desperately needed. From this point onwards, the alienation of the West and Syria from each other only became stronger.

Hafez al-Assad

Cometh the hour, cometh the man, and an unlikely looking man at that. Who would have thought that Hafez al-Assad, the minister of defence who had presided over the military disaster of 1967, would stage a coup three years later and then go on to rule Syria with a rod of iron until his death from leukaemia in 2000? The fact that he came from the minority Alawi community was not an insuperable obstacle in those days of Arab secularism and nationalism. Salah Jadid, the de facto military ruler he overthrew had also been Alawi, and there were many other senior Alawi officers in the military. Despairing at the way in which Syria was drifting, Hafez al-Assad had built up his own networks of officers who owed their positions to him. That was what enabled him to take control and stay in power.

As Hafez al-Assad's friend and foreign minister Abdul Halim Khaddam, a Sunni Muslim, put it, his rule was never that of one sect over others: it was the rule of a single man. The Syrian Ba'th party ceased to be an idealistic, revolutionary organisation and instead became a movement whose sole function was to keep the president in power. Alawis were disproportionately represented in his regime, especially in its officer corps and the vast security services that Hafez al-Assad built up to spy on the population and which used torture and worse whenever expedient. Many senior figures were recruited from his tribe and that of his wife (and were therefore Alawis). But when he fell ill in 1982 and had to appoint a kind of regency council to run the country until he recovered, its members all happened to be Sunni Muslims. This was despite a feeling by some Alawi generals that his brother Rif'at should have been made leader. This would probably have led to Rif'at taking over the country if Hafez al-Assad had not recovered.

Hafez al-Assad was a secularist through and through. He brought strong, authoritarian rule to Syria, which was welcomed by many after the years of chaos. He placed people in positions of responsibility because of their loyalty to himself, either through family or other ties, or because they owed him the positions they occupied. This inevitably meant that merit came second. It explains how Alawi cliques came to dominate the country, as well as his tolerance of corruption among many of those he appointed.

He also built up the armed forces, which proved their valour in a war with Israel in 1973 which Syria lost militarily but could claim as a moral victory. Although the American diplomacy of Henry Kissinger was to leave Syria to whistle in the wind for the return of the Golan Heights (the 1973 war only led to the recovery of Qunaitra), both Syria and Hafez al-Assad could now walk tall. Instead of being a weak state which provided a pond in which foreign actors could fish, Syria was a player that counted.

Israel had three objectives when it invaded Lebanon in 1982: to achieve hegemony over that bitterly divided country, to destroy the Palestinian nationalist movement, and to isolate Syria. But Hafez al Assad ensured that the eventual results were the opposite of what Israel had planned. After nearly a decade of further conflict, Lebanon came under the complete domination of Syria. All Israel's adventure had achieved was to replace the Palestinian guerrillas along its northern border with the far deadlier forces of the Shi'i militia Hizbullah, who would prove much more reliable friends for the Assad family across the decades than the Palestinians had ever been.

There were four systemic problems Hafez al-Assad would bequeath to his son Bashar on his death. Two have already been mentioned. These were the repression and corruption that made reform difficult. The others were the parlous state of the Syrian economy and the fact that militant Sunni Islamist politics had taken root in Syria. All four were linked.

During the 1950s and 1960s, Ba'thism (and Nasserism) had fallen under the influence of Soviet-style economics. The power of the rural landlords was broken and there was widespread nationalisation of business and finance. Much of Syria's commercial elite took whatever money they could carry and fled abroad. In the long term, this was a disaster for the country but central planning achieved some good results. There were many new infrastructure projects and an industrial base was created. Hafez al-Assad is entitled to the credit for spreading electricity, tarmac roads, education and health care across Syria. But the economy was choked by a corrupt bureaucracy created to provide jobs for Ba'th party members, while private sector investment was squeezed – unless it was by businessmen tied to and approved by the regime. On his death in 2000, he left behind a country without a single private bank and which operated almost as a cash economy with an unconvertible currency. The young people leaving school were now literate, but they found themselves let loose in a country where there were few opportunities open to them unless they had the right "connections."

The Growth of Religious Politics

The growth in militant, religious politics was to some extent a reaction against the economic path the country had taken. Hafez al-Assad managed to co-opt many Sunni businessmen and religious scholars to support his regime, but this could not compensate for the fact that most of the losers in the nationalisations and expropriations of the late 1950s and 1960s had been Sunni Arabs, especially the aristocratic land-owning families and the merchants in the *souqs* of the major cities. Syria's last freely-elected parliament had been overthrown in 1963, and under Hafez al-Assad democracy had been interred in a tomb. The Sunni Arabs were, perhaps, seventy per cent of the population, while the minorities which made up the rest (except for the Kurds) were disproportionately well represented in the Ba'th party.

An appeal to Muslim sentiment had served the cause of Syrian nationalism well during the great rebellion against the French. As we have seen, it had been a rallying cry that could unify Syrians of many different creeds. But over the decades since 1925, politicised versions of Sunni Islam had spread. These saw loyalty to Islam as akin to a national identity, and implicitly or explicitly excluded Arabs who were not Muslim. Their roots were the exclusivist Wahhabism of Saudi Arabia, the discourse of the Egyptian radical Syed Qutb who demonised Muslim secularists, and the triumph of the Islamic revolution in Iran which enabled some who felt disenfranchised to dream that the answers to the problems of the modern world lay in Islam, rather than in any western ideology.

In 1976, assassinations of prominent Alawis and bomb attacks on government targets began. In June 1979, a disillusioned Sunni Ba'thist brought militants into the artillery school in Aleppo to fire on fellow officer cadets. Those who were their targets were predominantly Alawis, and over thirty were killed. A year later, there was an attempt to assassinate Hafez al-Assad which would have succeeded if his bodyguard had not thrown himself on top of a grenade and sacrificed his life for that of the president. But the crunch came in 1982, when militants took control of Hama and executed over 70 Ba'thists in an attempt to spark uprisings across Syria. The regime's reaction was brutal and indiscriminate in the extreme. Hama was sealed from the outside world. Only Robert Fisk was able to penetrate the media blackout, and that happened by accident. In his book about Lebanon, *Pity the Nation* (1990), he recounts how he saw T-72 tanks pummelling the city into submission. The numbers killed are unknown, but the manner in which the city centre was rebuilt seems deliberately to have been designed to erase all traces of what had happened. The destruction of Hama was a success. Henceforth, the degree of repression in Syria would be stifling, but the country was at peace and became once again a safe place to travel around. It would remain so for nearly thirty years.

The Coming of Bashar al-Assad

The final years of Hafez al-Assad's rule were characterised by a general acceptance that change was needed, but the leadership at the top only allowed this to happen at a glacial pace. When he died in June 2000, the constitution was amended to allow a president to take office at the age of only 34 (the age of his son, Bashar). Bashar was groomed to succeed his father in the last few years of his life. Before then, he had been training to become an eye doctor – a fact that indicates he had not been initially marked out for a political career. Yet his succession to his father happened because the elite who surrounded the old president saw in the son a continuity candidate who would safeguard their interests. Bashar's instincts when he came to power may or may not have been reformist (the question was bitterly disputed by Syrians), but the truth was that he had little freedom of manoeuvre. When he allowed signs of political liberalisation in what was called the Damascus Spring, he was warned by the security services chiefs that this would lead to his overthrow unless he rowed back.

What Bashar did try to do was open up Syria to the world economy. There was some success – not least in the floating of the Syrian Pound, the appearance of the country's first private banks since the 1960s, the opening of a stock exchange, and spectacular growth in the tourism industry (from a very low base). GDP growth in some years rose to 5-6% (although in the years running up to the financial crash of 2008 that was not a particularly impressive rate for a country at Syria's stage of development). More reforms were contemplated, not least in the education system, but Bashar's efforts were ultimately defeated by two problems. The first was the unwillingness of the regime and its bloated and corrupt bureaucracy to lose control of anything; the other was the priority given to the favourites of the president and those close to him when economic opportunities arose.

Although the economic reforms created many new jobs and brought some prosperity to Syria, the gap between rich and poor grew ever wider. Bashar did not have his father's sure political touch, which had enabled Hafez al-Assad to use his peasant origins to retain much support across the Syrian countryside. Provincial capitals with rural hinterlands like Idlib, Der'a and Deir al-Zour had been strongholds of the Ba'th party, but under Bashar's rule alienation among traditional supporters set in. The president became associated with the new wealthy elites and was more dependent on close relatives than his father had been. When members of these elites abused their positions, he turned a blind eye – or was unable to make them change their ways. Thus it was that Bashar's cousin Rami Makhlouf was stated in an article in London's *The Financial Times* to control 60% of the Syrian economy while his brother was put in charge of internal security in Damascus.

Meltdown

The Arab Spring was slow to reach Syria. When spontaneous and uncoordinated demonstrations like those that had toppled the presidents of Tunisia and Egypt began in March 2011 and spread across much of the country, the regime could not claim it had not been warned. Many Syrians hoped desperately that Bashar would show that, after all, he was a reformer at heart. But when he finally addressed the Syrian Parliament (where he was guaranteed approval from an enthusiastic audience) on 30 March, his acknowledgement of the need for reform was vague and contained no specific proposals or milestones. Instead, much of the speech was taken up with assertions that the demonstrations had been orchestrated by hostile powers. Yet the reality was that the protesters were acting spontaneously. They certainly had no agenda beyond democracy, the rule of law, an end to corruption and the creation of an economy that could provide employment.

The security state had no idea how to control demonstrations without using live ammunition against crowds and rooftop snipers to pick off ring leaders. It also showed itself to be ill-disciplined. Syria slid ineluctably into violence. There are indications that Bashar genuinely did try to halt the slide into chaos and bloodshed in those early days, but he could not control the actions of his security chiefs and their henchmen. As they shed more and more blood in the months and years to come, he would stand by them and approve what they were doing in his name. The regime had always had an uncomfortable relationship with truth. It insisted that Syrians believed its propaganda, and often came to believe its own lies as well. Known Jihadi terrorists were let loose from gaol in the hope that they would alienate ordinary Syrians (and the international community) from what was fast becoming a revolution. A website was created that purported to belong to the Muslim Brotherhood so as to implicate the Brotherhood in violence. Indeed, throughout the crisis that began in March 2011 and has only got ever worse to this day, the regime has consistently shown itself to be a dab hand at the dark arts of spin.

As can be seen in the book *The Crossing* (2015) by the Syrian dissident Samar Yazbek, who travelled through the towns and villages of northern Syria which had slipped from the control of the regime in the first years of the revolution, there were brave, locally based attempts to build up a strong civil society which would prepare the country for democracy. The opposition Free Syrian Army was initially made up of soldiers who defected. They were joined by other groups which had driven out the regime's forces, but were poorly equipped and generally only locally based. The regime lacked the necessary number of troops even to take back control of places like Kafr Anbul, a vital town on the motorway south of Aleppo. Its response was indiscriminate bombing from the sky – including the notorious barrel bombs rolled out of helicopters. "Let them hate, provided that they fear," seemed to be the policy. Ironically, the regime's strategy echoed that of the outnumbered French in 1925.

The results were predictable. Millions of Syrians became refugees. Many fled into neighbouring Jordan, Lebanon and Turkey while others travelled further – especially to Europe after Germany opened its doors to them. Others retreated to the relative safety of the regime's heartlands: cities like Lattakia and Tartous on the Syrian coast, the villages and small towns of the mountains behind, and the centre of Damascus which, as I saw for myself in November 2014, remained under a tight lockdown.

Samar Yazbek's book is a story of the irrepressibility of the Syrian people. There are myriad other examples of this. One is the positive "can do" attitudes of many refugees in the Za'tari camp in Jordan which was highlighted in July 2016 in a documentary *The Refugee Camp: Our Desert Home* made by the BBC. Then there are inspiring stories of refugees who reached Germany such as Yusra Mardini, the eighteen-year-old swimming champion who competed at the Rio Olympics as a member of "Team Refugee." Back in Syria, civil society activity continues at a local level. One quite well-known example is the volunteer organisation called the "White Helmets" who provide emergency services in opposition-held areas in Aleppo and Idlib provinces. Its members risk their lives by rushing to the scene of explosions and searching the rubble for survivors. Less well-known are the volunteers who do what they can to preserve Syria's rich architectural heritage from destruction and plunder, such as walling up historic treasures to shelter them from bomb blasts. Their efforts demonstrate how the broad mass of the Syrian people only wish for the fighting to stop, and to be given the chance to rebuild their country and recreate it as a society and polity fit for the age we live in.

The Future

Yet that wish is being denied them. Yazbek's book does not end optimistically. In the summer of 2013 when she returned to the places she had visited in the areas outside regime control, she witnessed the remorseless pressure of Wahhabi-style Islamisation in the liberated communities, especially the marginalisation and segregation of women. This was not in response to local demands, but was brought by the foreign fighters who have flocked to Syria to create a "pure" Islamic state on Syrian soil and are willing to use coercive means to do so.

The regime has survived against the odds. It genuinely represents a substantial number of Syrians who prefer the devil they know to the many devils that they do not, but it would long since have collapsed without support from Russia, Iran and Hizbullah, as well as the Shi'i mercenaries or volunteers from Iraq, Iran, Afghanistan and elsewhere who come to Syria as auxiliaries to supplement the army's scarce manpower.

The revolution is backed by Saudi Arabia, the UAE and Qatar which decided in April 2012 to set aside money to pay Syrians who rose up against the regime. Another actor backing the revolution is Turkey. Once a good friend of Bashar al-Assad, Turkey's president Erdogan soon became an active supporter of the revolutionary cause. But like Iran and Russia, these powers have their own games to play.

For the Syrian revolution has turned into a proxy war. Just as in the 1950s, Egypt and Iraq each tried to pull Syria into their orbit so as to achieve dominance as the leader of the Arab world, today a new but much more grisly power play is taking place. In 1982, the religious militants who seized Hama were Syrian Sunnis who took their inspiration from the Islamic revolution in Shi'i Iran. Since then, however, the fault line between Sunnis and Shi'is has grown much wider. It has become a focus for identity politics, setting the members of one sect against those of the other as Saudi Arabia and Iran pose as their respective champions. The regime has now been so reduced that it has almost become an Iranian client state. This is despite the fact that the Syrian Alawis are only considered to be Shi'is in the broadest sense, while Syria remains a secular state and only one or two per cent of the Syrian population are Twelver Shi'is like those of Iran.

But the vicious actions of the regime since 2011 have bred anger, hatred and despair. Many of the most effective groups on the revolutionary side have a Sunni Islamist ideology. Different factions control the areas of Syria the regime has lost. Sometimes they combine against Bashar al-Assad, but they all have their own concerns and turf wars. The barbaric entity known in Arabic by its acronym Daesh, the self-styled Islamic State, purports to have created a messianic caliphate that has dissolved the old border with Iraq that Britain and France established all those years ago. It dismisses Syria as an entity that London and Paris created for their own purposes. Yet it has benefited from the regime's decision to release Jihadi prisoners, and has collaborated with the regime over the sale of oil. Observers have noted how Daesh usually seems to be low on the list of bombing targets for the Syrian and Russian air forces. The regime has been more than happy when battling opposition groups for Daesh to attack them from behind. In a similar way, opposition activists have noted how the regime largely withdrew without a fight when the Kurdish-led groups now styling themselves the Syrian Democratic Forces took control of large areas along the Turkish border and to its south.

Syria can never be restored to what it was before 2011. There is no simple answer to the country's plight. It can even be argued that attempts to broker ceasefires lead to an increase in fighting, as parties struggle to take control of whatever they can before they are finally forced to stop the bloodshed. Partition is certainly not a solution. Quite apart from anything else, to partition a sovereign state you need two sides who are prepared to negotiate the partition and to accept and implement its consequences. There are no two such sides in Syria today. The conflict will only end when there is the will on the part of the international community to wind it down. As of early September 2016, none of Russia and America, Iran and Saudi Arabia, or the Syrian regime and the opposition forces, seem to have reached this point. We can only hope and pray that that moment will come soon.

Blame for the disaster that is Syria today must be widely shared. This article shows that the disaster has many fathers. But there are salient facts about the regime and Russia's involvement that stand out, and should be stressed. Over ninety or ninety-five percent of those who have been killed have died at the hands of the regime, including women, children and other civilians. Its war crimes include not just ignoring the principles of proportionality and distinction when shelling or bombing areas over which it has lost control, but using starvation as a weapon of war and other forms of collective punishment – to say nothing of the widespread and arbitrary use of torture in its gaols. The shoots that have sprung from the hatred it has sown will be with us for decades.

The evidence suggests that Russia shares in these crimes. Yet perhaps Russia's greatest failure has been to ensure the prolongation of a conflict in which the parties were already close to exhaustion. Its prime motive seems to be to posture on the world stage in a way that will resonate with angry voters at home: those who dream the foolish dream of "making our country great again." Then it has more precise objectives: supporting what has become a client state, safeguarding its base at Tartous, and exploiting hydrocarbon concessions a desperate Syrian regime has granted it. For Syrians, their revolution is being crushed and their country shattered like a glass that has been tossed to the ground. When the revolution began, over forty years of Assad rule had ensured that no democratic forces existed that could challenge the regime. While blueprints for a democratic transition have now been forged by the exiles of the Syrian National Coalition, it has not been able – or, perhaps, has not been allowed – to act as a provisional government in the opposition-held areas. Instead, the fighters of the Free Syrian Army seem to be composed largely of disparate, locally-based groups which are often fluid. It has been the hardline Sunni Islamist groups that have received most arms and money and have often proved most effective on the ground.

Yet the international community is unable to cooperate to rescue Syria by finding a way to save the Syrian state, whilst disentangling the Assad family and their cronies from it. Worse still, the last five years show that the international community does not care very much – or, to be more precise, it really only cares about the issues that affect it directly, such as the risk of the spread of terrorism. Yet if people in the West paused for reflection, they would realise that the trauma Syria is undergoing today is just the worst and the most recent of a whole series of traumas that have been suffered by the peoples of the Arc of Instability since the First World War.

Is it any wonder that radical Islamism has an appeal to the disaffected and disinherited?

John McHugo received a degree in Arabic from Oxford in 1973, and subsequently did research into early Sufism at both Oxford and the American University in Cairo. After taking up law in 1977, he spent much of his career as a solicitor working on legal problems involving Arab countries, especially international boundary disputes; whilst also publishing work on legal aspects of the Arab-Israeli conflict, title to territory in international law, and the interpretation of treaties. He is the author of A Concise History of the Arabs *(revised second edition, 2016) and* Syria: A Recent History *(2015), both from Saqi. His next book,* A Concise History of Sunnis and Shi'is *(Saqi), is forthcoming in autumn 2017. He is currently a senior fellow at the Centre for Syrian Studies at St Andrew's University, and a board member both of the Council for Arab-British Understanding and of the British-Egyptian Society.*

WHY I GO TO ALEPPO

Samer Attar

Assad, Putin and *Obama – and the reckoning to come?*

I

The hospital where I work in Aleppo, Syria, is in a basement. The building above has been bombarded so many times that the top floors are too dangerous to use. Barrels and sandbags line the entrance to fortify it as a bunker.

Aleppo is a long way from my home in Chicago. That city, too, has its share of human suffering. Any Chicago surgeon who takes emergency duty can attest to the gun violence that plagues local communities. But the hospital where I work has state-of-the-art resources and some of the best doctors and nurses in the world. Scalpels are sharp, operating rooms are sterile, and specialists are abundant.

Aleppo, too, has some of the best doctors and nurses in the world, but there are so few left. They are exhausted, endangered, and they need help. That is why I volunteer for medical work in Syria; even the few weeks a year that I can offer provide some respite for the handful of surgeons who serve a population of 300,000 in a war zone. It is a heavy responsibility, but I feel I cannot ask world leaders to risk their citizens' lives to save people there if I myself am unwilling to take such risks.

My weeks in Aleppo are intense. In Chicago, where I specialize in surgical oncology, I see one patient at a time. In Aleppo, I see 20 at once. You live your life one massacre to the next: of children at school, or of families sleeping at home or shopping at a market. We hear the jets screech by, the helicopters whirring in the sky, the mortars launching, then the bombs exploding. Followed by sirens and screaming.

The screaming seems never to end, some days. So many people pushing through the entrance. There are never enough beds, so patients have to share gurneys or lie on the floor. Sometimes, there is no place to step, with patients lying on floors smeared with blood and strewn with body parts. There are few field hospitals left in Aleppo, so patients who are stuck outside and can't make it in sometimes die on our doorstep.

Then, abruptly, it ends. I walk away from all those patients. I am driven through sniper alleys, under airstrikes, and past checkpoints to cross the border into Turkey. From there, I fly home.

It crushes me every time. One moment, I'm in an underground hospital shaking from the blasts of missiles, saving whom we can, watching those we can't bleed to death. The next moment, I am at the airport coffee shop watching a man in a sharp suit cut the line or a woman berate the barista for putting too much ice in her tea. Nothing makes sense, and you feel like a ghost. Once you've been there, you never really leave Aleppo.

Back in Chicago, it's my patients who help me stay focused. I had a patient I'll call Sarah who had a sarcoma of the leg when she was eight. She endured a year of chemotherapy and had a portion of her fibula removed to excise the cancer, followed by radiation. The treatment stunted her leg's growth and deformed her ankle, but she wanted to be able to run track and play soccer.

On a ski trip to Colorado, she saw people skiing on prosthetics, and that's what she wanted. When she turned 11, she looked me in the eye and asked me to amputate her left leg. She showed such strength. She reminded me of Ahmad, a Syrian boy who had lost both legs, as well as his mother, when a bomb destroyed their home. He hoped one day to get robotic prostheses so he could walk again. His resilience was inspiring.

Each time I go back to Aleppo, though, conditions are worse. The pockets of life have become more tenuous with each visit. The markets, the children in the streets, the bustle of day-to-day living is replaced with rubble: apocalyptic wastelands of gutted buildings with collapsed roofs, exposed rebar and twisted staircases.

But people still live amid the ruins. You see them hanging laundry from a room on the third floor of a building cut in half. You see kids climbing over a 10-foot mound of rubble on their way home with some bread and water. Life has to go on, and people find ways to cope. They would rather face death at home than suffer in a refugee camp or risk drowning in a sinking boat.

For a surgeon in this setting, triage decisions mean the difference between life and death. A mother pleads with me to attend to her son; his skull is blown open, his brain exposed. He's gone. There's nothing we can do.

I move on to a girl with a lacerated artery in her amputated leg. She could bleed to death in minutes, but with pressure and a tourniquet we buy some time. Next to her is another young girl. Her right hand is obliterated: frayed tendons, twisted fingers, crushed bones. Her mother grips my shoulder, begging me to take her daughter to surgery first. But the girl is alive and she can wait.

This can last for hours. I lose all track of time. Eventually, the chaos dissipates. The floors are mopped clean. The dead are wrapped in white shrouds and laid in the street to make room for the next incoming tide of the wounded and dying.

You feel powerless. You can't stop it. There aren't enough hands to help, and you can't save everyone. Should we give all of our blood supplies to save one life? Or ration them to save five who all need some? The choices are impossible, yet we make them.

The Syrian medics and rescue workers in Aleppo have sacrificed everything, some even their lives. They show up to work every day despite all the horrifying brutality. Those of us who go to volunteer cannot stop the bombs, but we can serve in solidarity with Syria's full-time lifesavers. Who would I be if I could not support them and follow their lead for a few weeks a year?

They are among the most heroic, courageous and selfless people I have ever met – much like the New York firefighters I met on September 11, 2001. A medical student at the time, I squeezed into an ambulance with nurses and medics and we drove toward the smoke and ashes to help. I saw firefighters, paramedics, police officers and citizens rushing to the World Trade Center. That was the side I wanted to be on.

We wrote our names on the back of our scrubs with black markers in case our bodies needed to be identified. I was scared, but I was surrounded by good people doing the right thing.

I had never felt that way again until I went back to Aleppo in August 2013. I had visited Syria several times growing up, and knew Aleppo, but that was my first trip since the conflict started. The overwhelming sadness and dread I felt on September 11, I feel every day in Aleppo.

One night, we treated a child caught in an explosion who had the bone shards of obliterated bystanders embedded in his skin. An airstrike hit his school during a charity event to donate clothes to the poor. The last thing he remembered was seeing his best friend disintegrate in front of him.

The boy's father saw me and asked who I was, and why I was speaking in a strange language. A nurse explained to him that I was an American doctor. He told me that he had never met an American. He never thought he would. He never believed the day would come when an American doctor – one with Syrian blood but born and raised with the freedoms and luxuries of the United States – would come to Aleppo to help in a time of war.

That gave my work a new dimension of meaning: a palpable connection to alleviate the suffering of a people long abandoned. It lets them know that they're not alone. It has made me only more grateful for my life in America. It's also why I go back.

II

Aleppo is a resilient city, rich in history, older than New York, Paris and London. It is not a city of terrorists. It is a city full of ordinary people living everyday lives, people who want to put food on the table, send their kids to school and keep their families safe, just as anyone else in the world would want for their family. But its streets are literally flowing with blood. How can the world sit idle as the Syrian government, aided by Russia and Iran, brutalizes the people of Aleppo?

I saw this carnage for myself when I volunteered in an Aleppo field hospital in July. I was the last American to leave before Syrian government forces encircled and besieged the city.

On my first day, I saw a young mother newly paralyzed when a barrel bomb landed on her home. Her family pulled her from the rubble and brought her to the hospital. They were covered in blood and dust. As a last-ditch effort, Aleppo's only neurosurgeon attempted to open her spinal canal to relieve pressure on her spinal cord, but it didn't work. She would never walk again.

Next to her was another young mother on life support. A barrel bomb struck her home as well, killing her son and daughter. She had been pregnant, and the blast also killed her fetus. Her husband was working at his shop across the street. When he ran home after the first bombing, a helicopter dropped a second bomb that sent shrapnel into his head. Both father and mother survived, left only with scars and dead children.

On it went. The next two weeks were darker and more brutal. I saw human bodies dismembered, burned, crushed, ripped open, cut in half.

By my last day I was doing one surgery an hour. Then a driver risked his life to transport a few of us out on the Castello Road, the last supply route into Aleppo. Syrian government forces later permanently cut the road and besieged eastern Aleppo. Since then, unbelievably, things have got worse.

Aleppo has been pummelled with barrel bombs, chlorine-gas bombs, cluster bombs, bunker-busting missiles and even napalm. The hospital where I worked was so severely damaged by bombardment this past week that it is now out of service.

"In one day, we received 180 wounded civilians, including 72 children and 36 women. Many of them were critically injured," Mohamed Abu Rajab, a nurse with the Syrian American Medical Society, reported in September. "We had people dying in the ERs. Someone died because we couldn't get to him in time to save his life. The floor was overflowing with injured and blood."

The US, British and French air forces are already over Syria. Why do they do nothing to stop the Syrian government's attacks on homes, schools and hospitals? In their inaction, they have essentially green-lighted the war crimes of Bashar Assad's regime and its allies.

With every war crime, the Assad government grows emboldened to do worse. The Syrian and Russian actions are as much of a threat to world peace and security as the Islamic State of Iraq and the Levant. The bombs they drop kill innocent civilians and are radicalizing rebel forces.

US President Barack Obama and Secretary of State John Kerry speak of pleas and diplomacy. Why has it been so hard for them to see that they have been negotiating with thugs who laugh at their fecklessness? Since when does the United States plead with war criminals? How will Obama and the leaders of the world's powers explain themselves 10 years from now, when they look back and say that they did nothing?

Experts who have never set foot inside Syria say nothing can be done. I welcome them to spend one day volunteering in any Syrian field hospital amputating children's limbs. I encourage them to spend one day with the White Helmet rescue workers digging with bare hands through the rubble for survivors as helicopters drop bombs on them. Then see if they still say nothing can be done.

This is not a call for a US-led invasion of Syria. It is simply a call to protect civilians and the medics who are trying to save them from Assad's air force. With or without Russia, the United States and its allies must enforce UN Security Council resolutions — by grounding the Syrian air force, destroying runways and airfields if necessary, demanding an end to humanitarian sieges and implementing a global response if the Syrian government refuses. There can be no meaningful ceasefire or political solution as long as Syrian jets and helicopters rain hell from the skies.

The Holocaust, Cambodia, Bosnia, Rwanda, Syria – the genocide of our times keeps getting shoved out of sight and out of mind, but enough is enough.

Obama still has a chance to stand up for the Syrian people.

These articles appeared in the American press in, respectively, August and October 2016.

Dr Samer Attar qualified as an orthopedic surgeon at the University of Chicago and the Mayo Clinic. He works in several hospitals in Chicago.

FOUR POEMS FROM THE ARAB WORLD

—

Seán Lysaght

OVER SYRIA

My private screen shows a symbol of our plane
On the fine rule of its flight line,
Like spider gossamer, over Syria.
All the window blinds are down tonight
As passengers watch movies or try to sleep,
Some fully shrouded in their blankets.

Anyone looking up now would see us,
A hard star moving at altitude,
As I have stood in my plot after sunset
To watch a pin-gleam still in full light
At the head of a stream of contrails
Setting out across the Atlantic
And thought of guests there beyond contact
With cabin crew in the aisles like angels.

FLIGHT MODE

Dublin – Abu Dhabi, my first foray
Into space this free October,
I find my seat on a crowded flight
With IT folk and teachers and someone
Wearing a headrest like a Tudor ruff.
We stow our bags with common urgency,
A pledge that fate has no going back.
The plane joins the line for a lit runway
And that surge against the spine before take-off.

"Where can all the people be going?"
I wondered, in heavy weekend traffic
Out of Limerick forty years ago,
And my answer to myself, then as now,

Was, "Where are you going?"

ARABY

In the heat of day, I become a creature
Of the shopping mall and drift with others
Over the glazed floor. The local men wear
A white thowb, the women a black abaya
To keep this space their own. The Bedouin
Claimed he could go for a day on the skin
Of a date, for another day on the flesh,
And on the third he would live on the stone.

Now it's mall music to soothe a distracted soul.
Slow to spend, I follow my camera story
And ask a lady if I can photograph
What's stopping you?, a slogan on a hoarding,
And she answers with a laugh, "What's stopping you?"

OASIS

If the core of truth is a flame,
This is as close as I have come,
Stepping from the bus at Al-Ain
Into forty-three degrees.

The way cars pick up and disperse,
And people sit patiently under trees,
There can be only one knowledge now,
The sun and its fine pink sand
Running eternally under heaven.
Not that you ever get there.
There's only an empty street
Beyond the opening square,
A kaleidescope line of painted houses
To addle the senses, but for
One haven at lunchtime,
A restaurant for Asian builders
Where I can't read the menu,
I can't even speak.
A gesture of a hand
Directs me to a table. I sit and eat.

Seán Lysaght was born in 1957 and grew up in Limerick. He was educated at University College Dublin, where he studied French and English. He has published six collections of poetry and a biography of the naturalist Robert Llloyd Praeger (1865–1953), The Life of a Naturalist *(Four Courts Press, 1998). His recent collections include* The Mouth of a River *(2007), a celebration of the landscape of north Mayo, a volume of translations from Goethe,* Venetian Epigrams *(2008), and* Selected Poems *(2010) from Gallery Press. He teaches at Galway Mayo Institute of Technology, Castlebar and lives in Westport, Co Mayo.*

FROM THE HISTORICAL ARCHIVE:
ISRAEL AND THE ARROGANCE OF POWER

—

Avi Shlaim

Time for common human decency.

(Editor's Note: Complementing Avi Shlaim's six major works of scholarship, the following suite of reflections, essays and articles have been written over the past 15 years and constitute a brilliantly lucid and distilled overview of the Arab-Israeli conflict over the last half-century by one of the foremost scholars of the region. They are published here together for the first time.)

AN UNPUBLISHED LETTER TO SAMI MICHAEL
(29 January 2001)

From Ramat Gan to Golders Green — and beyond.

Today I am identified as a new historian or a revisionist Israeli historian and as someone who is highly critical of the state of Israel. But this has not always been the case. In these notes I shall try to trace the evolution of my attitude towards Israel.

I was born in Baghdad in 1945 to a wealthy Jewish family. My father was a very successful businessman who imported building materials from Britain. Among his clients were cabinet ministers who received on credit materials to build private houses but never paid their invoices. On the other hand, they gave my father government contracts and benefits and everybody was happy. My father also had a high social status and moved in elite circles which included prime minister Nuri al-Said and the regent, Abdul Illah. My mother was a lady of leisure. She was much younger than my father and this was an arranged marriage. We lived in a very large house and had about 15 servants. My memories of my childhood are very few and disconnected. But I have only happy memories of this early period in my life.

My family was well-integrated into Iraqi society and did not have any sympathy for, let alone involvement in, the Zionist movement. It was the establishment of the state of Israel which caused a backlash against the Jews in Iraq. As a result of this backlash, my family left Iraq in 1950, along with around 100,000 other Iraqi Jews. My mother's father was an interpreter for the British forces in Iraq during the Second World War and her two brothers were officers in British intelligence. So her side of the family all had British passports. My mother, her mother, my two sisters, and I, left Baghdad on a regular flight to Cyprus and we stayed in a hotel for several months before proceeding to Israel. My father had all his assets frozen and he had to leave Iraq illegally: he crossed the border into Iran on horseback with the help of some Kurds, and he joined us in Israel. It would not be true to say that we were refugees, but we were certainly the victims of the Arab-Israeli conflict. The whole family was suddenly uprooted and had great difficulty in adjusting to the new environment.

The effects of the upheaval were most devastating for my father. He was 50 years old when we arrived in Israel in 1950. He managed to smuggle a small sum of money which was enough to buy a flat in Ramat Gan and to live on for several years. But all his business ventures failed because of dishonest partners and he became unemployed. My mother who had never worked in her life became a telephonist in the town hall in Ramat Gan. My father also had great difficulty in learning Hebrew. At home he and my mother spoke only Arabic, and they both spoke to my sisters and me in Arabic and we would reply in Hebrew. But if one of my parents spoke to me in Arabic in the street in front of my friends I found it rather embarrassing.

There was a general sense in Israel at that time that anything to do with the Arab world was alien and inferior. I do not recall dissenting from this general view that everything Ashkenazi was superior to the language, culture, and social mores of the Jews of the Arab world. Nearly all the teachers at school were Ashkenazi. The Sepharadim were the bottom of the pile at school and in the rest of Israeli society. This seemed to be the natural order, and it never occurred to me to question it as a child. Indeed, I was very impressed with everything that I saw around me but I did not have a sense of belonging to it. Basically, I regarded the state of Israel as a clever Ashkenazi trick but I was not part of it. Nor did I really understand how it worked. Having said that, I should add that I never encountered any ethnic discrimination. I was subject, like so many other young oriental boys, to a sense of alienation.

At school I usually sat at the back of a very large class and rarely took part in class discussions. I was bored with the work and not engaged in what was going on around me. I hardly ever did any homework, and I often played truant. Once a teacher told my mother "his indifference makes me explode."

My form teacher was a woman from Germany who seemed rather aloof and snobbish, and hostile towards the Orientals in the class. At the age of 14 we all had to take a national test to determine whether we were good enough to go to high school. To my surprise I passed this test and evidently to her surprise as well. For she told me, rather unnecessarily in retrospect, that I only passed this test because of the allowances made for the underprivileged oriental sections of society. I did go on to a good high school, Gymnasia Dvir in Ramat Gan. I was still the bottom of the class in most subjects and I did not have a clue about English, having fallen hopelessly behind. So at the end of the first year I had a fail mark in English and I was due to take a resit at the end of the summer which I had no chance of passing. Had I stayed in Israel, that would have been the end of my academic career. My mother, however, was determined that I should be a success and she made arrangements to send me to school in England. I had an uncle in Newcastle who sold my grandmother's flat in Baghdad after the Second World War and deposited the money for her in a bank in London, and she agreed to pay for my education.

I arrived in London in 1961, age 15, and ended up as a student in the Jewish Free School and staying as a paying guest with the headmaster, Dr Edward Conway, at this home in Golders Green. It was cold and miserable, and I had no friends, and that was the turning point in my life. I started working day and night and making slow progress. It was more by dint of determination than natural talent that I achieved this progress. English I simply had to learn, because there was no other choice, although I found it an extraordinarily difficult language. At the end of the first year I took five O-Levels, passed three and failed two which I had to retake. In the sixth form I did four A-levels: History, Politics, French, and Classical Hebrew. By this time I was doing quite well and, with the help of my history teacher, got a place to read history at Jesus College, Cambridge. In those days one had to have a classical language at O-level in either Latin or Greek to take up a place at Cambridge. In my case classical Hebrew was considered good enough, though there had not been a precedent of this as a classical language. I never worked so hard in my life as I did during those three years in London. But I also felt that my family had sacrificed a great deal for me and that, in the end, I did not let them down. My attitude to Israel was not an issue for me during that period. I felt patriotic about the country and proud to be Israeli in a school of English Jews.

My school education completed, I returned home and went into the IDF to do national service. There was never any question of not returning to Israel or of dodging national service. My two years in the army were happy ones and carried me, after the basic training, into the signal corps where I became an instructor for wireless operators. There was no discrimination in the army, institutional or subtle and informal. In theory the IDF was meant to serve as a melting pot and that was the reality for me. I was very nationalistic in those days, and I held very conventional views about the Arabs as the enemy. I identified completely with the state of Israel and never entertained any doubts about the justice of its cause. My period in the army was from 1964 to 1966, i.e., before the territorial expansion of June 1967. It was a small and beautiful country, and it conformed to the image of an unequal contest between a little Jewish David and an overbearing Arab Goliath. But I have to say that already during this early phase in my life I did not have a monolithic image of "the Arabs," but discriminated between good Arabs and bad Arabs. The Syrians were the worst of the bunch and the Jordanians were the good ones. This I learnt from practical experience when doing field manoeuvres on the Judean Hills. These went on for three days and we were allowed very little sleep. One night my rifle was stolen by the sergeant from me in my tent, as well as the rifles of several other dozy members of the company. Our punishment was to march across the border into Jordan with high boots, full pack, ammunition pouches, but no trousers and no rifle. We were told that we are a disgrace to the motherland and that if we were shot by the Jordanians, then that is the fate we deserved. In fact, I never saw any Jordanians, and I concluded that they can't be quite as bad as they are made out to be. More than 20 years later I wrote a book with the title *Collusion across the Jordan: King Abdullah, the Zionist Movement and the Partition of Palestine*. In this book I argued that there was a special relationship between Jordan and Israel both before and after 1948.

Four days after demobilisation I turned up at Jesus College, Cambridge. It was a very abrupt transition from a highly structured and hierarchical environment, to one in which I had considerable freedom. Being a couple of years older than my contemporaries was a distinct advantage and enabled me to make the most of this freedom. The subject I studied was History which in those days was mainly medieval history, and even the modern history paper ended in 1914. So I knew very little about the twentieth century or about international relations. Yet, the only career that I had ever considered was a career as an Israeli diplomat. No other career options had ever crossed my mind. At the end of three very happy years at Cambridge, having ended up with an upper second degree, I went to say goodbye and thank you to one of my tutors, Mr Harry Hinsley, who later became Professor Sir Harry Hinsley. He said to me "Have you ever thought of doing a Ph.D., Shlaim?" I said I hadn't. He said "You should." "How does one go about doing a Ph.D.?" I asked sheepishly. Hinsley explained the procedure, offered to be my supervisor, and we settled on a topic for the thesis, namely, Britain and the European Balance of Power in the Inter-War Period. But I did not take up the offer of a place to do research at Cambridge since I was still set on a diplomatic career. Throughout my time at Cambridge, I retained my conventional and indeed nationalistic views about Israel and about the Arab-Israeli conflict. My views could be summed up in the phrase, "My country, right or wrong." In those days there wasn't the slightest doubt in my mind that my country was in the right.

In my third year at Cambridge I applied to the London School of Economics to do a one-year degree, the M.Sc. in International Relations. The reason for this application was purely vocational: I knew nothing about diplomacy and I wanted to do this course as a background and preparation to a diplomatic career. The degree consisted of a core course and two optional subjects, and I chose "International Institutions" and "The Politics of Western Europe." There was an optional subject on the Middle East but I did not take it because I had no particular interest in the Middle East at the time. I enjoyed the year at the LSE and ended up with a Distinction. My studies completed, I packed all my belongings to return home for good in the summer. My girlfriend, Mary Chamberlain, was on the same course and she too ended up with a Distinction. She came back to Israel with me for a holiday. Before leaving Britain, almost by accident, I applied for a temporary lectureship in International Relations at the University of Reading. To my utter surprise, I received a telegram in Israel offering me the job. I still had no interest in pursuing an academic career at the time. In fact, I was worried that I was not up to it and that I would be rumbled in the first week. On the other hand, I had not made contact with the Israeli Foreign Ministry yet, and there was no certainty that I would get in. Wanting to remain with Mary was another reason for accepting the offer. My thinking at the time was that I would apply to the Israeli Foreign Ministry from my position as a temporary lecturer at Reading and that this might help me to get in.

I took up my post in the department of Politics in the University of Reading in October 1970, and I was to stay there for 17 years. That is how

I became an academic. Right at the beginning, I made a decision to steer clear of the Arab-Israeli conflict. My main research interest was Britain and the origins of European unity. I taught a course on world politics in the department, and an M.A. optional course in the graduate school on "Political Integration in Western Europe." I never took a course on the Middle East at a University, nor taught a course on the Middle East until my move to Oxford 17 years later.

As a member of staff in the Politics Department I registered for a Ph.D. on Britain and the Origins of European Unity, but lost interest after a few years. After the first year, I was offered a permanent post at Reading. It was much easier to get university posts in those days than it is today. I had a keen teaching interest in the Cold War which gradually became my main research interest. In 1980 I eventually submitted a thesis on *The United States and the Berlin Blockade, 1948-1949: A Study in Crisis Decision-Making*. This was published as a book by the University of California Press three years later.

My interest in the Arab-Israeli conflict evolved very gradually, and my main source of information was *The Guardian*. From being strongly committed to the Israeli side at the outset, I became more detached, and eventually moved in the opposite direction. But this was a very slow process. Living in Britain gave me a sense of distance and perspective on my home country. It also exposed me to different points of view and brought me into contact with Arab academics and Arab students who challenged my pro-Israeli positions. Side by side with my research on European integration and the Cold War, I began to write the occasional article about the Arab-Israeli conflict. The more I studied the subject, the more I questioned the conventional Zionist version of the Arab-Israeli conflict, and this was reflected in my publications.

My dream when I was at Reading was to get a lectureship in International Relations at Oxford University, a fellowship at St Antony's College, and within St Antony's a room at the Middle East Centre. In October 1987 this dream came true. I was appointed Alastair Buchan Reader in International Relations and a Fellow of St Antony's College where I was attached to the Middle East Centre. My teaching caught up with my research interests. I stopped teaching an M.A. option on Political Integration and Western Europe and started teaching, for the first time, an optional M.Phil. course on the International Relations of the Middle East. All my research from now on centred on the Arab-Israeli conflict. *Collusion across the Jordan* which I had researched and written at Reading, was published during my first year at Oxford. From now on I was perceived as a Middle East area specialist and as a revisionist Israeli historian.

In 1988 three other books were published by revisionist Israeli historians: Simha Flapan, Benny Morris, and Ilan Pappé. Increasingly, we were identified as a distinct group which was said to have an anti-Israeli political agenda. There was no evidence for this, but that did not stop Israeli scholars and propagandists from attacking us and trying to discredit our work. The debate between the new historians and the old Israeli historians has been going on for twelve years, and it is still going strong. With the publication of *Collusion across the Jordan*, I acquired an international reputation as a scholar who is highly critical of Israel. The rest is history, one might say, new history.

A BETRAYAL OF HISTORY
(February 2002)

Propaganda of victors.

"A nation," wrote the French philosopher Ernest Renan, "is a group of people united by a mistaken view about the past and a hatred of their neighbours." By this definition, Benny Morris may now be counted as a true member of the Israeli nation. In his account of his "conversion" in yesterday's *Guardian*, Benny explains that, although he has not undergone a brain transplant as far as he can remember, his thinking about the current Middle East crisis and its protagonists has radically changed during the past two years.

Willingness to re-examine one's thinking is always a commendable trait in a historian. Unfortunately, in Benny's case the re-examination is confined to only one protagonist in the Middle East conflict: the Palestinians. As a consequence, his new version of the recent history of the conflict has more in common with propaganda than with genuine history. Like most nationalist versions of history, it is simplistic, selective and self-serving.

By his own account, Benny's conversion was a pretty dramatic affair. He imagines that he feels a bit like those western fellow travellers rudely awakened by the trundle of Russian tanks crashing into Budapest in 1956. But there is surely some mistake in this analogy. Benny could not possibly have heard the trundle of Palestinian tanks crashing into any Israeli city because there are no Palestinian tanks. What he might have heard is the sound of Merkava tanks invading Palestinian cities on the West Bank and refugee camps in Gaza in the most flagrant violation of a long series of agreements that placed these areas under the control of the Palestinian Authority. Another minor flaw in Benny's analogy is that the Palestinians, by any reckoning, can only be seen as the victims, while Israel is the aggressive and overbearing military superpower. If we are going to look for historical antecedents for this grossly unequal contest, it would make more sense to update the biblical image of David and Goliath: a Palestinian David facing an Israeli Goliath.

There is a historical irony in Benny's conversion to the orthodox Zionist rendition of the past, for he was one of the trailblazers of the "new history" which placed Israel's political and military conduct under an uncompromising lens. Indeed, it was he who coined the term "the new historiography" in order to distinguish it from the traditional pro-Zionist literature about the birth of Israel and the first Arab-Israeli war of which he was so savagely critical.

Three or four subsequent books consolidated Benny's reputation as the standard-bearer of the new historiography. The hallmark of his approach was to stick as closely as possible to the documentary evidence, to record rather than to evaluate. While his findings were original and arresting, he upheld the highest standards of historical scholarship, and he wrote with almost clinical detachment.

Sadly, the article in *The Guardian* does not display any of Benny's former scholarly objectivity or rigorous use of evidence. Instead of evidence we are treated to a rambling and self-pitying monologue, seething with contempt and hatred for the Arabs in general and the Palestinians in particular.

The message, pithily summed up in a long interview that Benny gave to *Yedioth Ahronoth* about his highly publicised conversion, is that "the Arabs are responsible." Where no evidence is available to sustain the argument of Arab intransigence, Benny makes it up by drawing on his fertile imagination.

According to Benny, what stayed the hand of Hafez Assad of Syria, and that of his son and successor Bashar, from signing a peace treaty was not quibbles over a few hundred yards but a basic refusal to make peace with the Jewish state. The evidence? Benny can see the father, on his deathbed, telling his son: "Whatever you do, don't make peace with the Jews; like the Crusaders, they too will vanish." It would appear that Benny can no longer tell the difference between genuine history and fiction or fabrication along the lines of *The Protocols of the Elders of Zion*. At this rate Benny is in danger of becoming what Isaiah Berlin once described as "a very rare thing – a genuine charlatan."

Most of Benny's venom and vitriol are, however, reserved for the Palestinians in what amounts to a remarkable attempt to blame the victims for their own misfortunes. He trots out again Abba Eban's tired old quip that the Palestinians have never missed an opportunity to miss an opportunity, blithely disregarding all the opportunities for peace that Israel has missed since 1967. But the main reason, we are told, around which Benny's pessimism gathered and crystallised was the figure of Yasser Arafat, the leader of the Palestinian movement since the late 1960s. Arafat-bashing has become a national sport in Israel of late, and Benny has a field day, calling him, among other things, an "implacable nationalist and inveterate liar." To be sure, Arafat is no paragon of virtue, but it is far too easy and too simplistic to place the entire blame for the failure of the Oslo peace process on the shoulders of one individual.

Like Benny, I was cautiously optimistic after Israel and the Palestine Liberation Organisation signed the Oslo accord in September 1993, but our interpretation of the subsequent history is very different. Oslo represented a historic compromise for the Palestinians: they gave up their claim to 78% of mandatory Palestine in return for a state of their own over the remaining 22%, comprising the West Bank and Gaza. Israel, for its part, recognised the PLO as the legitimate representative of the Palestinian people, and the two sides agreed to resolve their outstanding differences by peaceful means.

For Benny the principal reason for the collapse of this historic compromise is Palestinian mendacity; for me it is Israeli expansionism. The building of settlements in the occupied territories has always been illegal under international law and an obstacle to peace. Expanding Jewish settlements on the West Bank is not a violation of the letter of the Oslo accord, but it is most certainly a violation of its spirit. Israel's protests of peaceful intentions were vitiated by its policy of expropriating more and more Palestinian land and building more Jewish settlements on this land. By continuing to build settlements, Israel basically went back on its side of the deal that had been concluded at Oslo.

The main landmarks in the breakdown of the Oslo peace process are the Camp David summit of July 2000 and the outbreak of the intifada towards the end of September of that year. Israel's official history is full of myths, as Benny knows so well from the earlier stage in his career when he was in the business of exploding national myths and slaughtering sacred cows. The latest national myth is that of the generous offer that Ehud Barak is said to have made to Arafat at Camp David, only to be confronted with a flat rejection and a return to violence. There is a broad national consensus behind this myth, including the left and the peace camp, but popular support is not the same as evidence.

The role of the historian is to subject the claims of the protagonists to critical scrutiny in the light of all the available evidence. In this instance, however, Benny seems to have swallowed the official Israeli line on Camp David hook, line and sinker. The first-hand account of the American official Robert Malley is not even mentioned. It suggests that Barak mishandled the summit from start to finish. Benny also glosses over the fact that the al-Aqsa intifada, which has so far claimed the lives of 941 Palestinians and 273 Israelis, broke out not on orders from Arafat but in response to a provocative visit to Haram al-Sharif by the then leader of the opposition, Ariel Sharon.

Benny's account of the next phase in the "final status" negotiations is hopelessly inaccurate. On 23 December 2000, President Bill Clinton presented his "parameters" for a final settlement of the conflict. These parameters reflected the long distance he had travelled from the American bridging proposals tabled at Camp David towards meeting Palestinian aspirations. The new plan provided for an independent Palestinian state over the whole of Gaza and 94-96% of the West Bank (with some territorial compensation from Israel proper); Palestinian sovereignty over the Arab parts of Jerusalem, Israeli sovereignty over the Jewish parts; and a solution to the Palestinian refugee problem in which the new state would be the focal point for the refugees who choose to return to the area.

According to Benny, the Palestinian leadership rejected "the Barak-Clinton peace proposals of July-December 2000." In fact, they rejected Barak's proposals of July and accepted in principle Clinton's proposals of December, as did the Israeli leadership. Both sides had their reservations. On Jerusalem, the Israeli reservations were more substantial than the Palestinian ones. Benny not only conflates two entirely separate sets of proposals; he makes no mention at all of the negotiations at Taba in the last week of January 2001.

At Taba the two teams made considerable progress on the basis of the Clinton parameters and came closer to an overall agreement than at any other time in the history of this conflict. But by this time Clinton and Barak were on their way out and Sharon was on his way in. During the run-up to the elections, Barak hardened his line on Jerusalem. At this critical juncture, as so often in the past, the peace process was held hostage to internal Israeli politics. With Sharon's election, all the progress made at Taba towards a "final status" agreement was rendered null and void. A new and grisly chapter in the history of the conflict was about to begin.

Benny's conclusion follows naturally from his deficient and defective account of the history of the last decade, and especially of the last two years. His conclusion is that the root problem today is the Palestinian leadership's denial of the legitimacy of the Jewish state. The conclusion that I draw from my version of history is that the root problem today is the Jewish state's continuing occupation of most of the Palestinian territories that it captured in June 1967.

All the neighbouring Arab states, as well as the Palestinians, recognise Israel's right to exist within its pre-1967 borders. None of them recognises the legitimacy of the Jewish colonial project beyond the green line. Nor do I. This is where Benny Morris and I part company. His post-conversion interpretation of history is old history with a vengeance. It is indistinguishable from the propaganda of the victors. He used to have the courage of his convictions. He now has the courage of his prejudices.

This article was first published in The Guardian, *22 February 2002.*

WHEN HISTORIANS MATTER
(June 2008)

Jihadi onslaught – or ethnic cleansing?

Nationalist movements generate their own historical narratives in the struggle for statehood. These are, of course, usually distorted and self-serving. The official or semi-official history of the Zionist movement is no exception. Sixty years after the proclamation of the state of Israel, the origins of the state continue to preoccupy professional historians as well as the public.

The debate initially focused on 1948, on the birth of Israel and the first Arab-Israeli war. This debate is not so much between Arab and Israeli historians as it is between different groups of Israeli historians. And it has excited intense interest outside as well as inside universities, because it cuts to the core of Israel's image of itself.

Zionist historians have tended to portray Israel as the innocent victim of Arab aggression, as a peace-loving nation that resorts to military force only in self-defence. According to this school, the cause of the long-running conflict has been not Israel's occupation of Arab land, but the implacable hostility of the enemies of the Jewish state.

Over the last two decades, this argument has been critically scrutinised by a group of new Israeli historians. This re-evaluation was made possible by Israel's liberal policy of releasing its official documents to researchers after 30 years. It is very much to Israel's credit that, unlike the Arab states, it allows access to its archives, thereby making possible critical studies such as those written by the "new historians."

The original group included Ilan Pappé, Benny Morris and myself. All three of us published books in 1988, on the 40th anniversary of the creation of Israel. Our books deal with different aspects of the 1948 war. Pappé, in *Britain and the Arab-Israeli Conflict, 1948-51*, argues that Britain's real aim in the twilight of its mandate over Palestine was to abort the birth of a Palestinian state rather than to prevent the creation of a Jewish one. Morris, in *The Birth of the Palestinian Refugee Problem, 1947-1949*, sees many causes behind the Palestinian exodus, including deliberate Jewish political, psychological and military pressure. He therefore concludes that Israel bears at least a small share of the responsibility for the creation of the persistent Palestinian refugee problem.

My own book was called *Collusion Across the Jordan: King Abdullah, the Zionist Movement, and the Partition of Palestine*. I argued that the Arabs were not united in their desire to strangle the Jewish state at birth, and that one of them – the ruler of Transjordan – had a tacit understanding with the Jews to divide up Palestine between themselves at the expense of the Palestinians. All three of us relied on recently declassified official Israeli documents, and all of us depicted the Palestinians as the main victims of the war for Palestine.

The new history had a significant impact on a number of different levels. First, it influenced the way the subject is taught in Israeli schools. Textbooks were rewritten to incorporate some of the findings of the new historians. Students were exposed to different and conflicting interpretations of the birth of Israel.

Second, the new history helped Israelis to understand how the Arabs view them and the conflict. Third, to Arabs the new history was in line with their own experience instead of the one-sided account of the victors. And finally, the new history helped to create a climate, on both sides, in which the Oslo peace process could move forward in the early 1990s.

Palestinian negotiators at the Camp David summit hosted by Bill Clinton in July 2000, and in the bilateral talks held in Taba in the Gulf of Aqaba early the following year, referred to the work of the new historians, especially Benny Morris, in trying to establish Israel's share of responsibility for the plight of the 1948 refugees.

Shlomo Ben-Ami, a former professor of history at Tel Aviv University, was Israel's foreign minister at the time of these negotiations. He says, "the new historians definitely helped in consolidating the Palestinians' conviction as to the validity of their own narrative... the Israeli peacemakers also came to the negotiating table with perspectives that were shaped by recent research... But the introduction of new and powerful arguments on the 1948 war into the public debate in Israel became part of the intellectual baggage of many of us, whether we admitted it or not." In short, it was a history that made a difference.

The impact of history on politics, however, is not a one-way street. Just as the "new history" helped to promote the Oslo peace process, the breakdown of this process led some of the new historians to re-examine their beliefs. In the case of Morris, the consequences were far-reaching, effectively terminating his membership of the club. Following the outbreak of the second intifada in 2000, and more particularly the resumption of suicide bombing, Morris's view of the Israeli-Palestinian conflict changed radically. He no longer believes in the possibility of a peaceful solution. And he now thinks that it was a mistake on the part of Israel's founding fathers to allow even a small Palestinian minority to stay within the borders of the Jewish state.

The debate today on the origins of the Palestinian refugee problem is not between old and new historians, but within the ranks of the original group of new historians. Ilan Pappé maintains that in 1948 Israel acted on the basis of a master plan for the expulsion of the local Arabs. This conviction is reflected in the title of his 2006 book – *The Ethnic Cleansing of Palestine*. Benny Morris has just published another book – *1948: The First Arab-Israeli War*. He is now inclined to see 1948 not as a struggle between two nations over a piece of territory, but as a jihadi onslaught by the Muslim world against the Jewish community in Palestine. Pappé blames Israel for the expulsion and the dispossession of the Palestinians; Morris comes closer than ever before to blaming the Palestinians for their own misfortunes. Some arguments never end.

This essay was first published in Prospect Magazine, *Issue 147, June 2008.*

REFLECTIONS ON THE ISRAELI-PALESTINIAN CONFLICT
(March 2011)

Injustice is one-sided.

These are reflections about a subject which has preoccupied me for the best part of four decades. Most of these reflections are included in one form or another in my most recent book which was published by Verso a year ago in hardback and in October 2010 in paperback. The book is called *Israel and Palestine: Reappraisals, Revisions, Refutations.* It is not really a proper book, but rather a collection of essays on the theme of the Israeli-Palestinian conflict. These are articles and essays that I published over the past 25 years in different places and for different audiences. Some are scholarly articles with footnotes; some are more polemical comment pieces for newspapers; others are review essays which originally appeared in the *London Review of Books.*

The paperback edition of this book was reviewed by Rafael Behr in *The Observer* on 3 October 2010. Let me quote from this review:

> Several times in *Israel and Palestine*, his collection of essays on the Middle East, Avi Shlaim refers to Zionism as a public relations exercise. It sounds glib. But Shlaim … isn't talking about sales and marketing. He means a configuration of history that casts one side of a dispute as victim and the other as aggressor in the eyes of the world.
>
> In Zionism's case, the story told is of Israel restored to the Jews, carved from empty desert, "a land without a people for a people without a land." By extension, Arab hostility to Israel's creation was irrational cruelty directed against an infant state.
>
> It is a romantic myth requiring a big lie about the indigenous Palestinian population. Their expropriation was, in Shlaim's analysis, the "original sin" that made conflict inevitable. He also sees the unwillingness of Israeli leaders to recognise the legitimacy of Palestinian grievance as the reason why most peace initiatives have failed.
>
> There was a time of greater pragmatism, when ordinary Israelis at least were ready to swap land for peace. But that trend was crushed by a generation of turbo-Zionists from the Likud

party. Instead of trading occupied territory for normal diplomatic relations with the Arab world, they aggressively colonised it, waging demographic war to shrink the borders and diminish the viability of any future Palestinian state.

Palestinian leaders are not spared Shlaim's criticism. He singles out Yasser Arafat's decision to side with Saddam Hussein in the First Gulf War, for example, as a moral and political blunder. But most of the essays are about the cynical manoeuvrings of Israeli politicians. As a collection it is plainly one-sided; Shlaim does not aim at a comprehensive overview of the conflict so much as a running rebuttal of Israel's version of it; an insurgency in the public relations war.

So there you have it. This, in a nutshell, is what the book is really about. I couldn't have put it better myself! I also plead guilty to the charge of being one-sided. My sympathy is with the Palestinians because they are the victims of this tragic conflict, the victims of a terrible injustice. Injustice is by definition one-sided: it is inflicted by one party on another. I am a politically engaged writer and I believe in justice for the Palestinians. By justice I mean an end to the occupation and the establishment of an independent Palestinian state in Gaza and the West Bank with a capital city in East Jerusalem. The Palestinian state I envisage would be alongside Israel, not instead of Israel. In short, I am a supporter of a two-state solution. If this makes me one-sided, then so be it.

What I propose to do is not to try to summarise the book, but to offer you some reflections on the Israeli-Palestinian conflict from an historical perspective. Everything to do with Israel is controversial, so let me pre-empt misrepresentations by stating where I stand. I have never questioned the legitimacy of the Zionist movement or that of the State of Israel within its pre-1967 borders. What I reject, and reject uncompromisingly, is the Zionist colonial project beyond the 1967 borders.

I belong to a very small group of Israeli scholars who are known collectively as "the new historians" or "the revisionist Israeli historians." The original group included Simha Flapan, Benny Morris, and Ilan Pappé. We were called the new historians because we challenged the standard Zionist version of the origins, character, and course of the Arab-Israeli conflict. In particular, we challenged the many myths that have come to surround the birth of Israel and the first Arab-Israeli war.

The first thing to say about "old history" is that it is a nationalist version of history. The nineteenth-century French philosopher, Ernest Renan, wrote that "Getting its history wrong is part of being a nation." Nationalist versions of history do indeed have this feature in common: they tend to be simplistic, selective, and self-serving. More specifically, they are commonly driven by a political agenda. One political purpose they serve is to unite all segments of society behind the regime. The other common purpose is to project a positive image of the nation to the outside world. Conventional Zionist history is no exception. It is a tendentious and self-serving version of history.

The late Edward Said was not himself a historian, but he attached a great importance to the "new history," to critical historiography about Israel's past. The educational value of the "new history," he thought, is three-fold: first, it educates the Israeli public about the Arab view of Israel and the conflict between the Arabs and Israel; second, it offers the Arabs an honest version of history, genuine history which is in line with their own experience, instead of the usual propaganda of the victors; third, the "new history" helps to create a climate of opinion, on both sides of the divide, which is conducive to progress in the peace process. (One of the 30 essays in my book is on "Edward Said and the Palestine Question.")

There are two aspects to the Arab-Israeli conflict: the inter-communal and the inter-state. The inter-communal aspect is the dispute between Jews and Arabs in Palestine; the inter-state aspect is the conflict between the State of Israel and the neighbouring Arab states. The neighbouring Arab states intervened in this conflict on the side of the Palestinians in the late 1930s and they have remained involved one way or another to this day. In the late 1970s, however, President Anwar Sadat of Egypt began the trend towards Arab disengagement from the conflict.

The Zionist movement was remarkably successful in the battle to win the hearts and minds of people. Zionism is arguably the second greatest PR success story of the twentieth century – after the Beatles! Zionist spokesmen skilfully presented their movement as the national liberation movement of the Jews, disclaiming any intention of hurting or dispossessing the indigenous Arab population. The founding fathers of Zionism promised that their movement would adhere to universal values like freedom, equality, and social justice. Based on these ideals, they claimed to aspire to develop Palestine for the benefit of all these people, regardless of their religion or ethnicity.

A huge gap, however, separated the proclaimed ideals of the founding fathers from the reality of Zionist treatment of the Arab population of

Palestine on the ground. This gap was filled by Zionist spokesmen with hypocrisy and humbug. Even as they oppressed and dispossessed the Palestinians, the Zionists continued to claim the moral high-ground. In the face of overwhelming evidence to the contrary, they persisted in portraying Zionism as an enlightened, progressive, and peace-loving movement and its opponents as implacably hostile fanatics. One of the achievements of the "new history" is to expose this gap between rhetoric and reality.

From the early days of the Zionist movement, its leaders were preoccupied with what they euphemistically called "the Arab question." This was also sometimes referred to as "the hidden question" – the presence of an Arab community on the land of their dreams. And from the beginning, the Zionists developed a strategy for dealing with this problem. This was the strategy of the "iron wall," of dealing with the Arabs from a position of unassailable military strength.

A decade ago, I published a book under the title *The Iron Wall: Israel and the Arab World*. It covered the first 50 years of statehood, from 1948 to 1998. This is a fairly long history book but I can summarise it for you in a single sentence: Israel's leaders have always preferred force to diplomacy in dealing with the Arabs. Ever since its inception, Israel has been strongly predisposed to resort to military force, and reluctant, remarkably reluctant, to engage in meaningful diplomacy in order to resolve the political dispute with its neighbours. True, in 1979 Israel concluded a peace treaty with Egypt and in 1994 it concluded a peace treaty with Jordan but the overall pattern remains one of relying predominantly on brute military force.

The architect of the iron-wall strategy was Ze'ev Jabotinsky, an ardent Jewish nationalist and the spiritual father of the Israeli Right. In 1923 Jabotinsky published an article "On the Iron Wall (We and the Arabs)" with an analysis of "the Arab question" and recommendations on how to confront it. He argued that no nation in history ever agreed voluntarily to make way for another people to come and create a state on its land. The Palestinians were a people, not a rabble, and Palestinian resistance to a Jewish state was an inescapable fact. Consequently, a voluntary agreement between the two parties was unattainable. The only way to achieve the Zionist project of an independent Jewish state in Palestine, Jabotinsky concluded, was unilaterally and by military force. A Jewish state could only be built behind an iron wall of Jewish military power. The Arabs will hit their heads against the wall, but eventually they will despair and give up any hope of overpowering the Zionists. Then, and only then, will come the time for stage two, negotiating with the leaders of the Palestine Arabs about their rights and status in Palestine.

The iron wall was a national strategy for overcoming the main obstacle on the road to statehood. The Arab Revolt of 1936-1939 seemed to confirm the premises of this strategy. The point to stress is that this was not the strategy of the right, or of the left, or of the centre. Based on a broad consensus, it became the national strategy for dealing with the Arabs from the 1930s onwards. Regardless of the political colour of the government of the day, this was the dominant strategy under successive Israeli prime ministers from David Ben-Gurion, the founder of the state, to Binyamin Netanyahu, the current incumbent.

In my book I argue that the history of the state of Israel is the vindication of the strategy of the iron wall. First the Egyptians, in 1979, then the PLO, in 1993, then Jordan, in 1994, all negotiated peace agreements with Israel from a position of palpable weakness. So the strategy of "negotiations from strength" worked. The disappointment is that, in Israel's entire history, only one prime minister had the courage to move from stage one, the building of military power, to stage two, negotiations with the Palestinians. That prime minister was Yitzhak Rabin and the transition occurred during the secret talks in the Norwegian capital between Israeli and PLO representatives which produced the 1993 Oslo Accord.

In the rest of what I have to say, my reflections will revolve round four major landmarks in the history of the Israeli-Palestinian conflict: the 1948 war for Palestine; the June 1967 war; the 1993 Oslo Accord; and the Gaza war of December 2008.

The War for Palestine

The first Arab-Israeli war was, in fact, two wars rolled into one. The first phase, from the passage of the UN partition resolution on 29 November 1947 to the expiry of the British Mandate over Palestine on 14 May 1948, was the war between the Jewish and Arab communities in Palestine and it ended with a crushing defeat for the Palestinians and in the decimation of their society. The second phase began with the invasion of Palestine by the regular armies of the neighbouring Arab states on 15 May 1948 and it ended with a ceasefire on 7 January 1949. This phase, too, ended with an Israeli triumph and a comprehensive Arab defeat.

The main losers in 1948 were the Palestinians. Around 730,000 Palestinians, over half the total population, became refugees and the name Palestine was wiped of the map. Israelis call this "the War of Independence" while Palestinians call it the *Nakba*, or catastrophe. Whatever name is given to it, the war for Palestine marked a major turning point in the history of the modern Middle East.

The debate in Israel between the "new historians" and the pro-Zionist "old historians" initially revolved round the fateful events of 1948. There are several bones of contention in this debate. For example, the old historians claim that the Palestinians left Palestine of their own accord and in the expectation of a triumphal return. We say that the Palestinians did not leave of their own accord; that the Jewish forces played an active part in pushing them out. Another argument concerns Britain's intentions as the Mandate over Palestine approached its inglorious end. The old historians claim that Britain's main aim in the twilight period was to abort the birth of a Jewish state. On the basis of the official British documents, we argue that Britain's real aim was to abort the birth of a Palestinian state. There is another issue in dispute: why did the political deadlock persist for three decades after the guns fell silent in 1949? The old historians say it was Arab intransigence; we say it was Israeli intransigence. In short, my colleagues and I attribute to Israel a far larger share of the responsibility for the root causes of the Israeli-Palestinian conflict than the orthodox Zionist rendition of events.

It seems to me undeniable that the creation of the State of Israel in 1948 involved a monumental injustice to the Palestinians. And yet I maintain that the State of Israel within its original 1949 borders is legitimate. Some people say that this is inconsistent: how can a state built on injustice be legitimate? My answer to my critics is twofold. First of all, there was the all-important United Nations resolution of 29 November 1947, which called for Mandatory Palestine to be divided into two states, one Arab and one Jewish. This resolution constitutes an international charter of legitimacy for the creation of a Jewish state. Secondly, in the first half of 1949, Israel negotiated, under UN auspices, a series of bilateral armistice agreements with all its neighbours: Lebanon, Syria, Jordan, and Egypt. These are the only internationally recognised borders that Israel has ever had and these are the only borders that I still recognise as legitimate.

My graduate students at Oxford challenge me relentlessly on this point. In the first place, they claim that the UN partition resolution was unfair to the Palestinians because it was their country that was being divided. My reply is that this argument confuses fairness with legality. The partition resolution may well have been unfair but since it was passed by a two-thirds majority of the votes in the General Assembly, it cannot be regarded as illegal. A further argument that the students deploy is that even if Israel was legitimate at birth, its occupation of the rest of Palestine since June 1967 and the apartheid system it has installed there undermines its legitimacy in the eyes of the world. This argument is much more difficult to counter. By its own actions, by maintaining its coercive control of the occupied Palestinian territories, and by its callous treatment of innocent Palestinian civilians, Israel has torn to shreds the liberal image it enjoyed in its first two decades.

The June 1967 War

The second major watershed is the June 1967 war, popularly known as the Six Day War. The main consequence of that war was the defeat of secular Arab nationalism and the slow emergence of an Islamic alternative. In Israel, the resounding victory in the Six Day War reopened the question of the territorial aims of Zionism. Israel was now in possession of the Sinai Peninsula, the West Bank, and the Golan Heights. The question was what to do with these territories and to this question two very different answers were given. The moderates favoured the restoration of the bulk of these territories to their owners in return for recognition and peace. The secular and religious nationalists, on the other hand, wanted to hold on to these territories, and especially to the West Bank, which they regarded as an integral part of the Land of Israel.

The United Nations had its own solution to the conflict: Security Council Resolution 242 of November 1967, which proposed a package deal, the trading of land for peace. Israel would give back the Occupied Territories with minor border modifications and the Arabs would agree to live with Israel in peace and security. One feature of Resolution 242 which displeased the PLO was that it referred to the Palestinians not as a national problem but merely as a refugee problem. Resolution 242 has been the basis of most international plans for peace in the region since 1967.

History shows that this formula is sound. Whenever it was tried, it worked. In 1979, Israel gave back every inch of the Sinai Peninsula and it received in return a peace treaty which is still valid today. In 1994, Israel signed a peace treaty with the Hashemite Kingdom of Jordan and paid the price of returning some land it had poached along their common border in the south. This treaty, too, is still effective today. If Israel wanted to have a peace agreement with Syria, it would be within its reach through negotiations. But there is a price tag: complete Israeli withdrawal from the Golan Heights. The problem is that on the northern front, as on the eastern front, Israel prefers land to peace.

Quite soon after the ending of hostilities in June 1967, Israel started building civilian settlements in the Occupied Territories. These settlements are illegal, all of them, without a single exception, and they are the main obstacle to peace. Thus, as a result of its refusal to relinquish the fruits of its military victory, little Israel became a colonial power, oppressing millions of civilians in the Occupied Territories. It is largely for this reason that in the aftermath of its victory in the June 1967 war, Israel began to lose its legitimacy while the PLO began to gain in international legitimacy.

The Oslo Accord

Like all other significant landmarks in the history of the Israeli-Palestinian conflict, the Oslo Accord has generated a great deal of controversy. It was signed on the lawn of the White House on 13 September 1993 and it represented a historic compromise between the two warring peoples. The historic compromise was clinched by a hesitant handshake between Yitzhak Rabin and Yasser Arafat. Despite all its shortcomings, the Oslo Accord constituted a historic breakthrough in the struggle for Palestine. It fully deserved the over-worked epithet "historic" because it was the first agreement between the two principal parties to the conflict.

The Oslo Accord did not promise or even mention the brave phrase, "an independent Palestinian State." Its more modest aim was to empower the Palestinians to run their own affairs, starting with the Gaza Strip and the West Bank town of Jericho. The Accord is completely silent about all the key issues in this dispute. It says nothing about the future of Jerusalem, it says nothing about the right of return of the 1948 Palestinian refugees, it says nothing about the status of Israeli settlements in the Occupied Territories, and it does not indicate the borders of the Palestinian entity. All these key issues were left for negotiations towards the end of the transition period of five years. So Oslo was basically an experiment in Palestinian self-government.

For Yitzhak Rabin, Israel's security was the paramount consideration. Provided Israel's security was safeguarded, he was prepared to move forward and he did take another significant step forward by signing, on 28 September 1995, the Interim Agreement on the West Bank and the Gaza Strip, commonly known as Oslo II. Rabin's murder, two months later, dealt a body-blow to the fledgling peace process. We do not know what might have happened had Yitzhak Rabin not been assassinated. What we do know is that after his murder the peace process began to break down.

Why did the Oslo peace process break down? There are two conflicting answers. One answer is that the original Oslo Accord was a bad deal for Israel and that it was doomed to failure from the start. My answer is that Oslo was not a bad agreement, but rather a modest step in the right direction equipped with a sound gradualist strategy. The peace process broke down because Rabin's Likud successors, led by Binyamin Netanyahu from 1996 to 1999, reneged on Israel's side of the deal. There were other reasons for the breakdown of the peace process, notably the resort to terror by Palestinian extremists. But the single most fundamental reason was the continuing colonisation of the West Bank. This happened under both Labour and Likud governments after the signature of the Oslo Accord. It was a violation of the spirit, if not of the letter of the Oslo Accord.

The building of Jewish settlements on occupied land is not just a blatant violation of the Fourth Geneva Convention but in-your-face aggression against the Arabs who live there. So is the so-called "security barrier" that Israel is building on the West Bank. Settlement expansion on the West Bank can only proceed by confiscating more Palestinian land. It amounts to ruthless land-grabbing. And it is simply not possible to engage in land-grabbing and to pretend to be doing peace-making at the same time. Land-grabbing and peace-making are incompatible: they do not go together. It is one or the other and Israel has made its choice. It prefers land to peace with the Palestinians and that is why the Oslo peace process broke down.

The Gaza War

The fourth and final watershed in the history of the Israeli-Palestinian conflict on which I would like to offer a few reflections is the Gaza war unleashed by Israel on 27 December 2008. This was the climax of the strategy of the iron wall, of shunning diplomacy and relying on brute force to impose Israel's will on the Arabs. "Operation Cast Lead," to give the war its bizarre official title, was not really a war but a one-sided massacre.

On 7 January 2009, while the operation was in progress, I published a long article in the *Guardian*, in the G2 section. The title I gave the article was

"Israel's Insane Offensive" but the *Guardian*, typically, forgot to print the title. As will be clear from the title, I was extremely angry when I wrote this article. The article began by quoting a memo that Sir John Troutbeck, a senior official in the Foreign Office, wrote, on 2 June 1948, to the Labour Foreign Secretary, Ernest Bevin. Troutbeck castigated the Americans for creating a gangster state headed by "an utterly unscrupulous set of leaders." I used to think that this judgement was too harsh, but Israel's vicious assault on the people of Gaza, and the complicity of George W. Bush in this assault, reopened the question.

Very briefly, my view of the Gaza War is that it was illegal, immoral, and completely unnecessary. The Israeli government claimed that the war in Gaza was a defensive operation. Hamas militants were firing Qassam rockets on towns in the south of the country and it was the duty of the Israeli government to take action to protect its citizens. This was the objective of Operation Cast Lead. The trouble with this official line is that there was an effective ceasefire in place in the months preceding the war. Egypt brokered the ceasefire between Israel and Hamas in June 2008. This ceasefire had a dramatic effect in de-escalating the conflict. The average monthly number of rockets launched from Gaza on southern Israel in the first six months in 2008 was 179. After the ceasefire came into effect, the monthly average dropped to three rockets between July and October. It was Israel that violated the ceasefire. On 4 November 2008, the Israel Defence Forces (IDF) launched a raid into Gaza and killed six Hamas fighters. That was the end of the ceasefire. If all that Israel really wanted was to protect its citizens in the south, then all it had to do was to follow the good example set by Hamas in respecting the ceasefire.

The Egyptian-brokered ceasefire agreement also stipulated that Israel would lift the blockade of Gaza. After Hamas seized power in Gaza in June 2007, Israel started restricting the flow of food, fuel, and medical supplies to the strip. A blockade is a form of collective punishment that is contrary to international law. But even during the four months of the ceasefire, Israel failed to lift the blockade. Despite all the international protests, and despite all the boats organised by peace activists to carry humanitarian aid to Gaza, the savage blockade is still in force today.

During the war the IDF used its superior power without any restraint. The casualties of the Gaza war were around 1400 Palestinians, most of them innocent civilians, and 13 Israelis. In the course of this war, the IDF deliberately inflicted a great deal of damage on the infrastructure of the

Gaza Strip. It destroyed thousands of private houses, government buildings, police stations, mosques, schools, and medical facilities. The scale of the damage suggests that the real purpose of the war was offensive, not defensive.

It seems to me that the undeclared aims of the war were twofold. One aim was *politicide* – to deny the Palestinians any independent political existence in Palestine. The second aim of the war was regime change in Gaza – to drive Hamas out of power there. In the course of the war, war crimes were committed by both sides. These war crimes were investigated by an independent fact-finding mission appointed by the UN Human Rights Council and headed by Richard Goldstone, the distinguished South African judge. Goldstone found that Hamas and the IDF had both committed violations of the laws of war. The IDF, however, received more severe strictures on account of the scale and the seriousness of its violations.

My conclusion may come to you as a shock but it is not a conclusion I have reached lightly: Israel has become a rogue state. My academic discipline is International Relations. In the academic literature in this field, three criteria for a rogue state are usually put forward: one, a state that habitually violates international law; two, a state that either possesses or seeks to develop weapons of mass destruction; and three, a state which resorts to terror. Terror is the use of force against civilians for political purposes. Israel meets all three criteria and therefore, in my judgement, it is now a rogue state. It is because Israel behaves like a rogue state that it is well on the way to becoming a pariah state.

Dr Chaim Weizmann, Israel's first president, wrote in his autobiography that it is by its treatment of the Palestinians that Israel will be judged. It is accordingly by this yardstick that I judge Israel – and I find it sadly wanting. This is a melancholy conclusion to a rather depressing set of reflections. Let me therefore end on a more hopeful note. The hopeful note comes from a letter written in September 2010 by Eyad Sarraj, a psychiatrist from Gaza, to Lynne Segal, one of the sponsors of the Jewish aid boat to Gaza:

Dear Lynne,

You write to me, and I must tell you that I am very inspired by the coming voyage of a Jewish boat to break the siege on Gaza. I have helped and worked with and received other boats, but this is the most significant one for me, because it carries such an important message. It brings to us and tells the world that those we Palestinians thought we should hate as our enemies can instead arrive as our friends, our brothers and sisters, sharing a love for humanity and for our struggle for justice and peace. I will wait with anticipation to shake hands with them and hold them dear in close embrace. They are my heroes.

Please, never despair that you cannot bring peace, and never give up work for a just world. When I see, read, and relate to Jews who believe in me as an equal human being, and who tell me that their definition of humanity is not complete without me, I become stronger in my quest for justice and peace. I learnt long ago that there are Jews in and outside Israel who belong with me in the camp of friends of justice and peace. I have always strongly believed that we can live together, that we must live together. We have no other choice except to live together. It is because of people like you, and events like this, that I will never give up on the hope.

With my best and warmest,

Eyad Sarraj

This essay was first published in Asian Affairs, *Volume 42, Issue 1, March 2011.*

THE PERILS AND PITFALLS OF PATRIOTIC HISTORY
(February 2014)

Getting history wrong.

Michael Gove's perspective on the First World War is a classic example of a narrow, nationalistic, blinkered version of history. In an article in the *Daily Mail*, on 2 January 2014, the Education Secretary used the centenary of the Great War to declare war on "left-wing academics" whom he accused of peddling unpatriotic myths about Britain's role in the conflict.

For Gove this was a plainly just war, a patriotic war in defence of the homeland and freedom, a war forced on Britain by imperial Germany's "aggressively expansionist war aims." British soldiers, according to Gove, went to war in 1914 to defend "the western liberal order." Gove also argued that dramas such as *Oh What a Lovely War* and satires such as *Blackadder* enable left-wing myths to take hold, leading some people to denigrate the "patriotism, honour and courage" of those who fought and died for their country. Gove's article provoked a barrage of angry responses, including one from Baldrick, Blackadder's wily sidekick.

One of the fiercest counter-attacks on the education secretary came from the left-wing journalist Seamus Milne in an article entitled "An imperial bloodbath that's a warning, not a noble cause" (*The Guardian*, 9 January). Milne dismissed Gove's claims about the war and its critics as "preposterous nonsense." For Milne the 1914-18 bloodbath was not just a war: "It was a savage industrial slaughter perpetrated by a gang of predatory imperial powers, locked in a deadly struggle to capture and carve up territories, markets and resources."

Debates about the origins of wars have a habit of becoming highly politicized and very heated. The reason is that they cut to the core of a nation's image of itself as well as its image of the enemy. The stories that nations tell about themselves, like epic poems, are filled with heroes and villains and stirring events. As Michael Howard, the eminent British military historian, noted: such stories sustain us in difficult times but they are "nursery history."

In Michael Gove's simple view of the slide to war, the Germans were the villains and the British soldiers were the heroes. In Milne's Marxist view, none of the imperial powers who embroiled Europe in the catastrophe of 1914 was innocent or peace-loving.

Nationalist versions of history, whether British or German, French or Russian, Serbian or Austro-Hungarian, have one thing in common: they tend to be simplistic, selective, self-righteous, and self-serving. Nationalist movements always re-write history. A nation has been defined as a group of people united by hatred of their neighbours and a mistaken view of the past.

"Getting its history wrong is part of being a nation," observed Ernest Renan, the nineteenth-century French philosopher. The prevalence of stereotypes, inaccuracies, and distortions in nationalist historiography is not accidental; it is in the nature of the beast. Patriotic history is by definition partial and partisan history. It is driven not by an objective search for truth but by a political agenda, and most commonly by the desire to rally all segments of society behind the ruling party and to present a positive image of the nation to the outside world.

Historians who challenge the reigning orthodoxy about the past frequently arouse the ire of the political establishment of the day. "Historians are dangerous people," thundered Soviet leader Nikita Khrushchev, "they are capable of upsetting everything." And long may they continue to do so! For the task of the historian is not to buttress nationalist narratives but to subject the claims of both sides to rigorous scrutiny in the light of all the available evidence and to discard those notions, however deeply cherished, that do not stand up to such scrutiny. Indeed, it is the duty of the historian to hold a mirror to society, to convey uncomfortable home truths, and to speak truth to power. From an educational point of view, the subversive role of history is thus of supreme importance.

Loyalist historians, like Professor Anita Shapira of Tel Aviv University, lambasted the New Israeli Historians for our alleged pro-Palestinian bias, and regurgitated the conventional wisdom by portraying Israel as the wronged party, and as the innocent victim of Arab predators. Aharon Meged, a prominent novelist, went even further in an article in *Haaretz*, warning that we were leading our country towards collective suicide. Meged could at least claim poetic licence but some of the wild charges against us were of the kind that gives paranoia a bad name.

The debate quickly spilled from the academy into the public arena and initially it focused on 1948, on the conflict which Israelis call the "War of Independence." Politicians were particularly troubled by the prospect that our interpretations of Israel's birth and early years would affect the teaching of history in Israeli high schools. The new historiography was seen as thoroughly subversive.

Benny Morris, for example, drove a coach and horses through the Zionist claim that Israel was in no way responsible for the *Nakba* or the catastrophe, for turning over 700,000 Palestinians into refugees. Proof that Israel played an active part in creating the refugee problem entailed responsibility for solving it, a responsibility that Israel continues to deny to this day.

Another tenet of Zionist historiography was that the seven regular Arab armies that invaded Palestine in May 1948 did so with the united aim of strangling the infant Jewish state at birth and throwing the Jews into the sea. Our research revealed that the Arab rulers who made up the ramshackle coalition in 1948 were deeply divided among themselves and that one of them, King Abdullah of Jordan, was in fact in cahoots with the Jews against the Palestinians.

This was the thesis I advanced in my 1988 book *Collusion across the Jordan*. Abdullah and the Zionist leaders, I argued, conspired to divide up Palestine between themselves at the expense of the Palestinian national movement which laid a claim to the whole of Palestine.

Another cherished notion in the collective memory was that of a heroic struggle against overwhelming odds of the few against the many. We did not deny the courage or bravery of the Jewish fighters but we did point out that, in the Palestine theatre, they outnumbered all the Arab fighters, regular and irregular, put together and that their ultimate victory was not a miracle but the result of the military balance.

We also differed from the orthodox historians on the reasons for the persistence of the political deadlock after the guns fell silent. They claimed that Israel's leaders whole-heartedly strove for peace but there was no one to talk to on the other side. We demonstrated that on the other side there were pragmatic rulers eager to negotiate but that Israel's leaders were inflexible, rejecting any territorial compromise and denying the right of return of the Palestinian refugees. Our conclusion was that the quest for peace in the Middle East was frustrated more by Israeli than by Arab intransigence. Another sacred cow was slaughtered. The cumulative effect of all our books was to undermine the popular-heroic-moralistic version of the first Arab-Israeli war which was taught in Israeli schools.

The new history was a history that made a difference. What a decade earlier would have been dismissed as dangerous radicalism began to infiltrate into the intellectual mainstream. Our left-wing friends even started to tease us for having morphed from Young Turks into old jerks. But the Israeli political establishment remained adamant in rejecting the new interpretations.

In the run up to the elections of 2001, Ariel Sharon, the leader of the right-wing Likud party, was asked what changes he thought the education system needed. He replied: "I would like them to study the history of the people of Israel and the land of Israel…the children must be taught Jewish-Zionist values, and the 'new historians' must not be taught."

In most contexts, as in the British and Israeli ones, patriotic pride does not make for good history. The real value in studying history lies not in garnering evidence for conflicting nationalist narratives but in gaining a detached and unblinkered view of the past, and especially of the origins of wars. War is said to be too serious a business to be left to the soldiers. By the same token, military history is too serious a business to be left to the politicians.

When politicians pontificate about the past it is rarely in the disinterested pursuit of a complex truth and more often in order to score party political points. And when politicians invoke the "lessons of history" they usually have a hidden or not so hidden political agenda. People in power who assume the heavy responsibility of taking their country to war almost invariably claim that they had no choice. But in most cases the notion of TINA – there is no alternative – is false. Like patriotism, it can be the last refuge of the scoundrel. As Margaret Macmillan notes in the conclusion to her magisterial work on the outbreak of World War I – *The War that Ended Peace* – "There are always choices."

This slightly abridged essay was first published in OpenDemocracy, *7 February 2014.*

ISRAEL, HAMAS, AND THE CONFLICT IN GAZA (2015)

Securing Greater Israel (or: see you then and Shalom).

Zionism and the Arabs

"Operation Protective Edge" in the summer of 2014 was Israel's third major military campaign in the Gaza Strip in six years. It followed "Operation Cast Lead" of 2008-9 and "Operation Pillar of Defence" of November 2012. The name "Operation Protective Edge," like the names of so many of its predecessors, was intended to imply that it was a legitimate act of self-defence. The argument of self-defence is regularly cited by Israeli spokesmen to justify the resort to military force. It needs to be examined on a case-by-case basis. The evidence advanced for regarding "Operation Protective Edge" as a measure of self-defence is thin to non-existent. Like the invasion of Lebanon in 1982, the second Lebanon war of 2006, and the first two mini-wars in Gaza, it was an act of aggression, an offensive war undertaken by Israel in pursuit of broad but undeclared geopolitical objectives.

To make sense of "Operation Protective Edge" it is necessary to place it within the context of the Israeli-Palestinian conflict and in the wider context still of the emergence of Israel as a colonial settler-state. The State of Israel is the principal political progeny of the Zionist movement which was itself a product of the age of nationalism in late nineteenth-century Europe. Zion is one of the biblical names for Jerusalem and the Zionist movement's ultimate goal was to gather the Jews from "the four corners of the earth" and to build an independent Jewish state in Palestine in which Jews would constitute the majority. The principal problem with this project was that Palestine was already home to an Arab population that had lived there for centuries. There were two peoples and one land, hence the conflict.

Alongside the conflict on the ground in Palestine, there was the battle to win the hearts and minds of people in the world at large. Here the Zionist movement had a decisive edge over its rival. Zionist spokesmen skilfully presented their movement not as the ally of European colonialism but as the national liberation movement of the Jews, disclaiming any intention of hurting or dispossessing the indigenous Arab population.

In 1925 Jabotinsky broke away from the mainstream labour-Zionist movement led by Ben-Gurion to form the World Union of Zionist Revisionists. While the two movements were in agreement on the strategy for achieving a Jewish state, they differed in their territorial aims. Labour Zionists were deliberately vague about the borders of the state-in-the-making whereas the Revisionist Zionists insisted that it should stretch over the entire Mandate Palestine from the Jordan River to the Mediterranean Sea. When the Peel commission of inquiry first proposed the partition of Palestine in 1937, the Zionist movement was split but the official leadership eventually accepted it. Palestinian rejection sealed the fate of the plan. In 1947 the General Assembly of the United Nations voted for resolving the conflict by partitioning Mandate Palestine into Arab and Jewish states.

The Oslo Accord

The Palestinians believed that in return for giving up their claim to 78 per cent of Mandate Palestine, they would gain an independent state in the remaining 22 per cent with a capital city in Jerusalem. They were to be bitterly disappointed.

In 2000 the Oslo peace process broke down following the failure of the Camp David summit and the outbreak of the second intifada. Israelis claim that the Palestinians were responsible for the breakdown of the Oslo peace process because they made a strategic choice to return to violence and, consequently, there was no Palestinian partner for peace. Palestinian violence was indeed a contributory factor to the breakdown but not the main cause. The fundamental reason was that Israel reneged on its side of the deal following the assassination of Yitzhak Rabin. The Jewish fanatic who murdered Rabin also succeeded in derailing the peace train.

In 1996 the right-wing Likud Party returned to power under the leadership of Binyamin Netanyahu. Netanyahu had been elected leader of Likud in March 1993. That year, before the Oslo accord was concluded, he published a major book under the title *A Place among the Nations: Israel and the World*. The book was inspired by the teaching of Ze'ev Jabotinsky and by the fiercely nationalistic education he received from his father, the historian Benzion Netanyahu, who had been an adviser to Jabotinsky. The central element in Netanyahu junior's worldview was the right of the Jewish people to the whole Land of Israel. History was rewritten from a Revisionist perspective in order to demonstrate that it was not the Jews who usurped the land from the Arabs, but the Arabs who usurped it from the Jews. Britain was portrayed as no friend of the Jews, and the chapter on the British Mandate in Palestine was simply called "The Betrayal." The whole world was perceived as hostile to the State of Israel, and anti-semitism was said to be at the root of this hostility.

Much of Netanyahu's vehemence and venom was reserved for the Palestinians and especially for the notion that the Palestinian problem constituted the core of the Middle East conflict. For him the Palestinian question was not a genuine problem but an artificially manufactured one. He denied that the Palestinians had a right to national self-determination and argued that the primary cause of tension in the Middle East was inter-Arab rivalry. For Netanyahu, compromise with the PLO was completely out of the question because its goal was the destruction of the State of Israel, and this goal allegedly defined its very essence.

The change of government from Labour to Likud had profound implications for the peace process. The Labour Party is a pragmatic party whose position towards the West Bank is determined primarily by security considerations. Likud is an ideological party which upholds the right of the Jewish people to the whole "Land of Israel." Its position on the West Bank is shaped primarily by ideological rather than security considerations. Likud regards the West Bank – "Judea and Samaria" in its terminology – as an integral part of the historic homeland. In line with this view, it is opposed in principle to partition and in its electoral manifesto it explicitly rejects the idea of an independent Palestinian state alongside Israel.

As leader of the Opposition, Netanyahu made no effort to conceal his deep antagonism to the Oslo accords. He denounced them as incompatible with Israel's right to security and with the historic right of the Jewish people to the whole Land of Israel. Ever the opportunist, during the 1996 electoral campaign he toned down his criticism of the Oslo accords because they were highly popular with the Israeli public. Netanyahu won the elections by a margin of less than one per cent. Once ensconced in the prime minister's chair, however, he revealed his true face. And he spent his first term in office in a largely successful attempt to arrest, undermine, and bypass the peace accords concluded by his Labour predecessors. Rabin had been the builder of dreams; Netanyahu was the subverter of dreams.

Netanyahu also did irreparable damage to Israel's relations with Jordan by ordering the Mossad, in September 1997, to assassinate Hamas official Khalid Mash'al, a Jordanian citizen, in the Jordanian capital. King Hussein of Jordan was Israel's best ally in the Arab world. Whereas the peace with Egypt was a cold peace, Hussein did everything in his power to cultivate a warm peace with Israel. He was the only Arab leader with an active interest in normalizing relations with the Jewish state. In Itzhak Rabin Hussein found a genuine partner on the road to peace. In Binyamin Netanyahu he saw the negation of everything he had worked for. Following the signing of the peace treaty, a strategic dialogue was institutionalized between the two countries. In the context of this dialogue, Hussein conveyed to Netanyahu an offer from Hamas for a thirty-year truce. Netanyahu's response was the abortive attempt to assassinate a Jordanian citizen in Amman. Hussein was forced to conclude that the Likud leader was not a partner for peace but a saboteur and a menace to the Hashemite Kingdom of Jordan (Avi Shlaim, *Lion of Jordan: King Hussein of Jordan: A Life in War and Peace*, 2007).

Particularly destructive of the prospects of peace with the Palestinians was the policy of expanding Israeli settlements in the Occupied Territories. All Israeli governments, both Labour and Likud, built settlements in the Occupied Territories before and after 1993. But whereas Labour leaders tended to permit settlements mainly in areas of strategic importance that they hoped to keep permanently, Likud leaders took the view that Jews are entitled to settle anywhere they like in the Land of Israel. Although this was not explicitly stated, they also hoped that the settlements would become so firmly entrenched as to make territorial compromise impossible in the event of Labour returning to power.

Building civilian settlements beyond the Green Line (the 1949 armistice lines) does not violate the letter of the Oslo accord but it most decidedly violates its spirit. As a result of settlement expansion the area available for a Palestinian state has been steadily shrinking to the point where a two-state solution is barely conceivable. For the Palestinian population, these settlements are not only a symbol of the hated occupation, but also a source of daily friction and a constant reminder of the danger to the territorial contiguity of their future state.

For Raja Shehadeh, a Palestinian human rights lawyer and writer from Ramallah, the hills of the West Bank used to provide the setting for tranquil walks where he felt more freedom than anywhere else in the world. As a result of the Israeli incursion they became "confining, endangered areas and a source of constant anxiety." For many years, Shehadeh conducted exhausting legal battles in Israel's military courts to save the hills of Palestine from Jewish settlements:

> Now some twenty-five years later those times seem aeons away. How complicated and dismal the future has turned out, with the land now settled by close to half a million Israeli Jews, living in hundreds of settlements scattered throughout our hills and connected by wide roads crossing through the wadis. And more recently a wall has looped around the "settlement blocs," destroying the beauty of our hills, separating our villages and towns from each other and annexing yet more of our land to Israel, demolishing the prospect for a viable peace (Raja Shehadeh, *Palestinian Walks,* 2008).

The so-called "security barrier" that Israel has been constructing on the West Bank since 2003 is not only a blight on the Biblical landscape and a barrier to peace but also a blatant violation of international law. It was condemned by the International Court of Justice and by the UN General Assembly but construction continues regardless. The Wall's declared purpose is to prevent terrorist attacks on Israel and its West Bank settlements but it is as much about land-grabbing as it is about security. By building the Wall, Israel is unilaterally redrawing the borders at the expense of the Palestinians. The Wall separates children from their schools, farmers from their land, and whole villages from their medical facilities.

The rate of settlement growth in the West Bank and Israeli-annexed East Jerusalem is staggering. At the end of 1993 there were 115,700 Israeli settlers in the Occupied Territories. Their number doubled during the following decade. Today the number of Israeli settlers on the West Bank exceeds 350,000. Another 300,000 Jews live in settlements across the pre-1967 border in East Jerusalem. Thousands more settlement homes are planned or under construction.

The Oslo accord had many faults, chief of which was the failure to proscribe settlement expansion while peace talks were in progress. But the agreement was not doomed to failure from the start as its critics allege. Oslo faltered and eventually broke down because Likud-led governments negotiated in bad faith. This turned the much-vaunted peace process into a charade. It was all process and no peace. While failing to advance the cause of peace, it provided Israel with just the cover it was looking for to continue to pursue its illegal and aggressive colonial project on the West Bank.

The Unilateral Disengagement from Gaza

In August 2005 a Likud government headed by Ariel Sharon staged a unilateral Israeli pullout from Gaza, withdrawing all 8,000 settlers and destroying the houses that they had left behind. Hamas, the Islamic resistance movement, had conducted an effective campaign to drive the Israelis out of Gaza. The withdrawal was a victory for Hamas and a humiliation for the Israeli Defense Forces (IDF). To the world, Sharon presented the move as a contribution to peace based on a two-state solution. But in the year after the withdrawal, another 12,000 Israelis settled on the West Bank, further reducing the scope for an independent and territorially contiguous Palestinian state.

The real purpose behind the move was to redraw unilaterally the borders of Greater Israel by incorporating the main settlement blocs on the West Bank to the state of Israel. Withdrawal from Gaza was thus not a prelude to a peace deal with the Palestinian Authority but a prelude to further Zionist expansion on the West Bank. It was a unilateral Israeli move undertaken in what was seen as an Israeli national interest. Anchored in deep-rooted hostility to Palestinian national aspirations, the withdrawal from Gaza was part of the determined right-wing Zionist effort to prevent any progress towards an independent Palestinian state. American support was a major argument used in marketing the disengagement plan to the Israeli public. In an interview with *Ha'aretz*, Dov Weissglas, Sharon's closest aide and confidante, explained the motives behind the disengagement from Gaza:

> The significance is the freezing of the political process. And when you freeze that process you prevent the establishment of a Palestinian state and you prevent a discussion about the refugees, the borders and Jerusalem. Effectively, this whole package that is called the Palestinian state, with all that it entails, has been removed from our agenda indefinitely. And all this with authority and permission. All with a presidential blessing and the ratification of both houses of Congress. With the proper management we succeeded in removing the issue of the political process from the agenda. And we educated the world to understand that there is no one to talk to (Ari Shavit, *Haaretz*, 8 October 2004).

Weissglas resorted to clinical terms to explain how precisely the peace process would be frozen. The disengagement plan was the preservative, he said, of the sequence principle, which stated that there will be no political process until the Palestinians reform. The disengagement is "the bottle of formaldehyde within which you place the president's formula so that it will be preserved for a very lengthy period. The disengagement is actually formaldehyde. It supplies the amount of formaldehyde that's necessary so that there will not be a political process with the Palestinians." A lawyer by profession, Weissglas took particular pride in having secured American commitments in writing. "We receive a no-one-to-talk-to certificate," he claimed. "The certificate says: (1) There is no one to talk to. (2) As long as there is no one to talk to, the geographic status quo remains intact. (3) The certificate will be revoked only when this-and-this happens—when Palestine becomes Finland. (4) See you then and *Shalom*" (Ari Shavit, *Haaretz*, 8 October 2004).

Israel's spin-doctors repeatedly claimed that by withdrawing they gave the inhabitants of the Gaza Strip an opportunity to turn it into the Hong Kong of the Middle East. Gaza's inhabitants, however, saw no sign of this much-vaunted generosity. They were not freed from Israel's military grip nor were they given a chance to prosper. Israel's settlers were withdrawn but Israeli soldiers continued to control all access to the Gaza Strip by land, sea and air. Gaza was converted overnight into an open-air prison. From this point on, the Israeli air force enjoyed unrestricted freedom to drop bombs, to pursue with impunity the illegal practice of targeted assassinations, to make sonic booms by flying low and breaking the sound barrier, and to terrorise the defenceless inhabitants of the prison.

Israel likes to portray itself as an island of democracy in a sea of authoritarianism. But it has not done anything to promote democracy on the Arab side and it has actively undermined Palestinian democracy. Israel has a long history of secret collaboration with reactionary Arab regimes to suppress Palestinian nationalism. Appropriately enough, it also likes to play the old imperial game of "divide and rule" between rival Palestinian factions. In the late 1980s, it had supported the nascent Hamas in order to weaken Fatah, the secular nationalist movement led by Yasser Arafat. Despite all the handicaps of labouring under military occupation, the Palestinians succeeded in developing one of the few democracies in the Arab world. A major element in this success was the decision by Hamas to enter the political process.

Israel responded to the Hamas move by declaring the Gaza Strip a "hostile territory." It also enacted a series of social, economic, and military measures designed to isolate and undermine Hamas. By far the most significant of these measures was the imposition of a blockade. The stated purpose of the blockade was to stop the transfer of weapons and military equipment to Hamas but it also restricted the flow of food, fuel, and medical supplies to the civilian population. One American Senator was outraged to discover that pasta was on the list of proscribed items. The boycott applied not only to imports but, perversely, also to exports from Gaza. Why prevent the export of agricultural products and other non-lethal goods? It is difficult to avoid the conclusion that the hidden motive was to cripple Gaza's economy and to inflict poverty, misery, and unemployment on its inhabitants.

In its non-military aspects, the blockade constituted a form of collective punishment that is clearly proscribed by international law. Given the scale of the suffering inflicted by the blockade on the million and a half inhabitants of the strip, Israel could be considered guilty of "depraved indifference." The concept of "depraved indifference" in American law, or "depraved heart" under English common law, refers to conduct that is so wanton, so callous, so reckless, so deficient in a moral sense of concern, so lacking in regard for the lives of others, and so blameworthy as to warrant criminal liability.

As so often in the tragic history of Palestine, the victims were blamed for their own misfortunes. Israel's propaganda machine persistently purveyed the notion that the Palestinians are terrorists, that they reject coexistence with the Jewish state, that their nationalism is little more than anti-Semitism, that Hamas is just a bunch of religious fanatics, and that Islam is incompatible with democracy. But the simple truth is that the Palestinian people are a normal people with normal aspirations. They are no better but they are no worse than any other national group. What they aspire to, above all, is to live in freedom and dignity on what remains to them from Mandate Palestine.

Like other radical movements, Hamas began to moderate its political programme following its rise to power. It persisted in its refusal to recognise the Jewish state. But from the ideological rejectionism of its Charter and its call for an Islamic state over the whole of mandatory Palestine, it moved step by step towards pragmatic accommodation to a two-state solution. Its spokesmen repeatedly offered a long-term truce and they stated, in addition, that they would accept a Palestinian state within the 1967 borders if the peace deal is endorsed by a national referendum.

Operation Cast Lead

Ehud Olmert succeeded Ariel Sharon as prime minister and leader of Kadima, the party they formed after breaking away from the Likud. On 27 December 2008, the Olmert government ordered a major military operation against Hamas – "Operation Cast Lead." The thinking behind it was to weaken Hamas, cow the people of Gaza into submission, and crush the Islamic resistance to the Israeli occupation. The idea was to make life for the inhabitants of Gaza so hellish that they would revolt against their Hamas rulers, causing internal turmoil. Another objective was to restore the deterrent power of the Israeli army which had been severely damaged by the Second Lebanon War of 2006. Israel was intent on crippling Hamas because it knew that its leadership, unlike that of Fatah, would stand firm in defence of the national rights of the Palestinian people and refuse to settle for an emasculated Palestinian state on Israel's terms.

The Israeli authorities presented the Gaza war as an act of self-defence to protect their civilians against Hamas rocket attacks. The right to self-defence is enshrined in article 51 of the United Nations Charter. Implicit in this article is that a member state will use military means as a last resort to defend itself. For Israel, however, because of its broader political aims, military force was not the last resort but the preferred option. There was another, peaceful, option for stopping the rocket attacks from Gaza but Israel chose not to exercise it.

Rocket attacks had effectively ended in June 2008 as a result of an Egyptian-brokered truce between Hamas and Israel. The key element of the truce was that, on 19 June, the Gaza authorities would halt attacks by Palestinian armed groups against Israel and Israel would cease its military operations in Gaza. Another key element was an Israeli commitment to gradually ease the blockade of Gaza. The truce was due for renewal in December. The impact of the truce was dramatic. In the first six months of 2008, the monthly average of rockets fired from Gaza into Israeli territory had been 179. Between July and October the monthly average dropped to three. Hamas observed the truce but was unable to prevent other armed groups from firing the occasional rocket. Hamas officials explained that most of these rockets were fired by small militant groups and one group associated with Fatah, and Israeli officials did not dispute this explanation. On 4 November *(Editor's note: the evening of Barack Obama's first election as President)*, the IDF launched a raid into Gaza and the official reason given was to prevent the construction of a tunnel. But the tunnel was 540 metres inside Gaza. Building a tunnel was not a breach of the ceasefire but the armed incursion into Gaza definitely was. A fire-fight developed and six Hamas fighters were killed. Hamas retaliated to the unprovoked Israeli raid by renewing the rocket attacks.

Nor did Israel live up fully to its pledge to ease the blockade of Gaza. From July through September it permitted 200 trucks per day into Gaza. This was less than one third of the number of trucks promised in the Egyptian-brokered agreement. As the December deadline approached, Israel insisted that the rocket fire stop and Hamas demanded that Israel open the crossings to allow legitimate produce to go into and leave Gaza. Hamas offered to renew the truce on the basis of the original terms but Israel ignored the offer. On 27 December the IDF launched a massive air attack on Gaza and this was followed by a ground invasion on 3 January 2009. The stated aims were to stop rocket and mortar fire into Israel and to prevent the smuggling of weapons into the Gaza strip. The first aim, however, could have been achieved by pursuing the Hamas offer to renew the ceasefire. The conclusion is inescapable: the invasion of Gaza was not a legitimate act of self-defence but a disproportionate response to rocket attacks that were provoked by Israel in the first instance. Israel had a diplomatic option for defending its citizens but it made a deliberate decision to resort to military force.

For twenty-two days, the IDF shot, shelled, and bombed Hamas targets and at the same time rained death and destruction on the defenceless population of Gaza. Statistics tell only part of the grim story. Israel had 13 dead; the Gazans had 1,417 dead, including 313 children, and more than 5,500 wounded. According to one estimate, 83 per cent of the casualties were civilians.

Along with the heavy civilian death toll, there were serious economic, industrial and medical consequences. Gaza lost nearly two billion dollars in assets. Four thousand homes were totally demolished and another 20,000 were damaged. The IDF destroyed 600–700 factories, small industries, workshops and business enterprises, 24 mosques, and 31 security compounds. Eight hospitals, 26 primary health care clinics, and over 50 United Nations facilities sustained damage during the war. Overall, the savage assault drove Gaza to the brink of a humanitarian catastrophe. The indifference to the fate of the civilian population is difficult to comprehend unless it was motivated by a punitive streak.

The war crimes, allegedly committed by both sides, were another deplorable feature of this campaign. Israel's leaders claimed to target only Hamas activists and to make every effort to spare the life of innocent civilians. Yet throughout the war, the number of civilian casualties kept escalating. This was no accident but the direct result of applying a new IDF doctrine, the Dahiya Doctrine, which sought to avoid losses among its soldiers by the ruthless destruction of everything in their path. War crimes were investigated by an independent fact-finding mission appointed in April 2009 by the UN Human Rights Council and headed by Richard Goldstone, the distinguished South African judge who happened to be both a Jew and a Zionist (*Report of the United Nations Fact-Finding Mission on the Gaza Conflict*, 25 September 2009).

The IDF received more severe strictures than Hamas on account of the scale and seriousness of its violations. Hamas and other Palestinian armed groups were found guilty of launching rocket and mortar attacks with the deliberate aim of harming Israeli civilians: "These actions would constitute war crimes and may constitute crimes against humanity." The Goldstone team investigated 36 incidents involving the IDF. It found 11 incidents in which Israeli soldiers launched direct attacks against civilians with lethal outcomes; seven incidents where civilians were shot leaving their homes waving white flags; a "direct and intentional" attack on a hospital; numerous incidents where ambulances were prevented from attending to the severely injured; nine attacks on civilian infrastructure with no military significance, such as flour mills, chicken farms, sewage works, and water wells – all part of a campaign to deprive civilians of basic necessities. In the words of the report, much of this extensive damage was "not justified by military necessity and carried out unlawfully and wantonly."

In conclusion, the 575-page report noted that while the Israeli government sought to portray its operations as essentially a response to rocket attacks in the exercise of the right to self-defence, "the Mission itself considers the plan to have been directed, at least in part, at a different target: the people of Gaza as a whole." Under the circumstances the Mission concluded that what occurred just over three weeks at the end of 2008 and the beginning of 2009 was "a deliberately disproportionate attack designed to punish, humiliate and terrorize a civilian population, radically diminish its local economic capacity both to work and to provide for itself, and to force upon it an ever-increasing sense of dependency and vulnerability."

In the opinion of Goldstone and his colleagues, the grave breaches of the Fourth Geneva Convention committed by the Israeli armed forces in Gaza gave rise to individual criminal responsibility. They recommended that the UN Human Rights Council should formally submit their report to the Prosecutor of the International Criminal Court. But joint Israeli-American pressure on the Palestinian Authority and at the UN ensured that no further action was taken. There can be no doubt, however, that the Gaza war constituted a massive moral defeat for Israel and its army.

Most of the political objectives of Operation Cast Lead were not achieved. While the military capability of Hamas was damaged, its political standing was enhanced. The assault on the people of Gaza also had the immediate effect of radicalising mainstream Muslim opinion. The images shown by Arab and Muslim television stations of dead children and distraught parents kept fuelling rage against Israel and its superpower patron, effectively silencing critics of Hamas and legitimizing the radical resistance movement in the eyes of many previously sceptical observers. More than any previous Arab-Israeli war, this one also undermined the legitimacy of the pro-Western Arab regimes like Egypt, Jordan, and Saudi Arabia in the eyes of many of their citizens. These regimes stood accused of inaction or even complicity in Israel's crimes against the Palestinian people.

Internationally, the main consequence of the Gaza War was to generate a powerful wave of popular sympathy and support for the long-suffering Palestinians. As always, mighty Israel claimed to be the victim of Palestinian violence, but the sheer asymmetry of power between the two sides left little room for doubt as to who was the real victim. This was indeed a conflict between David and Goliath but the Biblical image was inverted – a small and defenceless Palestinian David faced a heavily armed, merciless, and overbearing Israeli Goliath. While leaving the basic political problem unresolved, the war thus helped to turn Israel into an international pariah. At home, however, Operation Cast Lead enjoyed the support of 90 per cent of the population who saw it as a necessary act of self-defence. This high level of popular support translated into a further shift to the right in the parliamentary election held the following month.

The Netanyahu Government

Likud returned to power under the leadership of Binyamin Netanyahu. With the emergence of a Likud-dominated government, the prospects of a negotiated settlement with the Palestinians virtually vanished. Netanyahu appointed as foreign minister Avigdor Lieberman, the leader of Yisrael Beiteinu, who had not only set his face against any compromise with the Palestinians but also favoured subjecting Israel's one and a half million Arab citizens to an oath of loyalty to Israel as a Jewish state – a move rejected by the Labour opposition and seen as borderline "fascist" and damaging to Israel's reputation. Netanyahu's coalition in his second term in office was arguably among the most aggressively right-wing and racist governments in Israel's history. It was led by a man whose ambition is to go down in history not as a peacemaker but as the leader who secured Greater Israel. The majority of the ministers were also wedded to an agenda of Greater Israel which was fundamentally at odds with the idea of a two-state solution.

In the worldview of Netanyahu, the brash scion of Revisionist Zionism, and of his even more extreme religious-nationalist partners, only Jews have historic rights over what they call "Judea and Samaria." The main thrust of their policy is the expansion of Jewish settlements on the West Bank and the accelerated Judaization of East Jerusalem. With such a focus, the government ensured that no progress could be made on any of the key issues in the Israeli-Palestinian conflict. Jerusalem, as always, lay at the heart of the dispute. By putting Jerusalem at the forefront of their expansionist agenda, ministers knowingly and deliberately blocked progress on any of the other "permanent status" issues.

Violence was the defining characteristic of the Netanyahu government's approach to Hamas. Like its predecessors it shunned diplomacy and relied heavily on brute military force. In doing so, it missed one opportunity after another to end the cycle of violence. In November 2012, it ordered the extra-judicial assassination of Ahmed Jabari, the chief of Hamas's military wing in Gaza, while he was reviewing the terms of a proposal for a permanent truce from Israeli peace activist Gershon Baskin (Nir Hasson, *Haaretz,* 15 November 2012). The timing of the assassination suggests a deliberate attempt to pre-empt the threat of a diplomatic solution. At any rate, Israel broke the informal ceasefire to launch Operation Pillar of Defence, its second major military operation against Gaza following disengagement. In eight days of intense aerial bombardment, 132 Palestinians were killed. The operation ended with a ceasefire brokered by Egypt. This specified that Israel and the Palestinian factions would stop all hostilities and that Israel would open the border crossings to allow the movement of people and the transfer of goods.

The sequel is described by Nathan Thrall, senior Middle East analyst of the International Crisis Group:

> During the three months that followed the ceasefire, Shin Bet recorded only a single attack: two mortar shells fired from Gaza in December 2012. Israeli officials were impressed. But they convinced themselves that the quiet on Gaza's border was primarily the result of Israeli deterrence and Palestinian self-interest. Israel therefore saw little incentive in upholding its end of the deal. In the three months following the ceasefire, its forces made regular incursions into Gaza, strafed Palestinian farmers and those collecting scrap and rubble across the border, and fired at boats, preventing fishermen from accessing the majority of Gaza's waters.
>
> The end of the closure never came. Crossings were repeatedly shut. So-called buffer zones – agricultural lands that Gazan farmers couldn't enter without being fired on – were reinstated. Imports declined, exports were blocked, and fewer Gazans were given exit permits to Israel and the West Bank...The

lesson for Hamas was clear. Even if an agreement was brokered by the US and Egypt, Israel could still fail to honour it (*London Review of Books,* 21 August 2014).

Operation Protective Edge

Hamas for its part continued to abide by the ceasefire to the satisfaction of Israel's securocrats for another eighteen months. But in April 2014 it committed what Israel considered an unforgivable transgression: it reached a reconciliation agreement with Fatah and proceeded, on 2 June, to form a unity government with responsibility to govern the Gaza Strip as well as the West Bank. Netanyahu immediately went on the offensive, denouncing the move as a vote not for peace but for terror and threatening Palestinian President Mahmud Abbas with a boycott of the incoming government. For him any sign of Palestinian unity or moderation poses a threat to the existing order and to Israeli hegemony. The unity government produced by the accord was in fact remarkably moderate both in its composition and in its policies. It was a government of Fatah officials, technocrats, and independents without a single Hamas-affiliated member. To escape isolation and bankruptcy, Hamas handed over power to the Fatah-dominated, pro-Western Palestinian Authority in Ramallah. The unity government explicitly accepted the three conditions of the Quartet (the United States, Russia, the United Nations, and European Union) for receiving Western aid: recognition of Israel; respect for past agreements; and renunciation of violence.

Israel responded to this promising development by what can only be described as economic warfare. It prevented the 43,000 civil servants in Gaza from moving from the Hamas payroll to that of the Ramallah government and it tightened siege round Gaza's borders thereby nullifying the two main benefits of the merger. Israel followed up its propaganda offensive and economic measures with a military assault on Gaza on 8 July 2014. It portrayed the attack as an act of self-defence in response to Hamas rockets launched against its civilian population. But these rocket attacks were themselves a response to a violent crackdown against Hamas supporters on the West Bank following the abduction and murder of three Israeli teenagers on 12 June.

Netanyahu stated that Hamas was responsible for the abduction and that Hamas will pay the price. He produced no evidence, however, to support the charge because there was no evidence. The murder was committed by a lone cell without the knowledge of the Hamas leadership. The Israeli authorities knew that the teenagers were killed soon after their abduction but they did not announce the death until eighteen days later. They used the intervening period to launch a powerful, worldwide propaganda offensive to denounce Hamas as a murderous organisation. At the same time, the IDF initiated Operation Brother's Keeper, ostensibly to search for the teenagers but in reality to deal a body blow to Hamas. As part of the operation, 350 Palestinians were arrested, including nearly all of Hamas's leaders on the West Bank. Netanyahu seemed to see an opportunity to destabilise the newly-established unity government and to undermine President Mahmoud Abbas. Reluctantly rising up to the challenge, Hamas responded with rockets. The sequence of events clearly indicates that the murder of the three Israeli teenagers was the pretext, not the cause, for the next onslaught on Gaza.

What were Israel's aims in launching this war? This question has no single, straightforward answer because the official war aims kept changing. First, in phase one of the war, which began with airstrikes on 8 July, the stated aim was to halt the rocket and mortar attacks from Gaza; then in phase two of the war, commencing in the late evening of 17 July with a full ground invasion lasting until 5 August, it was to destroy the "terror tunnels" that Hamas had dug under the border to launch raids inside Israeli territory; and subsequently it was said that war would continue until Hamas is completely disarmed. Behind these tactical objectives lurked undeclared geopolitical aims. First and foremost was the desire to reverse the trend towards Palestinian reconciliation and to undermine the unity government. This was in keeping with the policy of "divide and rule" and of keeping the two branches of the Palestinian family geographically separate. The aggressive practice of "*divide et impera*" in this instance demonstrates the falsity of the self-defence argument. Then there was the urge to punish the people of Gaza for electing Hamas and for continuing to support it in defiance of Israel's repeated warnings. Related to this was the irresistible urge to display Israel's raw military power. The overriding aim, however, was to defeat the struggle for Palestinian independence, to maintain the colonial status quo, and to preserve Israel's position as the imperial overlord.

The late Israeli sociologist Baruch Kimmerling coined a word to describe this policy: "politicide." Politicide is defined in a book with that title as "a process that has, as its ultimate goal, the dissolution of the Palestinians' existence as a legitimate social, political, and economic entity" (Baruch Kimmerling, *Politicide: Ariel Sharon's War Against the Palestinians,* 2006). In simpler language politicide means denying the Palestinians any independent political existence in Palestine. The idea is to make the Palestinians so vulnerable, divided, and exhausted by the struggle for physical survival that they would cease to constitute a coherent political community capable of asserting its right to sovereignty on even a fraction of historic Palestine.

Operation Protective Edge was the third Israeli attack on Gaza in six years, the fiercest in the firepower it deployed, and the most devastating in its impact. The aerial and naval bombardment of the enclave was followed by a large-scale land invasion. The toll on the Palestinian side after 50 days of intermittent fighting was over 2,200 dead, mostly civilians, and 12,656 wounded. 577 children were among the dead. 520,000 people, over a third of Gaza's population, were displaced. On the Israeli side the death toll was 67 soldiers and five civilians. Whereas the great majority of Hamas's victims were soldiers, most of Israel's victims were civilians.

The unleashing the full might of the IDF against the 1.8 million captive inhabitants of the densely-populated enclave suggests that the purpose of the operation went well beyond the targeting of Palestinian militants. Otherwise, how is one to explain the bombing of schools, universities, mosques, factories, hospitals, health clinics, ambulances, fire stations, and UN sanctuaries or the destruction of thousands of private homes and the flattening of whole neighbourhoods? Nor does the official line account for the deliberate targeting and destruction of the fragile civilian infrastructure that has not yet fully recovered from the damage done by the IDF in the 2008-9 attack.

Taken together the three wars in Gaza reflect a profoundly militaristic outlook, a stubborn refusal to explore avenues for peaceful coexistence, habitual disregard for the laws of war and international humanitarian law, and utter callousness towards enemy civilians. Israeli generals talk about their recurrent military incursions into Gaza as "mowing the lawn." By this they mean weakening Hamas, degrading its military capability, and impairing its capacity to govern. This operative metaphor implies a task that has to be performed regularly and mechanically and with no end. It also alludes to indiscriminate slaughter of civilians and inflicting the kind of damage on the civilian infrastructure that takes several years to repair.

Under this grim rubric, there is no lasting political solution: the next war is always just a matter of time. "Mowing the lawn" is a chilling euphemism but it provides another clue as to the deeper purpose behind Israel's steadfast shunning of diplomacy and repeated resort to brute military force on its southern border.

The conduct of the IDF during its 50-day military campaign in Gaza gave rise to questions about war crimes. Navi Pillay, the UN High Commissioner for Human Rights, pointed to a strong possibility that international law was violated in a manner that could amount to war crimes. She believed that Israel deliberately defied the obligations imposed by international law and demanded that the world powers should hold it accountable. The UN Human Rights Council appointed a three-member panel to investigate the allegations. Israel's past record suggests that it is unlikely to cooperate with any UN investigation. After Operation Cast Lead it denied access to the UN team headed by Judge Goldstone and, following the publication of their damning report, it engaged in character assassination of the principal author. Similar ad hominem attacks were launched to discredit Navi Pillay, the UN's then most senior human rights official.

These attacks are indicative of a general feeling among Israelis that the UN is biased, that the whole world is against them, that Israeli security overrides all other considerations, and indeed that Israel is above the law. To understand this attitude one has to delve into the political psychology of Israelis. Basically, despite their staggering military power, despite possessing the eleventh strongest army in the world and the strongest army in the Middle East, Israelis regard themselves as victims. As Uri Avnery, the veteran Israeli peace activist, wrote: the Israeli army is filled with "teenagers who are indoctrinated from the age of three in the spirit of Jewish victimhood and superiority" (Patrick Cockburn, *The Independent*, 2 August 2014). The same is true of much of the rest of Israeli society with the exception of individuals like Uri Avnery and courageous human rights groups. Feeling themselves to be the victims tends to blind the Israeli majority to the suffering they inflict on the real victims in this conflict – the Palestinians.

The subjective feeling of victimhood also blurs the distinction between enemy combatants and innocent civilians. Retired Major General Giora Eiland, the former head of Israel's National Security Council, published an article in *Ynet News*, claiming that there is no such thing as "innocent civilians" in Gaza and arguing that the citizens of Gaza share responsibility with their Hamas leaders for the violence against Israel. He even went as far as to compare Gaza under Hamas rule with Nazi Germany: "They are to blame for this situation," Eiland wrote, "just like Germany's residents were to blame for electing Hitler as their leader and paid a heavy price for that, and rightfully so" (Giora Eiland, *Ynet News*, 8 May 2014). Eiland was not reprimanded for expressing publicly these extreme views which are widely shared by the defence establishment and by the Israeli public at large.

The sense of permanent persecution, not to say paranoia, is understandable in the context of Jewish history. The American Jewish historian Salo Baron, spoke of "the lachrymose version of Jewish history" which sees the past as a worldwide and endless series of pogroms, culminating in the Holocaust. But this very preoccupation with security makes Israelis susceptible to politicians who are unscrupulous enough to manipulate the sense of threat and to inflate it for political advantage. The arch manipulator is Binyamin Netanyahu. He is the high priest of fear who never stops harping on the existential threats facing the country. His rhetoric about Hamas posing an existential threat to Israel is absurd when one examines the military balance between the two sides but it achieved the desired psychological and political effects. Ninety-five percent of Israelis supported the 2014 military campaign in Gaza with all its excesses, and many of them felt that it ended too soon. Netanyahu's popularity plummeted from 85 percent at the beginning of the operation to 38 percent when he agreed to a ceasefire "without finishing the job" (*The Times of Israel,* 28 August 2014).

Conclusion

The terms in which Netanyahu and his right-wing colleagues frame the conflict with Hamas are a mixture of half-truths, obfuscation, deception, and double-standards. Their narrative offers no peaceful way out of the conundrum. It is the problem, not the solution. It makes it impossible to tackle the real roots of the Israeli-Palestinian conflict. This is a political conflict for which, as the historical record conclusively demonstrates, there is no military solution.

It follows that if Israel adheres to its current policy, the result would be more of the same: more violence, more bloodshed, more terror, more wanton destruction, more human suffering, more wars, and more war crimes. In short, the Israeli narrative revolves round the demonisation of Hamas and demonisation leads directly to diplomatic deadlock.

The international community has both a moral and a legal obligation to protect the Palestinian civilians living under Israel's military occupation and to hold Israel to account for its persistent violations of the laws of war and of international humanitarian law.

The Western policy of refusing to engage with Hamas, of supporting Israel's abuse of the right to self-defence, and of supplying it with weapons that are repeatedly used to bomb a defenceless people is morally indefensible and therefore ultimately unsustainable.

UN secretary-general Ban Ki-moon called the Israeli attack on 1 August 2014 on Rafah in which a large number of civilians sheltering in UN schools were killed, "a moral outrage and a criminal act" (UN News Centre, 3 August 2014). This description aptly sums up Israel's entire policy in the conflict with Gaza.

The historical record of the last three wars in Gaza does not support Israel's argument that its resort to force is justified by the right to self-defence. By its own actions Israel has undermined any claim it might have had to dictate the terms in which the world should view its confrontation with Hamas. The international community urgently needs to develop a new narrative for addressing the conflict in Gaza, one based on the real facts of this tragic situation, international law, the norms of civilized international behaviour, and common human decency.

This essay is published here for the first time.

One of the foremost historians of the Arab-Israeli conflict, Professor Avi Shlaim is an Emeritus Fellow of St Antony's College and Emeritus Professor of International Relations at the University of Oxford. His books include Collusion across the Jordan: King Abdullah, the Zionist Movement, and the Partition of Palestine *(1988);* The Politics of Partition *(1990 and 1998);* War and Peace in the Middle East: A Concise History *(1995);* The Iron Wall: Israel and the Arab World *(2000, revised and expanded, 2014);* Lion of Jordan: The Life of King Hussein in War and Peace *(2007); and* Israel and Palestine: Reappraisals, Revisions, Refutations *(2009). He was born in Baghdad; grew up in Israel (1950-1961); attended school in London (1961-1964); served in the Israeli Defense Forces (1964-66); and has lived in England ever since.*

HASBARA IN ACTION

Dervla Murphy

Chips in a big mosaic.

(*Editor's Note: Last winter Dervla Murphy lived with Palestinians in Camp Hussein, Amman. When about to move to another camp, beyond the capital, she damaged her back and had to return to Ireland via London. What follows is a chapter – written first – of a Jordan-plus volume, entitled* Jordan from Afar. *See also Editor's Note on "Hasbara" on page 212.*)

While obeying the doctor's orders (99% immobility for a few days) I studied the newspaper cuttings saved for me by kind London friends. Soon my vocabulary had been expanded by one word – "Zios". Momentarily it baffled me, then I understood it to be a "nigger" equivalent, used by genuine anti-Semites in Britain and the US (apparently its place of origin) to taunt any Jew, regardless of their attitude to Zionism.

My file recorded that throughout the winter much trivial scratch-and-spit anti-Semitic quarrelling had distracted a minority of students in Britain. A young Muslim woman, Malia Bouattia, had angered fifty Jewish student societies by describing Birmingham University – a favourite of Jewish students – as "something of a Zionist outpost in British higher education." She also saw "Prevent," a much-mocked government programme to counter the "radicalization" of young Muslims, as "the product of a Zionist lobby" (Daniella Peled, *Haaretz*, 27 April 2016).

In mid-February, when the Oxford University Labour Club voted to support "Israel Apartheid Week," its co-chairman, Alex Chalmers, resigned, complaining, "Many members have some kind of problem with Jews" (Daniella Peled, *Haaretz*, 27 April 2016). This prompted the Oxford Jewish Society to publish details of the harassment of local Jews. And so it went on… One of my granddaughters asked rather impatiently, "Why waste time on silly student squabbles?" But she was quick to see the point: those little newspaper snippets were chips in a big mosaic depicting the contribution of *hasbara* to increasing instability in the Middle East – and elsewhere. Also, they well illustrated the ever-worsening terminology muddle. As Rashid Khalidi has observed more than once, in relation to the Palestinians, "The misuse of language has thoroughly corrupted both political thought and action" (*Brokers of Deceit*, 2014). Too much morphing has been going on since the turn of the century, a process greatly speeded up by the internet. Now the unwholesome conflation of anti-Semitism and anti-Zionism has been joined by the equally dangerous conflating of "Jewish" and "Zionist" in political speeches and written commentaries.

Britain's National Union of Students (NUS) is a confederation of 600 student unions with a 7-million membership – or so they say. Many of its past presidents have reached the top of various parliamentary and/or media greasy poles.

I was home in Ireland and semi-mobile by mid-April when Malia Bouattia was elected as president of the NUS. My heart sank; her having judged BDS "problematic," *because* it was "presented as a non-violent option" (Daniella Peled, *Haaretz*, 27 April 2016), had marked this young Muslim woman as no true friend of the Palestinians – and as an open goal for the *hasbara* team.

Next day Gabriel Gendler, a second-year Cambridge student, told Facebook, "I have never felt unsafe as a Jewish student until yesterday. I don't care what you think about the Middle East and I don't care if you're a brilliant liberation activist for other groups. Anyone who makes anti-Semitic comments has no place in anti-racist, anti-Fascist politics. And if Malia Bouattia can't listen to the voices of Jewish students then her politics aren't intersection at all." This message went viral and Russell Langer, the campaign director of the Union of Jewish Students (UJS) announced in painful student-speak – "I haven't called her an anti-Semite but her rhetoric has flirted with anti-Semitic discourse. She needs to address how she talks about Israel. When Jewish students raise legitimate concerns, people assume that it's a smear campaign. It's not Bouattia's anti-Zionist politics that make working with her challenging. The UJS supports the two-state solution but is committed to fighting any boycott of Israel. I sincerely hope that she will listen. She has caused a lot of distress. Most Jews have a connection to Israel whether or not their views of Zionism jibe with the radical perception of a colonial ideology. It's the responsibility of the president of the NUS to ensure that Jewish students feel comfortable on campus and the vast majority are Zionists. That's not to say they shouldn't be challenged on their opinions; that's part of being a student" (Daniella Peled, *Haaretz*, 27 April 2016).

Jake Cohen (first-year, University College London) described himself as "an activist with the liberal Zionist campaign group, Yachad" and noted,

"Over the past few years Jewish students have begun to feel that they were being expected to tolerate a significantly higher level of scrutiny than anyone else." He emphasised how few students vote in the NUS presidential election; Jews should not take Bouattia's victory too seriously. However – "This is the final nail in the coffin of me engaging with the Labour Party and other left-wing groups on my campus. Lack of understanding of anti-Semitism in itself isn't unforgivable but the refusal to listen and be educated is. This all leads to Jews being the only minority group that has to justify its accusations of discrimination and prove them to be correct. People feel if they want to join student politics they must leave their Zionism at the door and this is unreasonable" (Daniella Peled, *Haaretz*, 27 April 2016).

Then from Warwick University a pro-Bouattia, Lev Taylor, gave tongue – "She's a great improvement on the usually passive student leaders who always support the government line. I hope she will do what she can to mend bridges and Jewish students will do the same in return. Her comments on Zionism came from a place of ignorance rather than racism… She's been very active opposing the far right and Fascists. Much of the controversy is because she's a black Muslim woman. A white guy could have got away with it. It's fantastic to have a fighting leadership" (Daniella Peled, *Haaretz*, 27 April 2016)

Taylor disagreed that the new NUS president would make Jews feel unsafe on campus. "They'll be more galvanized. I met students who never cared about politics until someone criticized Israel, then they became a great defender of Israel, of women's rights, of gay rights. This doesn't undermine Jewish students, it's scary but not in a way that's unproductive."

A friend who can negotiate Facebook kept me in touch with this controversy and wondered – "Why is there so much ambiguity around?"

Why indeed! Except that ambiguity has always been an important tool in the *hasbara* kit, especially when major Israeli crises attract international attention. It's an easy tool to use, in conjunction with a glossary of double meanings: Democracy, Justice, Terrorism, Peace, Aggression, Rule of Law, Freedom.

What did Russell Langer mean by asserting, "The vast majority of Jews have a connection to Israel whether or not their views of Zionism jibe with the radical perception of a colonial ideology?" What does this "connection" mean to young British Jews? More than 50% of diasporic Jews have never visited Israel; I have no other statistics though my computer could no doubt provide them if I knew how to go about cyberspace explorations. Perhaps many Anglo-Jews have relatives in Israel and may often visit the country. But do any of them visit the OPT and watch Zionism in action? Within Israel, how many have talked with the Palestinian 20% of the population?

Malia Bouattia was savaged for complaining about "the Zionist-led media" though she was referring to a real phenomenon, not a conspiracy theory. And surely, if one-state is ever to come about, all such inconvenient truths, which have been buttressing Israel for generations, must be openly discussed in defiance of the "You're anti-Semitic!" threat. Israel's government spends lavishly on regulating how events in Palestine/Israel are presented to the world.

Often we hear or read about the thousands of rockets fired from Gaza into Israel – how often are we told precisely what damage they do? When our media report "terrorist" attacks on Israelis they rarely hold the balance by describing IDF "terrorists" blowing up the homes of suspects (SIC), or abducting juveniles from their beds in the small hours to take them for prolonged questioning without a parent or lawyer present. And how many BBC interviews challenge the slickly misleading statements of Zionist spokespersons? To learn about the routine facts of life in the OPT we have to rely on the Israeli daily *Haaretz* and the "alternative" media – *Counter-Punch*, *The Electronic Intifada* and the like.

The preservation of the West's Zionism-protecting status quo depends in part on an intricate web of deception so cunningly woven that Anglo-Jewish students can't be expected to understand why their loyalty to Israel provokes such vehement argument – and, too often, verbal abuse.

On 9 May 2014 Anshe Pfeffer informed *Haaretz* readers about the latest efforts of Israel's "national institutions" (World Zionist Organisation, Jewish National Fund, Jewish Agency, Keren Hayesod)

> to get in on the *hasbara* act, the new global frontier of Zionism. Two weeks ago, the National Information Directorate in the Prime Minister's Office held an unofficial gathering of *hasbara* organizations. "Members of over 30 private organizations came" said one of those present. Each group has heavy-weight donors, offices in Israel and abroad, a strong presence on the Internet and social media and a steely determination to conquer the battlefield of ideas – for Israel and the Jewish people. The hottest cause in the world of Jewish organisations is fighting the two-headed monster of anti-Semitism and the delegitimization of Israel.

"There's no crisis," says one Zionist activist, "but you have to keep the Zionist engines running, so you manufacture a threat." The Jewish state has never had so many self-appointed ambassadors to the world and the government's allocations for PR are breaking all records. Entire organisations, such as the WJC, have been refocused on *hasbara*. The WZO has beefed up its anti-Semitism department and hired a PR firm to draw journalists' attention to any and every odious utterance on the Internet. As in any war, facts go out the window. Research showing that anti-Semitism in Europe and North America has actually gone down is disregarded, as is the expert view that threats from delegitimization and BDS have been blown out of all proportion. Says one Israeli who works with American-Jewish organizations, "If you look at things from a historical perspective, nothing has changed. It's just the Internet that's magnifying the threat." The freelance organizations representing Israel all hew to a hard-right agenda, often creating absurd situations. Earlier this year, a group of British Jewish students, backed by the "Stand With Us" movement, expelled from the Israel Society at Oxford University Israeli students who were unhappy with their obsessive focus on fighting pro-Palestinian groups on campus. Says a British left-wing Zionist activist, "Only the right-wingers are on the front line. They've totally monopolized *hasbara* and it's all become very violent and theatrical. The whole world now believes the far-right represents Israel."

In 2003 Ephraim Nimni wrote: "The Zionist movement has shown a most remarkable ability to cover its own weaknesses by recourse to *Hasbara*, a sophisticated mechanism of lobbying and public relations capable of mobilising significant sections of the Jewish intelligentsia in the service of the national cause at home and abroad" (*The Challenge of Post-Zionism*, 2003).

The dark side of the Internet first became apparent to me in 2009 when I was living in Balata Camp, near Nablus on the West Bank. Around the time of Netanyahu's re-election as Prime Minister his son Yair, then aged 17, ran a Facebook campaign urging Israelis to boycott all Palestinian (he wrote "Arab") businesses and products. This message, quickly translated, went viral and had the predictable effect. Two years later Yair's Facebook mocked – "Terrorism has a religion and it is Islam." I wondered, did his father reprimand him for this incitement to violence? We all hoped no Palestinians were tempted to retaliate – "Terrorism has a religion and it is Judaism."

The absence of any mention of *Palestinians* during so many wordy student confrontations is puzzling until one realises that *hasbara* prefers to skirt around the mainspring of hostility to Zionism. It strives to keep the spotlight on *Jews*, as victims of anti-Semitism, and off the main victims of Zionism. Serious debates about the problem would defeat *hasbara's* purpose. Those aware of "the facts on the ground" recognise and despise *hasbara's* operations. But its target is the uninformed majority, people easily misled into confusing pro-Palestinianism and the generally abhorred anti-Semitism. Back to terminology: *hasbara* aims to avoid the honest equation – pro-Palestine equals anti-Zionist.

After 9/11 the English-language media avoided the Palestinian connection: as did the 9/11 "Commission Report." Later, Chairman Thomas Kean and Vice-Chair Lee Hamilton wrote in their memoir:

> This was sensitive ground. Commissioners who argued that al-Qaeda was motivated primarily by a religious ideology – and not by opposition to American policies – rejected mentioning the Israeli-Palestinian conflict in the Report. In their view, listing US support for Israel as a root cause of al-Qaeda's opposition to the US indicated that the US should reassess that policy. To Lee, though, it was not a question of altering support for Israel but of merely stating a fact that the Israeli-Palestinian conflict was central to the relations between the Islamic world and the US – and to bin Laden's ideology and the support he gained throughout the Islamic world for his jihad against America. (*Without Precedent: The Inside Story of the 9/11 Commission*, 2007)

That fact, so obvious to a minority in the West, attracted little notice among the majority who prefer not to look too closely at how the world is run – making them easy prey for *hasbara* teams and other opinion-formers.

Eventually it emerged that bin Laden, who frequently referred to the Palestinians' dispossession, had tried to persuade Khalia Sheikh Mohammed to reschedule 9/11 to coincide with Prime Minister Ariel Sharon's luncheon appointment at the White House. As a prisoner, KSM seemed calmly convinced that "9/11 would make America focus on the atrocities their country is committing by supporting Israel." I could quote twenty similar references to Palestine made by the al-Qaeda team as they planned their attack. In October 1999, at a friend's wedding, Binalshibh became inappropriately political and declaimed – "The problem of Jerusalem is the problem of the Muslim nation…the problem of every Muslim everywhere… Every Muslim has the aim to free the Islamic soil from the tyrants and oppressors." In July 2001, when an acquaintance wondered why Mohamed Alla rarely laughed, the response was – "How can you laugh when people are dying in Palestine?" However, for some hidden reason bin Laden neither directed attacks on Israeli targets nor funded Palestinian resistance groups. (See *The Eleventh Day* by Anthony Summers and Robbyn Swan, a labour-intensive, 800-page investigation of every aspect of 9/11.)

As Britain's *hasbara* bandwagon rolled on, some witless student threw himself under its wheels by demanding a global boycott of annual Holocaust Memorial Days. If only someone would organize an annual Nakba Memorial Day! Complete with before-and-after photographs and maps, poetry readings, videos, concerts, survivors' speeches, lectures, vividly presented tables of statistics…The opening events to be attended by prominent politicians, religious leaders, academics, writers and appropriate "celebrities." The lecturing historians (hand-picked, non-confrontational, of varied origins) could, among their many other tasks, gently ridicule Israel's complaint that anti-Semites would deny Jews the right to self-determination, allegedly granted to all other peoples (except the Tibetans, Kashmiris, Uigars, Chechens, Kurds and etc., etc.). When I put this idea to one Palestinian support group of London Jews and gentiles they asked dryly, "Where are the dollars?" But they saw my point. Most of the world's population know something about the Holocaust, comparatively few are aware of the Nakba's details or of its enduring consequences – Camp Hussein one of many examples. To prepare public opinion for one-state, that awareness has to be extended, not in any aggressive way, showing old wounds (been there, done that) but in as dispassionate a tone as possible, talking to the under-forties, quoting Shimon Peres, former President of Israel – "We have to do the peace process under new conditions, not so much between states as generations. Today if you want to do something you must turn to the young."

In the 1980s Rabbi Arnold Jacob Wolf of Yale University remarked, "It seems to me the Holocaust is being sold – it is not being taught" (Norman Finkelstein, *The Holocaust Industry: Reflections on the Exploitation of Jewish Suffering*, 2003). This Hillel Director had noticed some thimble-sized tip of an Everest-sized iceberg. Thirty years later several tomes had been devoted to the serial scandals of the Holocaust Industry: but you need a good head for figures to fully appreciate them. However, Raul Hilberg – who remains the pre-eminent Holocaust scholar – has found Norman Finkelstein's conclusions "trustworthy" and that's enough for me. I remember my father ordering *The Destruction of the European Jews* – an ex-Dachau friend of his had helped Hilberg with some research. But by the time this "definitive history" came out, in 1961, my father had died.

When Finkelstein's *The Holocaust Industry* first appeared in the US, in June 2000, no mainstream media outlet would acknowledge its existence. (They soon got a grip, when 130,000 copies of the German translation sold within weeks.) A Postscript fattened the paperback because in August 2000 the World Jewish Congress (WJC) announced that "$9 billion in compensation monies had become available for needy Holocaust victims." Hastily the WJC added that those monies belonged to "the Jewish people as a whole" – of whom the WJC happened be the self-appointed representative. Thus was born "The Foundation of the Jewish People" to subsidize Holocaust education. In celebration of this birth Edgar Bronfman, then WJC president, sponsored a black-tie "Reparations Banquet" in a New York hotel. President Clinton was among the guests and elderly impoverished survivors picketed the event. In Jerusalem in 2010, I talked with a member of the human rights organization B'Tselem who, aged 19, had joined this picket as a first-aid volunteer. She recalled that Hotel Pierre would not have allowed such down-at-heel oldies to use even its service entrances.

The US obsession with the Holocaust baffles many outsiders – and seems rather unhealthy. The *New York Times Index 1999* listed 273 entries for the Holocaust and 32 for the whole continent of Africa. Over 10,000 scholarly studies have analysed the Final Solution. Numerous State education authorities insist on Holocaust programmes in public schools. Numerous universities have endowed chairs in Holocaust Studies. The Holocaust is dragged onto the scene of numerous political causes – pro or anti this, that or t'other. Elie Wiesel deplored its association with "vulgar causes" (Norman Finkelstein, *The Holocaust Industry*, 2003). Peter Novick proclaimed, "The pretence that the Holocaust is an American memory is a moral evasion" (*The Holocaust in American Life*, 2000). Finkelstein was blunter – "Organized American Jewry has exploited the Nazi holocaust to deflect criticism of Israel's and its own morally indefensible policies" (*The Holocaust Industry*, 2003). Elsewhere he referred to "the symbiosis between the Holocaust Industry and Zionism's political agenda" (*The Holocaust Industry*, 2003).

Quickly the industry became multinational. In 2013 William Collins Donahue, Duke University Professor of German and Jewish Studies, visited Rwanda's Memorial Museum. The Professor is author of *Holocaust as Fiction*, regards the Holocaust as a useful teaching aid and was disconcerted by the museum's exorbitant admission and audio-guide fees. Also, he reckoned this memorial was premature – "Two decades have not healed the ethnic divisions." He didn't mention Israel's assistance to the Hutu killers so Rwanda's Holocaust education is incomplete.

On 26 January 2015 Professor Yair Auron wrote an open letter to Shimon Peres:

> In the early 1990s, you and the late Yitzhak Rabin stood at the head of the country's leadership. Those years were full of hope – hope that was cut off with Rabin's assassination. Yet you and Rabin sinned in all your actions concerning the acts of genocide that were perpetrated in Rwanda and Serbia. You approved the transfer of arms from the State of Israel – and not only through arms dealers – to Rwanda and the Serbia of Milosovic while genocide was in progress. The whole world knew about it in real time, and both of you also definitely knew. Attorney Itel Mack and I have been working to uncover the facts about the arms deals that were carried out after the UN had imposed an embargo on sales. It is clear that what the State of Israel did is nothing less than participating in war crimes and crimes against humanity. Rabin and you led this policy. Attorney Mack and I demand that the documents be made public that prove these crimes (and we have solid proof). But the justice system does everything to prevent this. In a hearing on the matter, the judge decided to accede to the Defence Ministry request not to release the documents that the Ministry conceded it had found – for security reasons. There are no security reasons to hide the crimes to which you were party – only moral reasons. Thus, you add insult to injury. You defile the memory of the Holocaust and its victims, which no one – certainly not we – have the right to do. On May 22 1994, at the height of the genocide, and after weapons shipments had already left Israel with your approval and that of

Prime Minister Rabin, the government released a statement: "The government of Israel is shocked at the genocide taking place in Rwanda. The Jewish people, who have experienced the bitterest of events, the Nazi Holocaust, and the State of Israel, cannot remain indifferent to the horrors in Rwanda."You are also responsible for that cynical and shameful statement. US President Bill Clinton, who did not try to stop the genocide in Rwanda – although he could have very easily prevented it – said at the 2013 event in honour of your ninetieth birthday, that he was to blame for what had happened in Rwanda 20 years earlier. Mr Peres, it is still not too late to ask for forgiveness and admit the crimes committed also in the name of the citizens of Israel – that is, in my name. These crimes will be remembered forever. (*Haaretz*, 26 January 2015)

In April 2016, *Haaretz* reported, "The Supreme Court on Monday upheld the denial of a Freedom of Information request to make public details of Israeli arms exports of Rwanda between 1990 and 1995." The panel ruled "Under the circumstances the disclosure of the information sought does not advance the public interest to the extent that it takes preference and precedence over the claims of harm to state security and international relations." International relations are lucrative. Israel had recently sold five billion dollars worth of Harop drones to Azerbaijan.

Professor Yair Auron is a well-known (though among Zionists not well-loved) scholar who specialized in the study of Israel's official attitude to other genocides. He apologized to the court for being so emotional. "I see this struggle as a kind of mission. I have been dealing with the Holocaust and genocide from the day I could think on my own, for 35 years. In 1948 Israel was established and then too the perpetrating and abetting of genocide were defined in international law as crimes against humanity."

Attorney Eitay Mack is young, wears a kippa and energetically opposes all Israel's arms dealing, whether free-lance or government-sponsored.

In the Supreme Court six experts from the Defence Export Control Agency (three men, three women) sat silently beside their attorney, Limor Ron, a young woman very sure of herself, knowing she couldn't possibly lose this case. One press reporter and no more than ten members of the public (usually only two or three) attended the various hearings.

Reading about Professor Auron's prolonged struggle took me back to Rwanda 1996. While collecting material for *Visiting Rwanda* (1998) I met several survivors who cursed the vicious foreign sources of Hutu weaponry. I winced to hear snide remarks about "those Jews making extra profit selling old grenades and rifles and bullets – their loot from '73" (the Yom Kippur War). My journal reveals that at the time I was even more upset by the unmistakable anti-Semitism ("those Jews") than by the arms trading.

The Israeli gun-runners were not alone. I quote now from *Visiting Rwanda* –

On 19 November "confidential" documents were found in a broken-down bus near one of ex-FAR's abandoned Goma bases. These revealed that a British company, trading as Mil-Tec Corporation, had supplied the genocidal government with £3.3 million worth of mortar bombs, grenades, rifles and bullets between April and July 1994. The shipment went to Goma via Albania and Israel, with Zairean end-user certificates, and began on 17 April – ten days after the start of the slaughter. According to British officials, these shipments broke no British law (though some broke the UN 17 May embargo) because they did not travel through British territory. A recent letter from Mil-Tec to the exiled former Minister of Defence requested the payment of debts totalling USD 1,962,375 and included invoices and bills for air freight. It concluded, "We have supplied your ministry for more than five years … You will realise that we have gone out of our way to assist your ministry in times of need." It soothes me to think of Mil-Tec losing $1,962,375.

In Gisenyi a French doctor praised Israel as the very first country to provide a fully equipped field-hospital for wounded survivors and more than 100 medical personnel. I already knew of this kindness; it had been widely publicised.

Towards the end of April a British Labour Party member, John McAuliffe, was suspended because of an "anti-Semitic slur" on his Facebook page. He had referred to the Holocaust being "used as a political tool of the Zionist government to establish a financial racket in the West" (Facebook) – not a startling revelation. He also mentioned the unnecessary level of poverty endured by many of Israeli Holocaust survivors; a sad reality beyond dispute. Roni Klinsky, CEO of the Foundation for the Benefit of Holocaust Victims in Israel, had complained in 2014 that 50,000 survivors (average age 86) were living in poverty – two-thirds of them women, many living alone. As McAuliffe pointed out "This paints a clear picture of the divide between Zionism and Judaism, and their incompatibility" (Yarden Skop, *Haaretz*, 24 April 14). Academics could spar for years over that statement (and some probably do) but to me it sounds like a decisively pro-Semitic attitude.

A day later (26 April) *Haaretz* printed an interview with Dr Anat Livni, for 30 years closely associated, as historian and teacher, with Tel Aviv's Holocaust Museum. She had concluded, "after carefully examining the situation," that "it is now time to change the agenda of Holocaust Memorial Day and to reduce the cost of the Tel Aviv ceremony – $133,000 this year." Her comments were in harmony with certain Israeli social media networks then sending out a manifesto calling for this money to be spent on survivors – John McAuliffe's idea in his "anti-Semitic slur."

Next came Naz Shah's Facebook reproduction of a map of Israel superimposed on a map of the US, originally shown in 2014 on Norman Finkelstein's blog and seeming to suggest that all Israelis should be transported to the US. I had a flashback to September 1992 when Prime Minister Rabin told a visiting Washington Institute delegation, "I would like Gaza to sink into the sea – but as that won't happen a solution must be found." Naturally no one expected Mr Rabin to apologize; many of us make similar remarks when exasperated. I've been known to exclaim, "Someone should strangle the lot!" – with reference to Ireland's present crop of political leaders. How come such mindless outbursts can now be used to provoke nationwide shock/horror?

Multiple public apologies were demanded of Naz Shah and when she had been suspended from the Labour Party Ken Livingstone hurried clumsily to the rescue with a completely irrelevant but not inaccurate linking of Zionism and Nazism in pre-Holocaust Germany. (One has to endorse Andrew Rawnsley's uncharitable summing up of London's former mayor – "a flippant, crass, muddled idiot" – in *The Observer*, 1 April 2016). When this intervention generated near-hysteria the Labour Party leader, Jeremy Corbyn, fumbled rather badly. To clarify Livingstone's incoherent mumblings he should have consulted Israeli historian Tom Segev's *The Seventh Million* (Picador, 2000).

I did just that and wrote to the *Irish Examiner* on 30 April 2016 –

Livingstone may not be everyone's pin-up boy but he does know his history

Ken Livingstone may not be everyone's pin-up boy but he does know his history. Shortly after Hitler gained power the Zionist leader, David ben-Gurion, felt the Nazis' take-over could become "a fertile force" for Zionism. A Mapai Party activist, Moshe Beilinson, soon visited Germany and reported – "The streets are paved with more money than we have ever dreamed of in the history of our Zionist enterprise. Here is an opportunity to build and flourish like none we have ever had or will ever have."

A senior Zionist official, Prussian-born Arthur Ruppin, then went to Berlin to bargain with the Nazis, to secure the transfer to Palestine of the property of German Jewish emigrants. Travelling on to Jena, Ruppin had a two-hour meeting with the prominent Nazi race theorist, Hans F.K. Gunther – who assured his visitor that he did not see Jews as "inferior" to Aryans, only "different." Therefore "a fair solution" must be found for "the Jewish problem." Back in Berlin, on 7 August 1933, Ruppin was well received at the Nazi finance ministry.

It was agreed that every German Jew emigrating to Palestine could take £1,000 sterling and merchandise worth at least 20,000 DM – perhaps more, were the finances handled by German and Jewish trust companies. In mandatory Palestine, £1,000 was the minimum capital essential to obtain British permission to settle. For this agreement the Hebrew term "haavara" ("transfer") was used in Nazi documents. It suited both the Nazis (Jews gone) and the Zionist (Jews arriving). *(Editor's Note: This arrangement is also described in detail by the Israeli scholar Yf'aat Weis in her article, "The Transfer Agreement and the Boycott Movement: A Jewish Dilemma on the Eve of the Holocaust," published by Yad Vashem, The World Holocaust Rembrance Center, in 2016).*

But, tragically, most German Jews were not then interested in the Zionist project though this transfer of people and property had been suggested by Theodor Herzl in *The Jewish State*, published a generation earlier. Many more details about those Nazi-Zionist negotiations may be found in Tom Segev's *The Seventh Million.*

And then I wrote an ignored letter to *The Guardian*:

> Mr Cameron finds it "quite extraordinary" that Naz Shah has been allowed to remain in the Labour Party after her reactivation online of Norman Finkelstein's deplorable 2014 "solution" of the Israel/Palestine problem: *Relocate Israel to the US*.
>
> On 9 March 2015 *Haaretz*, Israel's most reputable newspaper, reported that Avigdor Lieberman, then Israel's foreign minister, had declared that Arab citizens of Israel who are not loyal to the State should have their heads "chopped off with an axe." This immediately provoked social media demands for the beheading of Haneen Zoabi, one of the few Palestinian members of the Knesset. Around the same date, Lieberman had called for the transfer of *all* Palestinians from the OPT (Occupied Palestinian Territories). Presumably Mr Cameron also found it "quiet extraordinary" that Prime Minister Netanyahu did not at once replace his foreign minister. Naz Shah's message was measurably less shocking than Lieberman's. Relocated Israelis would keep their heads.

It seems young people, especially, don't bother weighing their words before going online. Naz Shah had two companions floundering with her in the hot water pool: the new NUS president, Malia Bouattia, and the 25-year-old Simone Zimmerman. Bernie Sanders had chosen Simone, a Conservative Jew, as his "Jewish outreach coordinator." (US politicians have strange appendages.) This was a brave choice. In 2014, during the Gaza carnage, Simone had organized a protest group. They recited the Mourner's *Kaddish* outside the Conference of Presidents' New York office, explaining that from Jewish prayers they seek inspiration and guidance. (Around the same time, in Bradford, Naz was having her intemperate Facebook reaction to all the bloodshed.) However, Sanders did not as yet know that his new aide had in 2015 described Netanyahu (Facebook again!) as "an arrogant, deceptive, cynical, manipulative asshole." Simone's political appointment brought about the inevitable "exposure" and Sanders came under "concerted and ultimately overwhelming pressure from American Jewish leaders" (The New York Times, 2016). And so he was forced to sideline this devout Conservative Jew.

The political commentator Peter Beinart (equally devout and Conservative) noted that she may have chosen the wrong words. Perhaps she should simply have quoted Leah Rabin, widow of Prime Minister Yitzak Rabin who was assassinated in 1995 by an admirer of Netanyahu's. Mrs Rabin had labelled the present Prime Minister – "a corrupt individual, a contentious liar who is ruining everything that is good about our society" (*Haaretz*, 18 April 2016). Or, Beinart suggested, Simone might merely have echoed Britain's succinct Foreign Office – "an armour-plated bullshitter" (*Haaretz*, 18 April 2016).

Beinart ends with a crucially important point, too often lost in these fogs of contrived anti-Semitism. "Simone cares about Israel and about the Jewish people. And she believes there should be space for moral opposition to Israeli policies, the kind of opposition once offered by communal leaders like Nahum Goldman, Rabbi Arthur Hertzberg and Rabbi Arthur Schindler… I'm not worried about Simone, she'll do fine. I'm worried about a community that punishes its children for challenging its lies" (*Haaretz*, 18 April 2016).

Back to Britain, where Sadiq Khan, on the eve of his election as London's mayor, was quoted in *The Observer* (1 May 2016) – "Corbyn had been too slow to act over Livingstone's remarks and those of Shah. He needs to act much quicker when allegations of these sorts are made."

My thoughts were then going in the opposite direction: "Why not take time to look into those cases before acting? And how stupid to summon all those sinister anti-Semitic wraiths out of Britain's shadows when we should be focussed on the very substantial Europe-wide threats of Islamophobia and fascism resurgent…"

For a week or so this rumpus managed to hog much of the mainstream media's attention, which won't have displeased those who work to minimize reporting on Israel's dirty deeds in the OPT. Amidst a welter of misinformation we heard John Mann M.P. asserting on BBC Radio that "Naz Shah's stupid remarks are also racist remarks and highly offensive." I groaned – aren't we confused enough already about anti-Semitism/anti-Zionism/anti-Israelism – why introduce "the racist slur?" How could anti-Semitism be a form of racism? The Jews are not "a race."

On my first visit to Israel it astonished me to find domestic race relations so severely strained. Approximately 63% of the Jewish population are Mizrahim (and 50% of Israel's total population) – aka "Orientals," officially called "descendents from Asia-Africa." They came from North Africa, the Middle East and, since 1990-ish, the Central Asian countries of the former Soviet Union: aka "the Stans." Some diasporic anti-Zionist

Mizrahi intellectuals call themselves "Arab Jews," which infuriates the Israeli Mizrahim. The Ashkenazim, of European extraction, make up some 30% of the population and have long been the dominant elite. That largely secular group are now beginning slightly to lose their grip as the ultra-Orthodox Ashkenazi, rooted in Eastern Europe, and right-wing religious Mizrahim increase numerically and gain more political power. Most of those in the earliest *Aliyas* (1882, then pre-1914) came from Russia and Yemen. Of the 2.5 million Jews who left Europe before the Great (!) War the vast majority sailed West. Very few were interested in Palestine (4 in 1,000) until the US ended mass immigration in 1924. The third and fourth *Aliyas* (100,000 immigrants from Eastern Europe) had doubled the size of Palestine's Jewish population by the early 1930s. At present the majority of Israel's Jewish citizens born in Israel (*Yelidei ha'aretz*) are Mizrahim because, until the mid-1970s, their birth-rate was by far the highest. Sadly though predictably they have always sided with the Ashkenazim against the Palestinians. However, Smadar Lavie, the Berkeley feminist and anthropologist who specializes in Egypt, Palestine and Israel, has hinted that it could be otherwise in a one-state Holy Land. At present, she explains,

> "the Mizrahi feminists" ability to challenge the regime is limited… They must speak the language of practice in order to help disenfranchised Mizrahi women resolve their daily problems in dealing with the regime's authorities, which, by default, are Ashkenazi. Thus, they have avoided intellectual possibilities for re-absorbing Mizrahim into Arab space. They have not pointed out that the early Ashkenazi-Zionist eugenic ideologies and practices against Mizrahim – such as forced sterilization, high-dose X-ray medical experiments without the subjects' consent and the removal of Mizrah babies for Ashkenazi adoption without the parents' consent – connect to the treatment of Palestinians (Hani Faris, ed, *The Failure of the Two-State Solution*, 2013).

And Dr Lavie goes on to reproach Ashkenazi feminists for "not merging the struggle for a just peace with the struggle against the racism experienced by the Mizrahim" (*The Failure of the Two-State Solution*).

Israelis come in all colours, some blue-eyed and blond, many Mediterranean olive, others Arabic handsome, a few red-haired and freckled, many indeterminate Central European or Slavic, an exotic minority glossy black like the 1,500 Abayudaya Ugandans due to arrive in Israel in 2016. About a century ago their ancestors began to identify as Jews and recently the Jewish Agency "recognised" them as belonging to the Conservative sect. The Law of Return ensures that Jews will immediately be granted Israeli citizenship and the exclusive right to buy land and property. Their race doesn't matter. Israel was established not as a homeland for one race but for one religion. The fact that political Zionism's founders visualised a mainly *European* colony in Palestine became tragically irrelevant after the Holocaust.

Prominent in that aforementioned welter of misinformation were the standard juvenile accusations of "consorting with terrorists" – Hamas and the like. Yet genuine peace-seekers, as distinct from "Quartet"-type charlatans, habitually engage in friendly and potentially healing discussions with the "other side" – and even attend ceremonies and visit locations of which the anti-terrorist establishment (its motives so often opaque) sternly disapprove. Listening to Jeremy Corbyn being excoriated for the company he keeps, and Sadia Khan cravenly apologising for his foolish youth and promising never to do it again, I thought of Washington's official outlawing of the PLO. After that, US security and political agents regularly met their PLO counterparts in Beirut. Kissinger admits, in *Years of Renewal* (1999), that a commitment was made to Israel in 1975 not to "recognize or negotiate with the PLO." Yet no one complained, four years later, when John Gunther Dean, then US ambassador to Lebanon, gratefully accepted PLO help to negotiate the release of the Teheran hostages. And, come to think of it, where would Ireland be in 2016 if nobody had consorted, twenty years ago, with our "terrorists"? Some of whom now enjoy cosy chats with Queen Elizabeth II…

On Skype, one of my London-Jewish friends told me about Avraham Burg, an observant Jew and former paratrooper, who was speaker of the Knesset from 1999 to 2003. He has now rejected political Zionism because of its core belief – dating back to the 1890s – that all gentiles, everywhere, have always hated Jews and will always hate them. The Jewish Agency, an ally of the Israeli government, funds the global propagation of this wicked message (among its many other enterprises) and my friend counted Britain's sporadic rows about anti-Semitism as one of its successes.

"A Zionist Israel is not a viable long-term project" (*The Guardian*, 29 December 2008). Did Nir Rosen's glimpse of the obvious provoke a Jewish Agency-sponsored sand-storm? Or, I wondered, was Britain's political atmosphere peculiarly unstable in the spring of 2016?

Rosen, in his much-quoted *Los Angeles Times* op-ed of 15 May 2009, diagnosed: "The problem is Zionism... If two decades ago comparisons to the South African apartheid system felt like hyperbole, they now feel charitable... The characterisation of anti-Zionism as an epidemic more dangerous than anti-Semitism reveals only the unsustainability of the position into which Israel's apologists have been forced."

A year later Henry Siegman noted despairingly in *The Nation* (25 January 2010) – "Israel has crossed the threshold from 'the only democracy in the Middle East' to 'the only apartheid regime in the Western World'... By definition, democracy reserved for privileged citizens is not democracy but its opposite." For years Mr Siegman has served as national director of the Synagogue Council of America and executive director of the American Jewish Congress – an unlikely anti-Semite. But how would this judgement have been received from a British public figure?

Ninety years ago Ze'ev Jabotinsky was honest in *The Shahak Papers* (No.31, p.16) – "If you wish to colonise a land in which people are already living, you must provide a garrison for the land, or find a benefactor who will maintain the garrison on your behalf. Zionism is a colonising adventure and, therefore, stands or falls on the question of armed force."Which neatly explains why Nir Rosen was right in 2008.

Britain's spasm of anti-Semitist agitation was nearing its climax when by chance (I suppose) *Haaretz* shed new light on Elie Wiesel, who for six decades featured regularly in such debates. His short first book, *And the World Remained Silent*, recorded his own and his family's sufferings during the Holocaust and was published in Yiddish in 1956. An even shorter version, *Night*, appeared in French two years later with a Foreword by François Mauriac, who had advised retitling and condensing the original. Mauriac hoped this slim volume would be as widely read as *The Diary of Anne Frank* – and it was. Translated into 35 languages it became a global best-seller, one of the most-quoted accounts of the Holocaust and mandatory reading for the schoolchildren of many countries.

For more than thirty years Wiesel laboured in Boston University, wrote many books and toured the world defending Human Rights, especially for Russian Jews. In 1986 he became another of those realpolitik Nobel Peace Prize winners who have made that award one of the world's worst jokes. His refusal to live in Israel antagonized quite a few of his fellow-Zionists, especially as Teddy Kollek, when Mayor of Jerusalem, had offered him a spacious "grace-and-favour" flat in the Old City.

In 2006 Oprah Winfrey boosted *Night* onto the shelves of another generation despite (or because of?) the controversies that eddied incessantly around its author. As a small sample – Wiesel always vigorously encouraged Zionist efforts to Judaise Jerusalem's Old City. He fought against the inclusion of Roma (or other non-Jewish) names on Washington's Holocaust Memorial. He supported the Reagan administration's crimes in Central America, rejoicing that Israel was the main weapons supplier for the Guatemalan thugs. He led the chorus likening Saddam Hussein to Hitler and frequently urged Bush Jr to get on with the illegal invasion of Iraq. On 4 August 2014 he took a full-page ad in *The New York Times* to condemn Hamas (the London *Times* refused to print his outrageous allegations). Then, to counter his rabid backing for Israel's 2014 attack on Gaza, 327 of his fellow survivors also invested in a *New York Times* page to deplore that barbarity.

Occasionally, over the years, friends have wondered at my reluctance to join whole-heartedly in their condemnations of Elie Wiesel. I never tried to excuse my uncharacteristic restraint; it would have sounded patronising to admit that I judged him too severely damaged to be held responsible for his vengefulness. Apparently he lost his compass, didn't know where to direct his rage. Perhaps, too, I was influenced, in some fuzzy way, by having once spent a week in his birthplace and there been repeatedly exposed to jagged anti-Semitism. For the first time I appreciated how deeply hurtful it can be, even when it's impersonal, retrospective, entirely dissociated from contemporary actions.

Elie Wiesel was born in 1928 in Sighetu Marmatiel (Sighet to you), capital of Maramuras in what was then known as the Kingdom of Greater Rumania. In 1990, soon after the Ceausescu deaths, I camped there during the first week of March, in the Tisa Hotel, a once-stately remnant of Austro-Hungarian glory. The tariff was £3.75 per night – cold nights, the bedding inadequate, the electricity feeble, the plumbing eccentric, the wind icy, the low sky stuffed with snow. In the nearby *Centru* stood three shabby churches – Orthodox, Roman Catholic, Calvinist – representing, as religious buildings often do, this region's centuries of cultural (and other) conflicts. I wondered where the synagogue had been; no one could or would tell me. Being less than a mile from the never-opened Soviet border, Sighet in 1990 had a pleasing end-of-the-road atmosphere. I enjoyed mini-treks through the roadless guardian mountains and strolls around the residential districts – long, straight, nineteenth-century streets of solid, one-story Magyar dwellings. Some were newly painted in contrasting pastel shades to celebrate the tyrants' exits, some had pairs of gaudy plaster gnomes grinning in porches, or comic wood masks, locally carved, hanging beside hall doors. Cocks crowed far and near, hens wandered across the streets, turkeys gobbled in little front gardens, invisible pigs grunted in sheds. In one such home the Wiesel family lived until 1944.

I learned that more than half of Sighet's 40,000 malnourished citizens lived in Soviet-style blocs around the periphery of the ancient Magyar town where, by the 1920s, 15,000 Jews were deeply rooted. That period, too, knew hunger; many Jewish families, left destitute after the First World War, received aid from US Zionist organizations, formed to "hasten the rebirth of a Jewish state in Palestine." I quote from the caption of a photograph showing a "Sephardic Girls' Embroidery Club, August 1927." That was among a fading collection in a fraying album belonging to Vicki, a young woman keen to improve her English. She had invited me into her granny's home for coffee (ersatz) and introduced herself as "an ethnic Hungarian." Granny had inherited the album from a Jewish neighbour and she cherished it because granddad (recently deceased) reckoned a museum might one day pay good money for it. Turning the pages I asked about the elaborate metal mesh defending shop fronts below Yiddish signs. Vicki translated Granny's explanation – the town's richest merchants were Jews, living aloof from the rest of the community and mistrustful of everyone.

At a World Women's Day party another of my new friends, after a certain amount of *tuica*, became autobiographical. "My mother was a baby when the Hungarians came to take the Jews. A Christian family hid her – very brave! – and she married a Rumanian. I've no memories, she died before I walk. You've met my father, in the Ethnographical Museum. *His* father had to work with the Hungarians, loading the trains, but he never liked Jews so he didn't mind."

Next day I met Mircea, a teacher at Sighet's biggest school and very happy to give the foreign writer a history lesson. When the Ottomans lost control, too many Jews moved in from Poland and Russia. Quickly they took over local trade, always had most money, ruined every small merchant. By law they couldn't buy land so all their savings went into commerce. When the nation of Rumania was established, in 1859, giving Jews equal rights was one of the conditions of international recognition. Soon that made more problems; too many Jews became stewards (known as land agents in Ireland) for wealthy absentee boyars who preferred city life –

Paris if possible. Stewards tended to be greedy and arrogant and as they became more numerous and powerful anti-Semitism flared higher and higher. Which was only natural…

By then I'd realised it was not tactless to question people about Sighet's Jews; Rumania's history of anti-Semitism had long since been "revised." Mircea never mentioned the mini-pogroms, or mega-terrorization campaigns, recorded around Moldavia (especially) in the 1920s. Mobs of students marched against Jews, broke Jewish shop windows and more and more frequently murdered Jews with impunity. Rumania didn't need Hitler; the League of National Christian Defence excluded all Jews from universities, not by law or force but through intimidation. One of the League's student leaders then founded the Legion of Archangel St Michael – aka the Iron Guard – soon to become one of the Nazis' most effective allies. Yet Mircea tried to give me the impression that only as a result of Nazi pressure did the Iron Guard become Jew-killers. And he never mentioned the anti-Semitic legislation passed by the Bucharest government in 1937. History revision was alarmingly easy in the Ceausescus' "intellectual prison." Several people assured me that Marshal Antonescu had done everything possible to protect Jews – including putting them on trains which were sent chugging round and round Rumania to deceive the Nazis into thinking their passengers had been delivered to the death-camps. My informants seemed normally intelligent, yet they resented this story's authenticity being questioned.

Dimitru was the Tisa hotel's elderly nightwatchman. He spoke surprisingly fluent English and had personal memories of the Hungarian police "coming to take them all away, to help the Germans. During the war the Hungarians ruled northern Transylvania again, including Marmures. Hitler gave it to them, to get their help. Then we got it back when Germany was beaten."

Deviously I asked, "So what happened to Sighet's Jews?"

"They never came back. Rumanians got their shops and houses, which was good."

"*Why* didn't they come back?"

"I think the Germans killed them. Hitler didn't like Jews – they had too many in Germany. And we had too many here, we were glad they went. Afterwards they were all sent to Palestine which was good for Europe."

Since the 1950s Elie Wiesel has been one of the most vocal Zionists on the world scene yet for decades one of his voices went unheard, lying dust-muffled in Boston University's archives. Not until 2009 did he ask his old friend, Dr Joel Rappel, one of Judaism's leading historians, to sort out the million or so papers stored in 330 boxes. Two and a half years later Dr Rappel came upon 150 manuscript pages apparently deleted from (or never included in) the famous Holocaust memoir. Those pages were quite easily deciphered but profoundly disturbing for a Jew to read. The 26-year-old Elie wrote:

> We believed in miracles and in God! And not in fate…and we fared very badly not believing in fate. If we had, we could have prevented many catastrophes… I stopped praying and didn't speak about God. I was angry at him. I told myself, "He does not deserve us praying to him." And really, does he hear prayers?… Why sanctify him? For what? For the suffering he rains on our heads? For Auschwitz and Birkenau?…This time we will not stand as the accused in court before the divine judge. This time we are the judges and he the accused. We are ready. There are a huge number of documents on our indictment file. They are living documents that will shake the foundations of justice. (Quoted by Ofer Aderet in *Haaretz*, 14 May 2016).

In other sections Elie condemned those Jews who, as he saw it ten years after his escape, were "false prophets," head-in-the-sanders able to convince themselves they'd be just fine, even after the 1935 Nuremberg Laws… He accused them of

> "paving the Nazis' way" to committing their horrors. "Eternal optimists"…it would not be an exaggeration on my part if I were to say that they greatly helped the genocidal nation to prepare the psychological background for the disaster. In fact, the professional optimists meant to make the present easier, but in doing so they buried the future. It is almost certain that if we had known only a little of the truth…we would have broken the sword of fate. We would have burned the murderers' altars. We would have fled and hidden in the mountains with farmers… We didn't know a thing in Europe, while they knew in the Land of Israel, and they knew in London, and they knew in New York. The world was silent and the Jewish world was silent. Why silent?

Why did it not find it vital to inform us of what was going on in
Germany? Why did they not warn us? Why? I also accuse the
Jewish world and its leaders for not warning us, at least about the
danger awaiting us in ambush so that we'd seek rescue routes.
(Quoted by Ofer Aderet in *Haaretz*, 14 May 2016).

Reading those words, I remembered that the last train left Sighet (many
were needed to transport 15,000) less than three weeks before the Allied
invasion of Normandy.

Elie dwelt in some detail on the attitudes of Sighet's gentiles during the
deportation.

All the residents stood at the entrances of their homes, with faces
filled with happiness at the misfortune they saw in their friends of
yesterday walking and disappearing into the horizon – not for a
day or two, but forever. Here I learned the true face of the
Hungarian. It is the brutal face of an animal. I wouldn't be
exaggerating if I were to say the Hungarians were more violent
towards us than the Germans themselves. The Germans tended
to shoot Jews… At the end of the war, I refused to return to my
hometown because I didn't want to see any more the faces they
revealed behind their disguises on that day of expulsion.
However, from one perspective I'm sorry I didn't return home.
At least for a few days, in order to take revenge – to avenge the
experts of hypocrisy, the inhabitants of my town. Then it would
have been possible to take revenge! (Quoted by Ofer Aderet in
Haaretz, 14 May 2016)

Most harrowing of all – at least to me – is Elie's recollection of what went
on "under the cover of night," in the cattle-cars.

There were some young boys and girls who had sexual
intercourse. The initial impact of the disaster was sexual. The
tension of the final days sparked the desires that now sought
release. And the heat also added its own touch, so that the sexual
scenes did not provoke protest in the carriage. Eat, drink and be
merry, for tomorrow we die. (Quoted by Ofer Aderet in *Haaretz*,
14 May 2016)

And tomorrow most of them did die, including Elie's parents and a sister.

Only readers of or near my age could fully appreciate the impact his last passage would have had sixty years ago, if included in *Night*. At that time there would have been much in common between priest-ridden Ireland (a belatedly recognised double entendre) and the prim Middle Europe communities of devout Jews. Had the lost MS been published when written, I can readily imagine how distressed, enraged, insulted and/or disbelieving many of Elie's co-religionists would have felt. What I can't begin to gauge, as a godless humanist, is the likely impact, then or now, of Elie's indictment of that God shared by the People of the Book.

The obvious questions are: why were those 150 pages never published? Why let them get lost for so long amidst a million others? Why were they written in Hebrew, not Yiddish? By the date of their discovery the recently deceased Elie was unable to answer such questions.

Dr Rappel, in whose Jerusalem library the MS is cherished, remarked to Ofer Aderet of *Haaretz* (14 May 2016) – "I wonder if someone wanted to make it disappear? Yet this is the version of *Night* that Wiesel wanted the *Israeli* reader to see. He didn't write it for anyone else. I believe he knew that someday someone would find it and leave it for the following generations."

Aderet wondered, "In that case, why did he store it away, deep in his archive?"

This may be only the first chapter of a rather convoluted story. However it unravels, those quotations seem to explain both Wiesel's refusal to live in Israel and my "patronising" intuition.

Long after certain diseases seem to have been eliminated, possible victims tend to remain on the alert lest the infections recur. During the immediate post-Holocaust years anti-Semitism was widely assumed to have been eliminated, though most Jews sensed that small shifts in the political (or in some regions economic) climate could reignite it. Is some such shift now threatening? It's easy to argue that the two "antis" are utterly different and in many cases they truly are. But when the Zionist state defines itself as a *Jewish* state, accepting only *Jews* as full citizens, and persistently discriminates against its *non-Jewish* population, and uses its army to oppress all *non-Jews* within the OPT, and illegally settles *Jews* on Palestinian land – then it's unsurprising, however regrettable, that some political anti-Zionists will eventually morph into emotional anti-Semites.

In the spring of 2016 Britain's opposition to anti-Semitism concentrated almost entirely on those individuals within one political party accused of having morphed. Clearly the countless yards of print and hours of over-heated yak-yakking had much more to do with domestic politics than with Jewish sensibilities. On the Palestinians' behalf I was very angry: this blurring sand-storm perfectly suited Israel. There was never a mention of IDF outrages while liberal Britain hunted *hasbara*-bred anti-Semites.

Meanwhile, an overlapping controversy had flared up in the Holy Land. During his Holocaust Day speech Major-General Yair Golan mentioned certain tendencies in contemporary Israel which reminded him of 1930s Germany. Said he: "If there's something that frightens me about Holocaust remembrance it's the recognition of the revolting processes that occurred in Europe in general, and particularly in Germany, back then – and finding signs of them here among us today in 2016."

This Major-General has been active since 1982. In 1988 he led a company during the merciless Operation Law and Order in Maydoun, Lebanon. In 2002 his infantry brigade behaved reprehensibly during Operation Defensive Shield; several of its permanently maimed victims became my friends in Balata and Nablus. In 2007 Golan was disciplined for using the "Neighbour Procedure," banned by Israel's High Court in 2005. This "procedure" sent relatives and friends, under false pretences, to the barricaded West Bank homes of "suspects." Palestinians don't like Golan. Nor did Netanyahu like him on Holocaust Day 2016. His speech, according to his Prime Minister, was "outrageous and unfounded." He had "wronged Israeli society and cheapened the Holocaust" – etc., etc. "Israel is a historical wonder and everyone is proud of the IDF" – etc., etc. Within very few hours, Golan was competing with Ken Livingstone in the global headlines.

Chemi Shalev reported in *Haaretz*:

> Within minutes of that speech, the right-wing spin machine leaped into action, inflating Golan's words, taking them out of context, blowing them up to diabolical proportions. Rather than challenging his assertion that disturbing trends in Israeli society evoke associations to (sic) Germany and Europe in the 1930s, his words were twisted to suggest that he had compared the IDF to the Wehrmacht, Israel to the Nazis and Palestinians, by logical extension, to persecuted Jews about to be carted off to concentration camps. With the ground thus prepared, politicians

started piling up on Golan, accusing him of defiling his own IDF, defaming the State and aiding and abetting BDS. The self-induced mass hysteria quickly turned into a virtual witch-hunt, which I can only assume Golan was prepared for; it is part and parcel of the ominous trends that he was warning against. (6 May 2016)

In Chemi Shalev's words there were echoes of the British scene a week previously. And I thought of Joel Kovel's 2013 observation – "The frenzy these days, that might be described as a 'Zionist thought police' trying to suppress any criticism of the Jewish state, is perhaps more a sign of weakness and doubt rather than the confidence of a truly hegemonic power." Soon the social media were howling for Golan's dismissal and dubbing him "Chief of the Wehrmacht." He was "a left-wing propagandist" who had "provided fodder" for Israel-haters abroad. A senior TV reporter noted that were he a British Labour MP "he'd have been suspended within the hour."

Some of my Israeli friends saw Netanyahu's turning on Golan, and his redoubled fear-mongering (popular now among politicians everywhere) as more evidence that he dreads defeat in his contest with the army "to shape the nation's values." One is reminded of Prime Minster Cameron's blethering on about "British values," without ever being able to specify even one value particular to Britain.

Then suddenly all was well in Israel. On 9 May Netanyahu informed a pre-Independence Day General Staff gathering – "The issue of the speech is behind us, a one-time incident – we're all going forward together." And he clapped Golan on the shoulder and shook his hand and they clinked glasses.

Two days later Amos Harel commented, "But in truth, the story is far from over. It's impossible to understand the furore roused by Golan's speech in isolation from the other storms that have hit the defence establishment's top brass in recent months... The wave of stabbings and car-ramming attacks that began last October has accelerated the outbreak of these disputes, all of which stem from the effects of Israel's ongoing control over the territories" (*Haaretz*, 11 May 2016).

I have on my desk a sheaf of reports about those "storms" but I'll mention only the killing in Hebron, in March 2016, of a Palestinian. Abdel-Fattah al-Sharif had confronted an IDF patrol, was wounded and, while lying immobile on the ground, was shot in the head at close range by a nineteen-year-old sergeant, Elor Azaria. Such deliberate killings are not unusual but when a video of this scene went viral Azaria was arrested and charged with manslaughter. At first Netanyahu condemned the killing, then he rang the killer's father to offer sympathy. This much-publicised phone call did something to soothe the angry thousands who were jeering online at the Defence Minister, Moshe Ya'alon, for his denouncing of Azaria. Later, pro-Azaria crowds in Tel Aviv, and outside Jaffa's military court, demanded the sergeant's pardon and release.

By then I had learnt that, astonishingly Chief-of-Staff General Gadi Eisenkot and I have something in common; in both our cases the social media penny took a long time to drop. Not until October 2015 did Eisenkot discover that a right-wing website, *0404*, was favourite viewing for his soldiers. Anxiously he deputed a relative to monitor that and similar sites and to keep him informed about his men's intake from cyberspace. What he was told and shown so alarmed him that he appointed a special task force to study the overall influence of the social media on Israel's army. In his youth, soldiers were allowed to communicate with the civilian world only once a week, using a public phone. Now they can contact anyone anywhere about anything at any time. While Eisenkot and his peers weren't looking – so to say – their IDF had become another sort of creature, its recruits no longer amenable to being moulded as they emerged from adolescence to adulthood. Here was a novel challenge for the top brass.

Eisenkot had already downgraded the IDF's chief rabbi, declaring that armies don't need rabbis to vet their operations or judge which commands should be obeyed. For this among other reasons, pessimists foresaw an IDF split – as perhaps Netanyahu did, when he spoke so cheerily of "all going forward together." Surreal fissures were plain to be seen: right-wing (pro-settlers) versus left-wing (end the occupation), to mention just one. The IDF has always boasted of being "the People's Army." It still is and its increasingly brutal behaviour throughout the OPT reflects that rapid moral retrogression of Israel society which prompted Golan's incendiary warning.

Immediately after the warning a distressed Chemi Shalev wrote:

> Netanyahu enables Israelis to deny reality and to fail to connect the dots, even if the evidence is under their noses. They have mastered the art of ignoring half a century of occupation and just as they have repressed memories of their blatant indifference to the carnage in Gaza in 2014, so they are now capable of overlooking the repeated and often well-documented pattern of

Palestinian assailants who are killed despite posing no danger, as well as the increasing public displays of dangerous racism and even genocidal agitation in the streets, in football stadiums and, perhaps most ominously, on social media. There thousands of Israelis call for ejecting, raping and murdering Palestinians, leftists and even plain old critics of the government. The cry of "Death to the Arabs!" which reverberates in radical right-wing demonstrations had become so routine that no one seems to notice anymore. (*Haaretz*, 6 May 2016).

No wonder Generals Eisenkot and Golan and their senior messmates are becoming apprehensive about the Zionist state's future. Occupying troops perforce spend long boring hours on the West Bank – at road blocks, settler (only) access points, Area barriers and so on. Consider how the attitudes and reactions of many impressionable and not too bright conscripts – conditioned from birth to distrust Arabs – are influenced when they switch on their cell phones to view *0404* and the like.

Are those Generals able to see that the IDF itself has sown most of the seeds of this menacing crop? We've now got to the "Shoot and Cry and Shoot Again" syndrome, first identified after the Six Day War in 1967. Then a small group of soldiers (men and women, aged 18 to 40, all "children of the kibbutzim") collaborated on a remarkable book, *The Seventh Day: Soldiers' Talk About the Six-Day War*. It was thoughtful, honest, moving and – re-read now – very sad. When I lent my Penguin copy to young friends in 1971 it inspired a few of them to become kibbutzniks for a year or so. The Israeli authors, having shot Palestinians, were very sorry and ready to cry – and then to shoot again. The Occupation was in its first year and to his friends Amos (Oz) said, "But can you live that way forever – with the feeling that every few years foreigners are going to be intent on killing you? Can you imagine living this way and still being the same person, the same nation, in a few years' time? Can it be done without our getting to the stage in which we'll quite simply hate them? Just hate them. I don't mean we'll take a delight in killing, or turn into sadists. Simply deep bitter hatred for them for having forced such a life on us." Amos' friend, Elisha, quoted Moshe Dayan, then a paratroop officer who had noted in 1967 – "Warfare is rapidly becoming the dominant *motif* in Zionism. While the battle against the desert and disease may have been the central concern years ago, war has become the central element of the past three decades" (*The Seventh Day*).

Dr Idan Yaron, an anthropologist who has often accompanied Israeli schools' Shoah tours, observed in May 2016 – "The obvious outcome of the story of the Holocaust as a Jewish story is often paranoia, and it is even dangerous. Israel is not cultivating the memory of the Holocaust properly. Instead they are creating fear. What's missing is empathy for the living" (*Haaretz*, 6 May 2016).

People who ask "What is the Holocaust Industry for?" should read *The Holocaust and Collective Memory*. In 2000 Peter Novick reckoned its chief use, in the US, is as a bonding agent, urgently needed because more and more Jews are "marrying out" and are united neither by religion nor politics. Reviewing this book, Rabbi Julia Neuberger uneasily noted "the inexorable growth of the Holocaust's importance as its historical closeness diminishes" (*The Observer* or *The Irish Times*). The intervening years have seen a steady increase in the organized and repeated exposure of young Israelis to the Shoah, an insistence that they must be aware of every detail, must be emotionally involved, must always regard themselves as endangered by their Jewishness.

And so we have Dr Yaron warning – "There's no doubt that the IDF is the beneficiary of the Shoah trips. The result of the messages of fear-mongering is an argument that something similar will not happen today because we're strong with an independent nation and army… The students need a moral viewpoint. I spend a lot of time in schools and see how prominent racism is in the lives of the young people. It's become more legitimate in recent years to say, 'We need to kill all the Arabs'."

On 1 May 2016 I wrote in my journal:

I don't envy Shami Chakrabarti – seems she's been set the task of "curing" the British Labour Party's alleged anti-Semitism. Let's hope she can do better than the 2006 all-party parliamentary group. When Israel's criminal assault on Lebanon provoked some mild international criticism the MPs were asked to report on Britain's problem of "resurgent anti-Semitism." They counted as anti-Semitic any incident or occasion "perceived" to be anti-Semitic by "the Jewish community." And they concluded that for student unions to promote BDS, and thus restrict the availability of kosher foods on campus, would be anti-Semitic.

This disease has taken many shapes over the centuries. Even its subdued current manifestations are very varied. Louts spit at Jews, slash car tyres, spray obscenities on synagogues. Occasionally murderers enjoy killing Jews – but they seem to be inflamed, nowadays, by Daesh & Co. with all that that implies. Then we have the well-spoken sophisticates whose anti-Semitism is so ingrained they themselves seem unaware of it – but it emerges horribly, in tiny ways that I personally find more unsettling than the louts' version. As for the social media trolls of whom we now hear too much – who and where are they? I can't imagine them but simply knowing they exist is unnerving. On another level, I'm worried by those who slyly masquerade as pro-Palestinians and do immense damage to the cause. Also there are the gormless Palestine supporters, enthusiastic, energetic and generous but alarmingly unaware of the complexities, therefore easily conscripted by the sly ones. They do sometimes morph from anti-Zionism to anti-Semitism, thus stoking the fires of animosity all round.

At present I feel I'm living in two quite separate worlds. The British media become more and more shrill and childish – are having a tantrum – kicking at those "hard-left" anti-Semites supposedly swarming through the Labour Party, threatening its very existence. There's never a mention of the Palestinians. In the other world, every morning *Haaretz* reports on the cruelties and injustices inflicted by the Occupation. If any British paper or broadcaster criticised Netanyahu's regime as some Israeli journalists do – but no, I can't bring that sentence to a coherent conclusion. Only to say – fear of the *hasbara* machine is a grimly effective gag.

On 14 May 2016 I wrote in my journal:

This date marks the end of the British mandatory role in Palestine and is celebrated by the Israelis as "Independence Day." If on 14 May 1948 a comparable (in numbers) religious minority (Parsees, Druse, Mormons, Yezedis or whatever) had proclaimed their right to take over another people's territory, driving most of the indigenes into exile, would that have been acceptable? Let's have a bit of over-simplification. It's time to refer to the king's nudity. Why go on pandering to those who pretend that once upon a time the ancestors of those now identifying with Judaism were promised, by some god or other, ownership in perpetuity of what has been, for very many centuries, the land of the Palestinians? True, there never was a nation-state called "Palestine." Nor were there nation-states called Turkey, Syria, Iraq, Lebanon, Jordan, Saudi Arabia – or Italy and Germany, until 1871 and 1870. But most Italians had lived in Italy and most Germans had lived in Germany – and most Palestinians had lived in Palestine until the Zionist colonists invented "Israel." The "international community's" refusal to see that naked king serves only one set of interests, those of the US. It has not provided "a safe haven" for the world's Jews.

Speaking in New York on 17 April 1938, Albert Einstein said it all:

> I should much rather see reasonable agreement with the Arabs on the basis of living together in peace than the creation of a Jewish state with borders. Apart from practical considerations my awareness of the essential nature of Judaism resists the idea of a Jewish state with an army, and a measure of temporal power no matter how modest. I am afraid of the inner damage Judaism will sustain – especially from the development of a narrow nationalism within our own ranks, against which we have already had to fight strongly, even without a Jewish state.

However, this is 2016. It's time to stop crying over spilt blood, razed villages, burnt olive groves and despoiled holy places. Millions of Jews have forcibly settled in Palestine and continue that operation even as I write. Like the European settlers in North America, Australia, New Zealand and South Africa they can't be uprooted. Unlike those earlier genocidal settlers, their mid-twentieth century activities were exposed to some (not enough) public scrutiny which left them with an awkward residue of displaced indigenes. Those Palestinians, whether in exile or in the OPT "Native Reservations," are not going away. Hence increasing support for one-state – support as yet beyond the confines of the institutionalized "international community." Zionism hasn't worked. The malign Netanyahu regime represents its dying kick and without that incubus it's possible most Israelis – given generous incentives – may allow a peaceful funeral for the dead Zionist state. The Mizrahim majority might show least flexibility – need extra incentives. Or, having experienced the flimsiness of Zionism's utopian promises, they might suddenly see the Palestinians as natural allies in the creation of "Palis" or "Ispal" or (my favourite despite the objections of political geographers)

"Canaan." This new country could be very rewarding on several levels. As intermarriage came to be taken for granted, the mixed gene pool would surely produce an exciting new culture, intellectually and aesthetically creative beyond anything achievable now, while so many are entrapped in a misery of uncertainty and poverty. Material poverty for most Palestinians and many Jews, other sorts of poverty for the elite.

Perhaps that's a silly dream? But, to advance, human beings have always needed dreams...

Editor's Note: In Hebrew, the word "hasbara" simply means "clarification" or "explanation". As used by the Israeli government and its supporters, it refers to public relations, public diplomacy or overseas image-building that aims to explain policy or disseminate positive information about Israel in the face of criticism, especially in the press. For the opponents of Israeli policy, especially as regards the Occupied Palestinian Territories, it is simply a euphemism for massive pro-Zionist propaganda or "soft power" that seeks to explain and/or spin all actions of the State of Israel (both pre-'67 "Israel Proper" and post-'67 "Greater Israel"), whether or not they are justified.

See bionote on page 15.

WE ARE (STILL) LIVING IN CAGES

Lara Marlowe

I

Interview with Mahmoud Darwish

Grass growing on a wall.

(2000)

WHEN HE WALKS AWAY

The enemy who takes tea in our shack has a mare in the smoke
And a daughter with thick eyebrows, hazel eyes, and hair as long as the
    night of songs on her shoulders
And her image never leaves him when he comes to our home to ask for
    tea …
In our shack, the enemy takes a rest from his rifle
He leaves it on my grandfather's chair, and eats our bread
Like any guest
He dozes for a while on the wicker chair, strokes our cat's fur and says to
    us always:
Do not blame the victim
We ask: *Who is the victim?*
He answers: *Blood that the night never dries.*
The buttons of his uniform shine when he walks away
Goodnight! Say hello to our well and the patch of fig trees
Walk softly on our shadow in the oat fields
Say hello to our cypress trees overhead
And don't forget to close the gate at night
Remember that the horse is afraid of aircraft
And say hello to us over there, if you find the time.

Translated, from the Arabic, by Elias Sanbar and Lara Marlowe.

He is the voice of a stateless people, the man widely regarded as the finest
living Arab poet. But each time journalists knock on Mahmoud Darwish's

door to ask about recurring rumours that he will win the Nobel Prize for literature, he tells them: "Go home. I know I am not going to get it. I don't deserve it. I've achieved nothing until now."

Over the past four decades, Darwish has published twenty books that gave expression to the despair and dispossession of the Palestinians. Longing for the lost fig and olive trees of his native Galilee is the leitmotif of Darwish's oeuvre. But his is a sensitive, wounded narrative, never a tirade. "Against barbarity," he has written, "poetry can resist only by conforming its attachment to human fragility, like a blade of grass growing on a wall while armies march by." It is a message that interests French, Spanish and even Israeli readers more than the English-speaking world. Most of Darwish's books have been translated into Hebrew, far fewer into English. He was recently invited to Paris by the French culture ministry for its "Springtime of Poets," and to launch a new collection of his work published by Gallimard.

A frail-looking, ascetic fifty-nine-year-old whose work includes as many love poems as it does odes of exile, Darwish wrote the 1988 Palestinian declaration of independence. Five years later, he resigned from the PLO's Executive Council because of what he saw as the sloppy, hurried way in which the 1993 Oslo accords were being negotiated. "I am very sorry to see I was right," he says. "After seven years, the accords have not been implemented." But his mood lightens when our conversation turns to the poets he admires: the tenth-century Arab wanderer Al-Moutanabbi, Derek Walcott, Joseph Brodsky and Seamus Heaney. Darwish's life changed one summer night in 1948, when his mother woke him in a panic. His family ran through the forest, along with hundreds of inhabitants of his village, El Birwa. "Bullets were whistling over our heads, and I didn't understand what was happening. After walking all night, we arrived in a foreign village with children I didn't know. I asked innocently 'Where am I?' and I heard the word 'Lebanon' for the first time."

After a miserable year in a refugee camp, Darwish's parents decided to sneak back into northern Israel – something forbidden by the Israelis. They returned to El Birwa to find it had been razed. Darwish grew up in Israel, and was imprisoned for political activities five times between 1961 and 1967, before being banished in 1970. A long period of wandering then began, from Beirut to Damascus, Paris, Tunis and Cairo.

In 1995, after twenty-five years of exile, Israeli authorities allowed Darwish to return for the funeral of his friend, the writer Emile Habibi. He now lives in the West Bank town of Ramallah. The Israelis renew his multiple reentry visa twice a year, enabling him to visit his mother and family in Galilee.

It was in Ramallah that Darwish recently watched five hours of Israeli Knesset debates, broadcast live on television. The education minister, Yossi Sarid, had requested that three Darwish poems written in Israeli jails become optional texts in Israeli schools. "To My Mother," about the young poet's longing for his mother's bread, coffee and tenderness, is an Arab classic, made famous by the Lebanese singer Marcel Khalife. Although the poems were written thirty-four years ago, Sarid's suggestion nearly brought the Israeli government down and prompted an Orthodox rabbi to call the education minister a "satan whose memory must be erased."

Darwish says he was indifferent to the internal Israeli dispute over his texts, but he was obviously amused by it. "They were all carrying poems in their hands!" he laughs. "A woman from the Labour Party read my poem 'I am a woman, not more not less …' to prove that I wasn't a misogynist. It took them two sessions – two hours plus three hours. Did this ever happen in history? Five hours of parliamentary debate about poetry!"

Although he is a former communist who considers the Bible to be mythology, Darwish said that Pope John Paul II's March 2000 visit to Israel and the Occupied Territories gave Palestinians great moral encouragement. "He mentioned our fifty years of suffering, which means he named the victim. The Israelis are obsessed about monopolising the status of victims: they don't want anyone else to be victims. What the Pope said changed the way people see history: it recognised that we were here before the state of Israel."

Palestinian leaders, Darwish says, are wondering if now, fifty-two years after what they call "the catastrophe," they are any closer to a solution. "What is clear is that the period of dreams and illusions is over. We are more realistic now. We know that it will be impossible to obtain justice, that history does not dictate just solutions. But even the possible peace we are trying to achieve is ambiguous for us, because of the conditions that the Israelis are imposing." Those conditions, Darwish says, are the refusal to consider allowing Palestinians to return to the land they left in 1948 (the sacrosanct "right of return" enshrined in UN General Assembly resolution of 1948), the continued building of Israeli settlements in the Occupied Territories, and the insistence that "united" Jerusalem remain Israel's capital alone.

Of the three, the settlements are the most palpable. "When I was outside Palestine and Israel and I heard about settlements, I thought they were like army camps that could be dismantled," Darwish explains. "But when I went to live in Ramallah in 1996, I was deeply shocked. We have small ghettos separated by settlements that are actually towns and I don't think the Israelis will remove them. These three obstacles make our dream of independence very humble."

Darwish fears that a final accord on Israel's terms will fail. "Peace between Israel and any other Arab country is possible, because they are neighbours," he continues. "But Israel and Palestine are not neighbours; Israel is built not next to Palestine but on top of Palestine." Ideally, he would like to see a single, secular democracy for Palestinians and Israelis alike. "But this will be very difficult to realise because the Israelis are obsessed by the purity of their identity," he says. "There is a contradiction between their claim to be democratic and their identity as the Jewish state. If they want a pure Jewish state, they should have no Arabs, yet from the beginning there were Arabs in Israel. If they want to be democratic, then they must have Arabs."

A less satisfactory solution, Darwish says, is for Israel to withdraw from the entire West Bank and Gaza Strip. "If we don't get that much, it cannot work. What Likud and Labour have offered us is less than 50 percent of the Occupied Territories." He explains how the Israeli-occupied land is divided up into zones A, B and C. Zone A represents the centre of towns and villages under the control of the Palestinian Authority. Zone B, under joint Israeli-Palestinian control, comprises the suburbs, including the main Palestinian university at Bir Zeit. Zone C applies to the connecting roads, which are under complete Israeli control.

"We are living in cages, and all around the cages is Israel," he says. "Every time they make a closure, all life stops; we cannot move. How can you call this a state?"

Ramallah is a hot, lacklustre town; I ask Darwish if he is happy living there. "I am unhappy everywhere," he says, before revising his answer. "I feel happy rarely, but really happy when I finish a new work. I feel useful. But these moments are very unusual." Many of Darwish's poems are about the women he has loved, whose names are Hebrew as well as Arabic. "I'm not interested in whether a woman is Jewish or Muslim or Christian," he says. "I loved many Israeli girls. It is the person, not the nationality, that interests me."

Darwish says he has not abandoned the theme of dispossession. "But there is a change of focus. I am trying to normalise my life, not to be jailed by what the [Israeli] occupation decides for me by writing only about Palestinian land. I am liberating myself through language, because the most dangerous thing is to stay where others decide to put you."

When Mahmoud Darwish died on 9 August 2008, Palestinian President Mahmoud Abbas declared three days of mourning. Darwish was given the equivalent of a state funeral in Ramallah, where he is buried on a hilltop overlooking Jerusalem.

This interview was first published in The Irish Times *on 4 April 2000.*

II

Epilogue

Worth the hassle.

Over three and a half decades, I have written dozens, perhaps hundreds of articles about the Israeli-Palestinian conflict. For me, the one that came closest to the poignancy of Mahmoud Darwish's poetry was the story of a Palestinian family who were driven out of their village in northern Galilee in 1948.

Seventy-six year old Naif Kawash, the patriarch of the branch that ended up in Jordan, remembered a place of fresh milk and honey, and roses in profusion, where the Jewish caretakers of an ancient shrine lived peacefully alongside Arab neighbours. There were groves of apricot and olive trees, lentil and tobacco crops, watered by springs flowing down to Lake Tiberias. The livestock came back from the meadows each evening, and the wheat harvest was a time of celebration.

Kawash sat at a table in his prosperous restaurant in Amman and wept, saying, "Mirun, Mirun, I cannot forget you."

I drove from Amman to northern Galilee. Kawash's cousins had been forced out of Mirun, but I was able to accompany them on a pilgrimage to the village now called Meron. It was indeed a beautiful place, wooded with pine and olive trees.

Mohamed Abbas, then 65, showed me the ruins of the family's Ottoman stone houses. He grew anxious when a rabbi walked down the hill towards the village's ancient synagogue.

Rabbi Haim Levy was from Morocco, and conversed with me in French. He told me that a Talmudic sage had sought refuge there in Roman times, and looked suspiciously at my Arab companions.

What happened to the Arabs who lived here until 1948? I asked Rabbi Levy. "This land was given to us by God 2,000 years ago," he replied. "There were never any Arabs here."

The article had been commissioned by my editors at *Time* magazine, shortly after the September 1993 Oslo accords. It was never published because it didn't mesh with their euphoria over the doomed agreement.

The experience drove home that, as Darwish put it, "Israel and Palestine are not neighbours; Israel is built not next to Palestine but *on top* of Palestine." It was also a lesson in the near impossibility of explaining the conflict to an American audience that did not want to know. This was one of the reasons why I moved from *Time* magazine to *The Irish Times* in 1996.

Though my editors at *The Irish Times* are braver, I've encountered howls of protest from the Israeli Embassy in Dublin each time I've reported from Israel and the Occupied Territories. Prominent politicians and journalists in the US, France and Ireland have told me it just isn't worth the hassle of criticising Israel.

This intimidation extends to the highest levels of government. "America will not turn our backs on the legitimate Palestinian aspiration for dignity, opportunity, and a state of their own," President Barack Obama said in Cairo in June 2009. But faced with the anger of Prime Minister Benyamin Netanyahu, and painfully aware of Netanyahu's influence over US politics, Obama gave up.

"We are living in cages," Darwish told me in 2000. The Palestinians are still "living in cages" 16 years later, in the world's largest prison in Gaza, in the chopped up zones A, B and C of the West Bank, where Israel holds exclusive control over 60 per cent of the land.

Some harbour a fantasy that Obama, in his two remaining months in office, could refrain from vetoing a UN Security Council resolution demanding an end to settlement-building. Since 1978, the US has used its UN Security Council veto 44 times to defeat resolutions unfavourable to Israel. There are now more than 700,000 Israelis on land seized illegally since 1967. Yet Israel has not once been brought to account by the "international community."

Mass protests failed to stop three Israeli assaults on Gaza that killed more than 3,800 Palestinians between 2008 and 2014. The Boycott, Divestment, Sanctions (BDS) movement that was launched in 2005 to force Israel to leave the West Bank was modelled on the campaign that brought down apartheid in South Africa.

The Israeli government has never distinguished between legitimate criticism of its policies and anti-Semitism. Now it has convinced some western leaders that BDS is "anti-Semitic." On a visit to Israel in May 2016,

France's Prime Minister Manuel Valls said, "We know well what's behind this boycott: not only contestation, but also hatred for the state of Israel, hatred for a Jewish homeland, and for all Jews."

Peaceful protest against Israeli policies is increasingly penalised. In France, "the country of human rights," it's now illegal to call for the boycott of Israeli products.

France's supreme court, the Cour de Cassation, upheld the conviction of 14 militants from the BDS campaign who held a peaceful protest outside a Carrefour supermarket near Mulhouse, on the grounds of "provocation to discrimination, hatred or violence." They were sentenced to pay €28,000 in damages to civil plaintifs, plus a suspended fine of €1,000 each.

In March 2016, a BDS campaigner was arrested simply for wearing a T-shirt with the words "Boycott Israel Apartheid" printed on it. Lawyers say the French ban on BDS violates freedom of expression and association and the right to peaceful protest. They have taken the case to the European Court of Human Rights.

Ireland's Minister for Foreign Affairs, Charlie Flanagan, has said the government "does not agree with attempts to demonise" BDS supporters. Yet there's a sense that Ireland no longer leads on Palestine. When Frank Aiken was Minister for External Affairs from 1957 until 1969, he made support for Palestinian rights a mainstay of Irish policy. In 1980, Brian Lenihan Senior made a famous speech as foreign minister, supporting recognition of the PLO and self-determination for the Palestinian people. It led to the EU's Venice Declaration.

By contrast, the Irish government used the pretext of European solidarity to explain its abstention in a 2014 vote in the UN Human Rights Council on setting up a commission of inquiry into the Israeli Gaza offensive that killed more than 2,000 Palestinians.

And although both houses of the Oireachtas have recognised the state of Palestine, the Irish government has not. The government of Sweden showed more courage.

Alon Liel, a former director-general of the Israeli Ministry of Foreign Affairs, campaigns for European governments to recognise Palestine. "Only such recognition can level the diplomatic playing field," Liel wrote in 2015. "Only the creation of a Palestinian state will save us from continuing down the slippery slope leading to an Israeli apartheid."

Netanyahu has imposed three pre-conditions: Palestinians must recognise Israel as a Jewish state; negotiations must be direct and bi-lateral;

and a settlement must *precede* recognition of independent Palestine. By passively accepting Netanyahu's pre-conditions, western governments consolidate and perpetuate the injustice to Palestinians. Netanyahu has snuffed out all attempts to address settlements and statehood.

In 2014, the Palestinian President Mahmoud Abbas floated a UN Security Council resolution that would have set a December 2017 deadline on final status negotiations and an end to the occupation of the West Bank. Washington ensured the resolution did not pass. The former French foreign minister Laurent Fabius planned a similar resolution, with an 18-month deadline for completing negotiations on a "two-state solution." If it failed, the French government was to have recognised Palestine.

The Obama administration threatened to veto the French resolution, so Fabius's successor, Jean-Marc Ayrault, convened a preliminary peace conference in June 2016, in the hope of persuading the Israelis to attend a second conference by the end of this year.

By refusing to participate, Israel sabotaged that plan too. On November 7, Netanyahu did not have time to receive Pierre Vimont, the senior French diplomat who is trying to salvage the initiative. Netanyahu met instead with the prime minister of Fiji. His office announced that advisors told Vimont "in no uncertain terms" that progress could come only from direct, bilateral negotiations between Netanyahu and Abbas.

As Henry Siegman, the former head of the American Jewish Congress and the president of the US/Middle East Project, wrote in the *New York Times*, "It is now certain that a two-state agreement will never emerge from any bilateral Israeli-Palestinian negotiations."

Now, thanks to Donald Trump's election, Netanyahu will no longer have to go through the theatrics of stonewalling. "Trump's victory gives Israel the chance to renounce immediately the idea of the creation of a Palestinian state," Education Minister Naftali Bennett crowed on November 9.

Trump has subcontracted his Israel policy to Jason Greenblatt and David Friedman, New York real estate lawyers and fervent Zionists. He's expected to appoint Friedman as ambassador to Israel. Friedman says he's "tremendously skeptical" about a two-state solution.

This hopeless impasse for Palestinians coincides with two landmarks on the march of the Zionist movement next year: the 50th anniversary of the Six-Day War that started the occupation, and the 100th anniversary of the Balfour Declaration that lead to the creation of Israel.

Though ignored and virtually forgotten, Palestine remains an open wound, in Darwish's words, "the blood that never dries."

Lara Marlowe is currently the France correspondent of The Irish Times. *Born in California, she holds a BA in French from the University of California, Los Angeles, and a Masters in International Relations from Oxford. She worked 15 years as journalist for* Time *before moving to* The Irish Times *as the paper's US correspondent. She is the author of two books,* The Things I've Seen *(2010) and* Painted with Words *(2011), both from Liberties Press. She lives in Paris.*

Mahmoud Darwish was born in 1942 in British Palestine, in al-Birwa, Galilee, a village that was occupied in 1948 and later razed by the IDF during the formation of Israel. Because they had missed the official Israeli census, Darwish and his family were considered "internal refugees" or "present-absent aliens." Darwish lived for many years in exile in Beirut and Paris. Influenced by Iraqi poets as well as Rimbaud and Ginsberg, he was the author of over 30 books of poetry and eight books of prose, all in Arabic, and awarded many prizes. He was, and is, widely regarded as the Palestinian national poet and his work has been translated into over 20 languages.

Of his work, the Palestinian-American poet Naomi Shihab Nye has written that Darwish "is the essential breath of the Palestinian people, the eloquent witness of exile and belonging…" Of his view on the possibility of peace, he remarked to Haaretz: *"I am patient and am waiting for a profound revolution in the consciousness of the Israelis. The Arabs are ready to accept a strong Israel with nuclear arms – all it has to do is open the gates of its fortress and make peace."*

Of his role as a Palestinian symbol and literary spokesman for the Arab opposition within Israel and the Occupied Palestinian Territories, he rejected accusations of anti-semitism: "The accusation is that I hate Jews. It's not comfortable that they show me as a devil and an enemy of Israel. I am not a lover of Israel, of course. I have no reason to be. But I don't hate Jews." Darwish also spoke English, French and Hebrew.

Darwish once described Hebrew as a "language of love." He considered himself to be part of the Jewish civilization that existed in Palestine and hoped for a reconciliation between Palestinians and Jews. When this happens, "the Jew will not be ashamed to find an Arab element in himself, and the Arab will not be ashamed to declare that he incorporates Jewish elements." The "Rita" of many of his poems was a Jewish woman whom he loved when he was living in Haifa.

Mahmoud Darwish died in 2008 in Houston, Texas. He had lived two-thirds of his life in exile.

TWO POEMS

Andrew McNeillie

On Twitter's perch.

INTIMACIES

And so we sit here for a while together
an ancient couple in their gazebo
rediscovering truth in a glass or two
making the most of freak warm weather.

We do what we can with what we have
written through us, and what we dream,
we dream, or run to ground in stolen time
like this, those intimacies for which we live.

Searching for solace in a broken world –
bewildered by too much information,
sidelined by the techno generation,
their devices no sooner new than old.

Their lives a solipsism where means are ends,
where speed and scale are deities,
hubristic billionaires dictate new pieties
and folk they've never met are friends.

All of whom are called and all chosen
and who would argue with that
or risk going viral among the trolls? And yet
it still remains what's odd can never be even.

We pour another glass, each to their tipple.
The evening light begins to thin and fail.
House martins dart announcing their arrival.
We wonder for another year at this miracle of April.

Until I start up about the rise of Islam.
The cue for you to totter down the lawn
knowing that very soon I'll move on
to my party piece about the fall of Rome.

MEMORANDUM TO MACNEICE

Should I say I saw you in a vision? —
glimpsed your shade in my rear-view mirror,
my head cocked, like a budgerigar,
as I drove in your far-near country:
McNeillie calling MacNeice . . . MacNeice
are you there, still travelling
the fuchsia'd roads from Cleggan to Clifden
by Omey and through Claddaghduff . . . ?

While history, the morning after,
the night before, weather reeling in the sea's shadow —
its eyes turned down upon now
and nothing as lasting as bronze,
repeats itself again as farce,
a throwaway on Twitter's perch,
a thing of little consequence
quaint as thought or going to Church.

We are the ghosts in the machine
(and scarce your shadow cast at noon),
how right you were. Yet premature:
Rome's immortal story
still goes hurtling on, to ever greater ruin.
We are defined by differences
and our doom is bottomless
is all we know and all we need to know.

The train was ever off the rails
rattling through galaxies of inert stars,
the strings false all along.
And so you sang and whistled in the dark
and so I hear you as I go
west in Eden on a day in June
the perch still burning,
and budgie in full song.

Andrew McNeillie was born in 1946 in North Wales, where he was raised and educated. He read English at Magdalen College, Oxford. His recent publications are a memoir, An Aran Keening *(The Lilliput Press, 2001), and a collection of poems,* Winter Moorings *(Carcanet, 2014). He is the editor and publisher of both Clutag Press (which he founded in 2000) and the literary magazine* Archipelago. *He lives in Thame, Oxfordshire.*

TWO PALESTINIAN POEMS

Cathal Ó Searcaigh

DOMHNACH I MÍN A' LEÁ, DOMHNACH I NGAZA

Ar an Domhnach lách seo
i Mín a' Leá
agus mé ar mo sháimhín só
sa gharradh
tá mo mhacasamhail i nGaza
rite as anáil
agus é ag impí
go ndéanfaí é a tharrtháil
ó ruathar na ndiúracán
agus ó bhrúcht na bpléascán.

Ar an Domhnach shítheach shóch seo
i Mín a' Leá
titfidh an oíche chun ciúnais
agus éireoidh an ghealach
ar aer an tsuaimhnis
ach i nGaza
lasfaidh an spéir
ina craos tine
is déanfar conamar de thithe
is smionagar de chnámha an duine.

Ar an Domhnach chiúin seo
i Mín a' Leá
is domhsa is fusa a bheith
ag mairgneach faoi Ghaza
is mé i mo suí go sócúlach
sa gharradh
ag baint sú as boladh úr
an fhéir ghearrtha
gan de chaitheamh orm
ach dán a dhéanamh.

Gan de chaitheamh orm
ach dán a dhéanamh?

SUNDAY IN MÍN A'LEÁ, SUNDAY IN GAZA

A gentle Sunday
in Mín a'Leá
I'm unperturbed
in the garden
my counterpart in Gaza
running out of breath
pleading
to escape
the next missile attack
the fallout of explosions.

A soft slow sleepy Sunday
in Mín a'Leá
night will fall into silence
a moon will rise
relaxing in the air
but in Gaza
the sky will ignite
in burning flames
houses will crumble
bones shatter.

On this quiet Sunday
in Mín a'Leá
how easy it is
to mourn Gaza
as I sit in the garden
comfortably
enjoying the scent
of newly mown grass
not a care in the world
but the making of a poem.

Not a care in the world
but the making of a poem?

DO MHOHAMMED ABU KHDEIR

Buachaill Palaistíneach a dódh ina bheathaidh i gcoillidh lámh le Iarúsailéim

D'aghaidh bheag shnoite dhea-chumtha
chomh cnámhach le héan;
gealbhan glas na coilleadh nó colmán.

Bhí tú chomh héadrom ar do chois
le beochán gaoithe, chomh seangéasca
i do sheasmhacht le slat na saileoige.

An mhaidin sin, mar ba ghnách, chuir tú
lúcháir ar d'athair agus ar do mháthair
le bláthfhleasc álainn do gháire.

Sula dtug tú d'aghaidh ar an Mhosc
le go ndéanfá na trátha a ordaíodh duit
an feacadh agus an t-umhlú a rialaíodh duit sa Leabhar.

Ach a dhíograis, d'fhuadaigh siad leo thú
chun na coilleadh; ógánaigh fhuilchraosacha
a tógadh i dTiomnacht an díoltais.

In éiric na ngasúr dá gcineál, dá gcine
a maraíodh go fealltach, bhí cúiteamh uathu.
Dhaor siad tusa, a chroí, ar altóir na híobairte.

Tchím thú faoi dhlaoi tiubh d'óige,
na bladhairí ag bearnú do ghéaga,
ag creachadh do shé bliana déag de ghnaoi.

Mar dhearcáin ag réabadh, pléascann
do phutóga, stollan d'fhéitheoga
agus iad i do dhódh, 'do loscadh agus tú beo.

Tá na Leabhair Bheannaithe gan bhrí,
ceann faoi orthu as a bheith fuilchiontach.
Tá focail na bhfáithe báite i do chuid fola.

Inniu agus cuma thuartha ar gach ní, an mhaidin
ar liathadh an cholmáin, cluinim uaillghol
do chuid fola i bPalaistín bhuartha mo chroí.

A Mhohammed Abu Khdeir, tá gach litir
de d'ainmse, a mhaicín chaoin gan choir,
ag éamh in aibítir téachta seo an léin.

TO MOHAMMED ABU KHDEIR

A Palestinian boy burnt alive in the woods outside Jerusalem

Your little shapely-carved faced
bony as a bird's;
a green linnet or dove.

Light-footed as a gust of breeze
and lithe, supple
as a sally rod.

That morning, like other days,
you delighted your father and mother
with your blossoming smile

before setting off for the mosque
to perform your rituals,
the kneeling and bowing required by the Book.

But, dear one, they whisked you away
to the woods; bloodthirsty delinquents
reared on the testament of revenge

to pay for the youths of their own race
treacherously murdered, they sought what was theirs.
You were condemned, dear heart, on the altar of blood.

I see you with your youthful locks flowing,
flames engulfing your limbs,
your sixteen years of loveliness in torment.

Your innards explode
like acorns, sinews
ripped apart as they burn you alive.

The Sacred Books are wilting,
bent low in shame,
the words of the prophets splattered and stained with your blood.

Today the world is blanched, morning
is a grey dove, I hear the savage moan
of your blood, in Palestine of many a weary heart.

Mohammed Abu Khdeir, every letter
of your name, sweet innocent child,
cried out forever in the congealed alphabet of pain.

Translated, from the Irish, by Gabriel Rosenstock.

Cathal Ó Searcaigh is the Irish Language Editor of this journal. He was born in 1956 and raised in Meenala, near Gortahork, an Irish-speaking district in Co Donegal. He has published 15 poetry collections over 40 years, most recently Gúrú i gCluídíní *(Cló Iar-Chonnacht, 2006),* An tAm Marfach ina Mairimid *(Arlen House, 2011),* Aimsir Ársa *(Arlen House, 2013),* Na Saighneáin *(Arlen House, 2014), and* An Bhé Ghlas *(Leabhar Breac, 2016). His prose works include* Seal i Neipeal *(Cló Iar-Chonnacht, 2004),* Lights on Distant Hills: A Memoir *(Simon & Schuster, 2009), and* Pianó Mhín na bPreáchán *(2011). He is also the author of several plays in Irish, and a selection of English translations of his poetry,* By the Hearth at Mín a' Leá *(Arc), appeared in 2005. He is currently completing a novel in Irish,* Thugmar Féin an Samhradh Linn. *He continues to live in Meenala and is a member of Aosdána.*

POEM AND PROSE

Naomi Shihab Nye

Old news.

BEFORE I WAS A GAZAN

I was a boy
and my homework was missing,
paper with numbers on it,
stacked and lined,
I was looking for my piece of paper,
proud of this *plus* that, then multiplied,
not remembering if I had left it
on the table after showing to my uncle
or the shelf after combing my hair
but it was still somewhere
and I was going to find it and turn it in,
make my teacher happy,
make her say my name to the whole class,
before everything got subtracted
in a minute
even my uncle
even my teacher
even the best math student and his baby sister
who couldn't talk yet.
And now I would do anything
for a problem I could solve.

Note: Naomi Nye's father, Aziz Shihab (1927-2007), a Palestinian from Jerusalem, was made a refugee in 1948. He became one of the few Arab newspaper journalists in the US. He was the author of two books, A Taste of Palestine *(Corona, 1993) and* Does the Land Remember Me? A Memoir of Palestine *(Syracuse University Press, 2007).*

WHERE WE ARE NOW

News of the World (2016), by Paulette Jiles, is the best novel I have read in a very long time – a National Book Award finalist that did not "win" but will win hearts of everyone who reads it. A compact little book, with a finely luminous cover like an old hand-tinted photograph, two hugely appealing main characters, the rough, richly beautiful rural landscape of early Texas after the Civil War, small towns called Dallas and Durand, horses and swollen creeks and unknown people who might wish you harm lurking everywhere. But it's also funny. It's endearing and mesmerizing and suspenseful.

How comforting to read news of a world other than our current own.

Here in Texas going on two weeks after the election, some of us are shocked and embarrassed. We are ashamed in ways it is hard to put a finger on. A lot of blame flying around, lighting on telephone wires, lifting off. Where is my pack horse, please? Where is my battered wagon? Why are these thick-bellied white men in boots and hats strutting around DFW airport more aggressively than usual, speaking so loudly, why are the Mexican-American citizens of my majority Mexican city looking so downcast and quiet as they stand waiting to cross a street?

It's a new world. No, it's an old world. My Arab friends in the United Arab Emirates, where I spent Election week, wished me "safe journey back to your changed country."

This morning I had a new thought, new for me, anyway, after the most exhaustingly tedious, melodramatic build-up to a Presidential election one ever did witness.

Maybe a few more Americans are about to find out what Palestinians and many other people of color and oppressed histories have known for 70 years – that unfairness, ugly injustice, cruel domination, have a lot of power. Public relations does too. These inequities are not necessarily dissolved by intelligence or information. Something else is going on. Jimmy Carter and Bernie Sanders tried to talk about it openly and honestly. Why only them?

Recently I was heartbroken to hear that the smartest president of my whole lifetime, President Barack Obama, had overseen a 38-billion dollar gift of more weaponry from our nation to Israel, though the screams and cries of Gaza children, the brutal massacres of two summers ago, still ring in our ears. What? How could he do this? He is smart, gentle, wise! He has a great memory!

Of all the wonderful things President Obama has done, it seems so sad that an indiscriminate reward for terrible behavior has been given to the racist leader Netanyahu who doesn't care a bit about whom he offends or overlooks or ruins. Netanyahu has been saying ugly things about Arabs for years, and continues being rewarded. Netanyahu jails people without due process. A young Palestinian woman is under house arrest for months because she wrote a poem saying "Resist." He built a wall and it's a nightmare. He seizes land and plans to seize more. Just read Miko Peled, an Israeli telling the truth, if you don't believe me.

Now a man who seems to hate openly and bully happily has seized the votes of the Electoral College in our own nation and we have something and someone else to think about for the next four years. But I cannot say his name, look at him, or bear hearing his voice for one more minute.

Where is that book I am reading?

For some of us who didn't vote for him, this sad state of affairs may seem less shocking than for the rest of us who also didn't vote for him. It's not a first. It's old news, really.

(*Editor's note:* Peled is the author of *The General's Son: Journey of an Israeli in Palestine, 2012.* Born in Jerusalem in 1961, Peled grew up in Motza Illto to a prominent Zionist family. His grandfather, Avraham Katsnelson, signed Israel's Declaration of Independence; his father, Mattityahu, fought in the 1948 war and served as a general in the war of 1967.)

Naomi Shihab Nye was born in St. Louis, Missouri in 1952. Her father was a Palestinian refugee and her mother an American of German and Swiss descent, and she spent her adolescence in both Jerusalem and San Antonio, Texas. She is the author of nine volumes of poetry and two works of prose, as well as numerous books for children and young adults. She continues to live in San Antonio.

TRILINGUAL ELEGY
(Irish, Polish, English)

Simon Ó Faoláin

Translated by Justyna Mackowska, John Kearns & Paddy Bushe

CAOINEADH HENRYK PIOTROWSKI

A bhráthair ón oirthear
is trua liom d'oidhe,
ba thusa mise
ar chonair eile,
nár mhinic 'bhíos prioctha
ag meach na buile
chun ruathair a thabhairt
fén ndoras is siúil
an bóthar amach,
is droim a thabhairt
le gach a bheartaíos,
le clann, le grá,
le cairde, tír,
le gach a d'aithníos,
fiú an dóchas

Nuair – ainneoin
an uile aisce,
áilleacht, eitilt,
síor-chlaochlú –
bhraitheas nach fiú
faic mo bheo
gan chiall, gan sprioc,
tiománta ag duibhe,
ag daille, ag easpa
tuisceana,
ag slí a bhraitheas
mo shaol 'bheith curtha
ar fán iomlán,
ag slí a bhraitheas

gur teipeadh orm,
is ag gach urchall
coirp is samhlaíocht'
gan dul a ghearradh.

A bhráthair ón oirthear,
tuigim d'oidhe.

Nó cad is fiú
aon taise duitse
nach féidir dod'
chluas mharbh a chloisint,
's nár thig dod'
chluas bheo a thuiscint?
D'fhair an saol ort
thar tréimhse fhada
le súil ghéar,
fuarchúis fiolair,
tá breithiúnas tugtha
ag an margadh,
ba ró-shoiléir
meafar an údair
a d'fhág do chorp
i gcarn bruscar,

ach a bhráthair ón oirthear,
is trua liom d'oidhe.

Canaim dóibhsan
gan rath le bronnadh,
Canaim dóibhsan
nach fiú a moladh,
Canaim dóibhsan
gan chlú, gan leaba,
Canaim dóibhsan
nach geal le dia,
Canaim dóibhsan
le claí 'na n-aigne

nach ligfidh dóibh
dul abhaile,
Canaim dóibhsan
féin-damnaithe
ag an iomarca
d'fhéin-aithne,
Canaim dóibhsan
gur cam, gur claon,
gur saofa a gcúrsa
tarraingthe
trén saol, ó bharróg
bhaclainn máthar
go barróg idir
gialla cruacha.

A bhráthair ón oirthear,
is trua liomsa d'oidhe.

TREN KU CZCI HENRYKA PIOTROWSKIEGO

O bracie ze wschodu,
zasmuciła mnie
Twoja śmierć tragiczna.
Byłeś mną
na innej ścieżce,
nie raz czułem ukłucie
żądła szaleństwa
gnającego mnie
ku drzwiom i dalej,
na drogę, by porzucić
wszelkie plany,
rodzinę, miłość,
przyjaciół, ojczyznę,
wszystko, co znajome,
nawet nadzieję

Kiedy – pomimo
każdego z darów,

piękna, wzlotów,
nieustannych przemian –
czułem, że moje życie
grosza nie warte,
bez sensu, bez celu,
napędzane ciemnością,
może zaślepieniem,
brakiem zrozumienia,
poczuciem bezgranicznego
w życiu zagubienia,
poczuciem, że zawiodłem
oraz każdym potknięciem
ciała i ducha,
którego powstrzymać nie mogłem.

O bracie ze wschodu,
rozumiem Twoją
śmierć tragiczną.

Lecz cóż warte
dla Ciebie współczucie,
którego ucho martwe
nie usłyszy,
a którego żywe
zrozumieć nie mogło?
Obserwowano Cię
przez długi czas
z wnikliwością,
beznamiętnością orła,
rynek wydał wyrok
i zbyt banalna była
metafora autora,
który ciało Twe cisnął
na śmietnisko.

Mnie jednak,
o bracie ze wschodu,
zasmuciła Twoja śmierć tragiczna.

Śpiewam dla tych,
co nie mogą dać wiele.
Śpiewam dla tych,
co niegodni są chwały.
Śpiewam dla tych
bez honoru, bez łóżka.
Śpiewam dla tych,
co bogu nie mili.
Śpiewam dla tych,
którym myśli spętane,
wrócić do domu
nie pozwolą.
Śpiewam skazanym
przez własną świadomość.
Śpiewam dla tych,
których kurs życia popchnął
z czułych objęć
matczynych ramion
w zimne objęcia
stalowych szczęk.

O bracie ze wschodu,
zasmuciła mnie
Twoja śmierć tragiczna.

Translated, from the Irish, by John Kearns and Justyna Mackowska.

THE LAMENT FOR HENRYK PIOTROWSKI

Comrade from the east
I mourn your downfall,
you might have been me
on a different road,
I also was goaded
by the sting of madness
to make a dash
for the door and to

take off down the road,
to turn my back
on all I had planned,
on family, on love,
on friends, on homeland,
all things familiar,
on hope itself

When – in spite of
all good fortune,
flights of fancy,
of transformation –
I felt my life
was a zero sum
of pointlessness, aimlessness,
driven by darkness,
blindness, bereft
of understanding,
such that
my out of control
world was in a downward spin,
such that I felt
I had been abandoned,
and every tether
on my body and soul
tightened beyond release.

Comrade from the east
I understand your downfall.

For what good to you
is any compassion
which your dead ear
may not hear
nor your living ear
have understood?
The world observed you
for a long time
keenly,
with an eagle's cold eye,

evaluation is finished
by the market,
no subtle author
created the metaphor
that dropped your body
on a garbage tip,

but comrade from the east
I pity your downfall.

I sing for those
with no wealth to share,
I sing for those
who earn no praise,
I sing for those
with no name, nor place to stay
I sing for those
whom god has turned away,
I sing for those
with a fence in the mind
closing them off
from home and kind,
I sing for those
who condemn themselves
to endless digging
within themselves,
I sing for those
for whom slant, skewed,
perverted is the course
that is plotted
through life, from the embrace
of a mother's arms
to the embrace
of those iron jaws.

Comrade from the east
I grieve for your downfall.

Translated, from the Irish, by Paddy Bushe.

Henryk Piotrowski (born 1943) was a homeless person who came to Ireland from Poland in search of work. Whilst asleep in an industrial bin, he was crushed to death by a commercial waste pick-up truck. He had been sleeping rough after a hostel for Eastern European migrants in Dublin city centre was closed. His body was subsequently found in a waste management depot on the outskirts of the city.

———

Simon Ó Faoláin was born in Dublin in 1973 and raised for the most part in Paróiste Mhárthain in West Kerry. He is a professional archaeologist and has written, or co-written, several books and articles on the subject. He holds two degrees from University College Galway, and has spent various periods working and living in Galway, Wales and Achill Island. He has published three books of poetry: Anam Mhadra *(Dog's Soul, 2008),* As Gaineamh *(Out of Sand, 2011), and* Fé Sholas Luaineach *(By Unsteady Light, 2014), all with Coiscéim, as well as an illustrated chapbook,* Baile do Bhí *(A Home That Was, 2014) with Púca Press. He is Literature Officer in An Lab Arts Centre in Dingle and the Director of the Féile Bheag Filíochta, a bilingual poetry festival which takes place each November in Ballyferriter. He lives on the Dingle Peninsula with his wife Zoë and their son Ruaidhrí.*

Paddy Bushe was born in Dublin in 1948, and now lives in Waterville, Co. Kerry. He writes in both Irish and English, and has published eight collections of poetry, most recently To Ring in Silence: New and Selected Poems *(The Dedalus Press, 2008), a bilingual volume, and* My Lord Buddha of Carraig Eánna *(The Dedalus Press, 2012).*

A lecturer in translation at the Kazimierz Wielki University in Bydgoszcz, Poland, John Kearns is General Editor of the journal Translation Ireland. *He has edited* Translator and Interpreter Training: Issues, Methods and Debates *(Bloomsbury, 2008).*

Justyna Mackowska is a qualified Court and Community Interpreter with a Chartered Institute of Linguists' Diploma in Translation, a Certified Translator (from English to Polish and from Polish to English), and a Professional Member of the Irish Translators' and Interpreters' Association. Based in Ireland since 2002, she lives in Kilkenny.

THREE POEMS

Ciarán O'Rourke

POSTCARDS FROM PALESTINE

The tidy wars you planned
above my body's shrinking map,

the scars your bullet-mind unlatched,
and hatched, and loosed across my land,

the stench of metal on your boots,
the brutal compass in your hands,

(my south of buried villages,
my east of risen moons) –

they all go into it, shards
of the voice, or lines in the air,

into the remnant which you fear,
my torturer, will escape from here

to rectify the echoes, redirect the breeze…
that ghost, that almost emptiness,

in which your symphonies of dread
have dared me to believe.

~

We know our land
when the soldiers send us
to the border camps,

and press our mouths
into the ground.

We knew our home
when the fugue of drones
began to float,

rising, falling,
above the roof.

We'll know our names
from the numbers
they assign to us,

our every death apportioned
by a decimal of grief.

~

Not the body only,
but my poetry
and dreams they killed —

the presidents and generals,
the governments
of nations,

the scientists
and educators
standing to attention,

the nimble-
minded bureaucrats
whose fingers typed extinction.

I mark them all
as profiteers
of massacre and rubble.

And to the others,
opening clear windows
to tomorrow's sun, I say:

look for me
among the vanished faces
of my people.

~

Remember my words,
as if they were warmed by the blood in my wrist,
as if they were cut from the coil of my tongue.

Remember my song,
as if it contained the bricks of my city,
or rang with the sound of the sea on the rocks,
as if it resisted a world without pity,
or was wrung from the breath of my life's skeleton.

Remember the sun
that lent me a shadow to plant in the ground,
that gave me the right to delight in the clouds,
that watched as I fell at the flash of bombs,
that burns on the flesh of the bone-brittle homes.

Remember my poems,
as if in accusation of the architects of pain,
when seeking for the future that the olive branch proclaims.

GUATEMALA, 1967

In memory of Otto René Castillo

Say nation,
and the deer and moon
unlatch a shadow;

the darkness
quickens;
a candle blows.

Say water,
and thirst assumes
a human shape:

the man
whose mouth
defied the desert,

whose lips
the owners of the rain
would govern,

whose throat
the street-patrolling
prison guards would smash.

Say pain,
and the concrete
barracks' walls

are politic with light:
in the blood-loud night
the shutters glisten,

the darkened windows
flash and gleam;
next door, nearby,

across the world, a thousand
silences conspire
to regulate the scream.

Say beauty,
and perhaps, my love,
I'll find your form again,

my tongue journeying
the valleys, my fingers
rivering the slopes,

in search of quietness,
of storms,
and the real dawn

always gaining,
to burn the blue half-
sleep of it to air.

Or perhaps it's you
I'll see, my country,
with a hope grown vivid

at the edge of vision:
in the slum, in the mud,
on the stricken hills,

in the book of laughter,
in the nameless streets,
in the fists

of language lifting
with the stars and sun,
in the flickered flame.

Say poetry,
and the voices
of the sick

might rise tomorrow,
the faces of the earth
might smile.

THE KILLING MARCH
In memory of Miklós Radnóti

Each day permits
the old atrocities
anew —

the necessary deaths,
the far-off scream
come near,

the itch of madness
spreading
on the hands and hair.

History is one
disaster, feeding
off another, or

what poems are made
to witness
and withstand.

You taught us that;
or someone did,
whose teaching stemmed

from what he saw,
from the hunger hushing
through him like a mist,

his head adrift
with grief, or sleep,
but not dead yet

on the killing march.
Against all murderous
decrees, and against

the unreturning cities
razed, the angel
drowning in the bricks,

the roads
where beggars roam
and drop, it's true:

the oak trees
still are breathing,
and the fist,

which ice and metal
hammered once,
can furl

to feel the winter
easing
in a luff of rain.

So it is, poet,
in this barbaric language,
built from pain,

I imagine echoings
to be enough
to raise

your sightless eyes
and famine face,
and faith

in breath, a force
to conjure
youth again –

that place
of which, you say,
the music speaks

in mutter-tongues
and morse. Love poet,
eternal pastoralist,

in the din of one more
ending world,
I commemorate your corpse.

One of the greatest Hungarian poets of the twentieth century, Miklós Radnóti (1909-44) was born in Budapest to a Jewish family. He was killed during a fascist death march and was buried in a mass grave near the village of Abda, Hungary. When his body was exhumed 18 months later, a small notebook of final poems was found in the front pocket of his overcoat and published in 1946 as Foaming Sky. *It is now widely considered a masterpiece of Holocaust literature.*

Ciarán O'Rourke was born in 1991 and studied English and History at Trinity College, Dublin. He received a Masters in English and American Studies from Oxford in 2014. His poems have appeared in a number of publications, including Poetry Ireland Review, Poetry Review, The Irish Times, The London Magazine, New Welsh Review, The Spectator, *and* The SHOp. *His pocket-pamphlet* Some Poems *was published as a Moth Edition in 2011.*

TROUBLED BELFAST

Mrs Powell: "Well, Doctor, what have we got, a republic or a monarchy?"
Benjamin Franklin: "A republic, if you can keep it."
1787

———

Provincia – always near the beast's lair.

Miroslav Krleža

———

One day in June 2007, I was driving from Belmullet, County Mayo, on the far western seaboard, to Belfast, on the eastern. With me in the car were the critic Patricia Craig, the poet Michael Longley and my teenaged son, Jacob. We were exiting, with some relief, from a few days at a small literary festival, held in the midst of the bleak, windswept, scraggy flatland of northernmost Connaught. It was a soft day, as the expression goes in the West (from the Irish, *lá bog*), meaning clement, pleasant and gentle – even if, more often than not with the weather of those oceanic parts, also cloudy and misty.

The trip across the island would take us about six hours, perhaps more with stops, and the growing prospect of a day of conversation, free-wheeling narratives, passing scenery, jokes, comebacks and repartees seemed, by turns, to animate each of us. After the slight claustrophobia of another ego-laden literary weekend – one of an archipelago of such gatherings now dotted across virtually every county – we were freed into the vivid island itself. We had nothing but time and the company of ourselves – and the result ("the trek from Belmullet") has always struck me since as a shorthand image, or personal parable, for why it is easy, first to fall for Ireland, then to stick with it.

In Ireland, counties do indeed still count, in a way now lost or waning on "the other island." They have antique roots in a remote tribal past but are still the loci of various loyalties, from sport to creameries, politics to ancestral kinship. Likewise the four provinces – or five, if the huge Irish diaspora is made a metaphorical coccyx. To which, interestingly, only three of the cardinal points of the compass are ever superimposed in common island parlance: the *North*, *South* and *West* of Ireland. The Irish lexis somehow shuns the *East* in any demotic self-definition; it must surely be because that zone is straddled by Partition. But it was to the *East of Ireland* – the dense population and industrial zones of Belfast and Dublin, with its long historical tilt to Britain, a mere hundred miles apart – to which our talkative car-trek was now headed.

Michael, in the back, got going. He expatiated on the beauties and uses of swearwords, offering a number of choices of purely personal provenance, then suggesting some applications. Patricia, in the passenger seat, out of her phenomenally well-stocked cultural and literary mind, from time to time threw a quip over her shoulder as a perfect foil. Jake, who was attending Michael's school *alma mater* fifty years later, incited the latter into a rendition of the transgressive school-boy ditty still in currency. And so on – and on. As I drove to this brilliant sound-track, I must have felt – hence its sticking power – that a "day like this," to paraphrase "Van the Man," was, in some ineffable way, one that simply could not *be* (or be replicated) outside Ireland.

Soon enough we were travelling through the vast blanket boglands of remote North Mayo. They are exquisite, their muted subtleties of colour morphing and blazing through the seasons. Even in winter their rusts, mauve-greys and bleached greens are radiant in low sunshine. They have, of course, been hand-cut for home turf for at least four centuries; at sunset, the resulting bank-trenches of cutaway bog are darkling pools of western light. All over Ireland they have preserved a living museum of extreme archaicness: the vestiges of Neolithic farmsteads; trunks of oak and bog-bodies, steeped in the aspic of their anaerobic reticulations; hoards of golden torcs, brooches and bowls; altar vessels and reliquaries; even butter centuries out-of-date first buried for the bog's coolth.

Over the past half-century, however, peat extraction has also been heavily mechanized, for industrial purposes, by a state enterprise, Bord na Móna. So it was not long before we entered the now-desolate, stripped prairie-zone around the turf-fired power station at Bellacorick, even then being fed by several tractor-towed caterpillar-tracked millers in the surreal distance. Its huge, rusted tower looked a Lilliputian version of one of the cooling towers at Drax, Yorkshire's vast power complex. As our silver Cruiser sped by, Michael – the most ecological of poets – revved up again and murmured drolly, to my son's huge amusement: "so this is the Irish space programme ..."

"That's the Irish people all over," wrote Sean O' Casey in his play on the events of the War of Independence, *Shadow of a Gunman,* "they treat a joke as a serious thing and a serious thing as a joke." But since this theatrical gag is placed in the mouth of an unreliable blabbermouth, we can't be sure if, well, O'Casey was serious about his now-stereotypical utterance.

So too, writ large, the stereotypical "West of Ireland": it has become the repository of every romantic or Celticist cliché you care to name *re* "the real Ireland." Yet despite all the over-development and atrocious imagery, the modern West *is* marvellous for its endless dovetailing of natural beauties and cultural fascinations: the sea-girt landscapes, the Irish language, the vestiges of an older material and social way-of-life – to name the obvious ones.

More, the stereotypes about the West of Ireland do point to a decisive historical role in upholding a sense of Irish cultural and national distinctiveness after the 1801 Act of Union. That Victorian anthem of a resurgent Irish nation, "The West's Awake," by the Young Irelander Thomas Davis, suggests as much. It could be said – and has been often – that the Easter Rebellion would never have occurred without the Gaelic Revival, whose living linguistic base lay primarily in the Western counties. As the Kilkenny essayist Hubert Butler would put it a generation after independence, "the mainspring of our freedom was not political theory but the claim that Ireland possessed and could develop a unique culture of its own." Much the same discourse has now taken wing in Scotland.

On an island the middling size of Ireland, however, no cardinal point is very far from its three fellows. This is particularly true of the six counties of Munster, with its South-West axis; but also the nine counties of Ulster, with its North-West axis straddling (unlike the other points) the long, meandering and rural border between Northern Ireland and the Republic.

The extent to which Partition was felt to be a fracturing of not only an island, but an antique province, is perfectly embodied in the contested lexicon for the new Northern state. The republican nomenclature – "the six counties" or (still more old-fashioned) "the wee six" – reflects "an Ulster of the mind" that sees, therein, the lost limb of an imagined 32-county nation. The "North of Ireland," tending to be shared by nationalists or centrists of all stripes, avoids the British constitutional terminology, which, of course, is embraced by mainstream unionists in the abbreviated form, "Northern Ireland." Militant loyalism uses the incorrect "Ulster" for the same native territory. Even in the rest of the United Kingdom, it is often not appreciated that the word "United" in the state's name refers specifically to the Union with a rump Ireland, not with Scotland and/or Wales. Only the rather poetic "the North" receives easy assent across such petrified national and sectarian divisions.

I couldn't say now whether Michael's joke was the trigger, but I recall distinctly that the talk turned to the state of the island, its despoliations and follies, its foibles and stupidities, North and South (meaning: the two jurisdictions). What is perhaps most telling about such perennial ruminations is the instinctive, near-universal assumption that the island somehow remains a fractured whole, a cultural and geographical unity underlying all constitutional and economic arrangements.

More glorious Mayo landscape shot by. Michael, reaching for the closure of a punch-line, delivered the *coup de grace* to our antic critiques: *The Irish don't deserve Ireland, I'm beginning to think* ... All caveats notwithstanding, we knew exactly what he meant – even if, in truth, the same might be said of every place where natural beauty is despoiled by human activity.

If the East of Ireland seems somehow bifurcated by the two states, the West suffers no such psychic partition. Donegal, in particular – where the West and North crosshatch – is widely felt to be the seamless hinterland of Northern Ireland, a fact evident in much of the most important imaginative literature to have emerged coevally with the Troubles. In a clutch of Brian Friel's plays, the fictional townland of Ballybeg in Donegal becomes the Chekhovian locus of an extended history of this "imagined community" and, by subtle proxy, of the West of Ireland itself – in sharp contrast to several of his others dealing overtly with the politics of a turbulent Ulster.

More widely, Seamus Heaney's magisterial poetry volume, *North* (Faber, 1975) – perhaps the single most influential book written in the shadow of Troubled Ulster – plumbs the boglands of the North and West as a rich metaphor for the continuum of violence, ancient and modern. Patricia herself, in her splendid memoir of teenage hi-jinks in the fifties, *Asking for Trouble* (Blackstaff, 2007), shuttles between the gritty backstreets of Belfast and a Donegal Gaeltacht's authoritarian charms. For Michael too – witness a half-century of poems – Belfast and Mayo are the twin poles of his imaginative zodiac.

As we crossed the Border, the craic dwindled and silence descended – whether from the vanished West, conversational fatigue or nightfall (or all three), I could not have said even then. But I have often had this feeling of a slow landing as my son and I hurtled home on a motorway from a spell in

Donegal. In that movement from time in the West to life in the North, would it be too much to see something epigrammatically human? Peace and violence? The ordinary and the extraordinary – or *vice versa*? The rural and the urban? The vital and the petrified? "Days like this" and the daily grind?

In any event, the car-trek from Mayo had ended and the mean streets of a still-troubled Belfast were the first to meet us.

———

I grew up in the liberal milieux of East Coast America, but I have spent almost my entire adult life (36 years) in Ireland. Is it *strange destiny* to have fallen so far from the trunk of origins?

For the first two decades or so, I often thought so, particularly intensely in relation to Belfast. That changed, decisively, with the birth of my two children. Now, like so many immigrants, I am much more sanguine about the experience of departure from my life's "first narrative" and the unexpected arrival into a second, indeed a third. As the English poet (and lover of orchards) Michael Hamburger once remarked – his family fled from Nazi Germany when he was nine – it is trees, not humans, which have roots. Viewed in the round, acknowledging the original risk of a mistaken cul-de-sac and the many subsequent difficulties, I have no doubt whatsoever now that my Irish flit was a good opening gambit for a second narrative. Without it, no Jacob and Miriam – and that, of course, settles the question, especially in retrospect. *Destiny Ireland*, it turns out, has been very good indeed for me. In life, says an elderly Sarajevo friend who survived the siege, *always expect the unexpected*.

Why, at first, did I come? There was a push and there was a pull. The push was from the United States in the 1970s: I had become somehow disenchanted with those "milieux," for a complex and suffocating mix of family, class, cultural and personal reasons (another story!). The intense proto-professional pressures of boarding school and an Ivy League education had exhausted me by the summer of '79, and indeed – I see now very clearly – I feared proceeding further along an unknown route to a known professional fate for which apparently I had been prepared, but to which I had never really inwardly assented. I needed a pause. I feared above all, after graduation, I would now say, the danger this unreflectively preordained path posed to what had already become a central literary aspiration.

Outside the dominant familial and educational zones before university, I had had, moreover, important extended experiences, mainly in the summer, in rural Vermont, Rhode Island and the Adirondacks of New York, as well as in peasant Mexico and circumpolar Labrador. These constituted a composite alternative universe and anti-suburban formation – of which I was very emotionally and aesthetically aware, from an early age. In such supposed backwaters, the small-scale, the remote, the intimate, the natural and the wild, and of course the older, were revelatorily present. From early on it became a kind of grain within me, where I most distinctly felt more fully at home, happier and clearer, and so more fully myself.

The pull came from Europe. I had spent a transformative gap year (1974-75) studying French language and literature at the Université d'Aix-en-Provence, followed by two memorable summers in Ireland (1977-78), where I did some contact-scouting in the North for a Harvard professor writing on the Troubles, and so acquired an incipient interest in Irish writing. Without any post-graduation plan whatsoever, I defaulted to another summer on Block Island, Rhode Island, where I worked as a night watchman. My plan was to write in the wee hours; but I mostly slept on duty and wrote, I think, only a sentence or two before my one idea expired.

But Ireland, it seemed, was unfinished business – and the vague desire to return gelled over a Thoreauvian summer and early fall on that ecologically radiant island. I had no commitments and made some money renovating an old summer shack. *Now or never!* I expected to stay a year or two.

I arrived in Ireland on 29 September 1979, via a Laker flight to London and the ferry from Holyhead to Dun Laoghaire, the route used by generations of immigrants to Britain, whether leaving or returning. It's not that I didn't know that the Polish Pope was arriving in Dublin the same day; it's just that, like the rest of the island, the scale of the crowds and the collective euphoria greeting him in the Republic was beyond my ken. Off the boat, I took the last packed train through a completely emptied city, to Phoenix Park, where John Paul II performed his first Mass, a tiny speck in the raised distance, before 1.2 million people – the largest single mass of humanity I have ever experienced.

Looking back, those three days of the first papal visit to Hibernia strike me now as a perfect symbolic threshold between the old and the new Ireland – between the 63 years succeeding the Proclamation of the Irish Republic, and the 37 since. With further masses to the West, South and North, the Pope's triumphal trip did not prove the well-spring of enduring Eucharistic renewal, as many in the Church hoped and expected, so much as an autumnal, ebullient celebration of the mighty magisterium and its faithful grip on the *res publica* and much of its citizenry.

Yes, in the figure of Karol Wojtyla, former athlete and passable poet, the Church was at its liturgical, verbal and ethical best – but there was something, too, of the last unselfconscious hurrah for a monolithic political Christianity, *Irish Catholicism,* that had so hijacked that state and its evolution. Within a decade, its authority was in sharp decline, rocked by a relentless series of scandals, heading rapidly towards the Irish separation of church and state that now mainly obtains. Meanwhile, the North – in its usual time-lag time-warp – would have to wait another two decades for its own great glacial shift: the Good Friday Agreement.

Four days later, I was on the train from Dublin to Belfast, wondering whether I had made the right decision. As we passed a row of ruined houses along a grim Portadown siding – due, possibly, to the turmoil of the Troubles – I had my first real stab of adult fear. What was I doing here, intending this time to stay? Why had I not stuck to the beaten American track? Would it, ultimately, be dangerous?

That first Belfast, in 1979, was almost wholly devoid of immigration in the usual sense. Naturally, there were numbers of English and Scots, fellow citizens, as well as Southerners, who had come for work or personal reasons; there was even a sprinkling of immigration from Hong Kong and the Subcontinent, mainly centred on the restaurant business. Outside Queen's University Belfast, however – with its longstanding tradition of overseas students – the city had achieved as close to nil inward immigration as would be possible in a post-colonial, multinational state like Britain.

As the stalemate of the violence dragged on through the eighties, a small trickle of EEC nationals did begin to arrive, often for particular reasons – to teach as *assistants* in schools, say, or to man the new cosmopolitan restaurants that began to burgeon as the politico-military situation began to "stabilize." Amazingly, I remember reckoning, at some point in the early eighties, that I knew of only two Afro-origin people living in Belfast; one had grown up on the Shankill Road with a white mother, the other was a strikingly elegant, salt-and-pepper West Indian residing right in the middle of loyalist working-class East Belfast.

My future wife, who grew up in Armagh, first saw a black person when she emigrated to London at the age of 18. Ethnically speaking, the early troubled North amounted to a near-autarky – certainly compared to the vast polyglot cities (Boston, New York, Providence) I grew up with. Apart, of course, from the rotating regiments of the British Army, lodged in ring-fenced bases.

So the common joke with me during my first years in Belfast was that I had somehow come in the wrong direction. From the outset of the Troubles in 1969, the North had been haemorrhaging people, especially from the Protestant community, and the young. In the early eighties, the Southern economy had tanked after the comparative prosperity of the sixties and seventies, triggering new large waves of Irish emigration to America, the Continent and Australia.

Metaphorically speaking, the exit/entrance was getting crowded and I was moving against the flow. In time, though, I would find that the Belfast cultural scene, however constricted by the Troubles, had a distinct international dimension; and that, even earlier, there had actually been a small but fascinating émigré artist tradition in interwar Belfast. I soon got to know the Mexican painter Alfonso Monreal; the Iranian gallery owner Jamshid Fenderesky; and the extraordinary Czech choreographer, writer and Auschwitz-survivor Helen Lewis (1916-2009).

Now Belfast has "changed, changed utterly" in the matter of diversity. Since the historic political settlement in 1998, large-scale immigration has increased by leaps and bounds. The obvious first arrivals were from the Balkans, Africa and Romania; then, with the 2004 EU accession of the Eastern states, large numbers of Poles, Lithuanians, Slovaks and Roma, along with many Western Europeans (especially Portuguese), have settled in Belfast and the North.

At the weekly market under the clock and glass-roof of St George's – in dereliction during the Troubles, where once over 900 corpses were laid out after the Belfast Blitz, on Easter Tuesday, 1941 – a new and vibrant multiculturalism shows its full face. Not since the "plantation" of Ulster by Lowland Scots and English in the seventeenth century has there been such an overseas influx of population to the Belfast environs; it was, in fact, this foundational Protestant colonization that gave birth to the city around an older native ford.

In the long-term, this enormous shift in the human character of the city may be the most momentous of the all the changes following the Troubles. Some of the new arrivals, especially non-European refugees, may maintain a loyalty to Britain for the asylum granted; others from nations characterized by independence struggles, like Poles and Lithuanians, may come to identify with Irish nationalism. One thing is certain: they and their

(Continued after Portfolio *on page 257)*

PORTFOLIO

Mark Cousins

Salt and Sweet

(stills and voice-overs from I am Belfast*)*

A wise woman
"I can see more clearly now."

A filmmaker, film critic, writer, presenter and wanderer, Mark Cousins was born in Northern Ireland in 1965 and has lived in Edinburgh since the 1980s. His filmography includes The First Film *(2009),* The Story of Film: An Odyssey *(2011),* What is This Film Called … Love? *(2012), and* Here Be Dragons *(2013). He took the Edinburgh Film Festival to Sarajevo during the siege of that city in the early 1990s, and is the author of* The Story of Film *(Pavilion, 2011) and* Imagining Reality: The Faber Book of the Documentary *(Faber, 2006). His acclaimed, landmark and richly poetic cine-essay,* A Story of Children and Film *(2013), was one of* The Official Selection 2013 *of the Cannes Film Festival.*

His latest and highly celebrated film is I am Belfast *(2015), from which the following photographic stills and texts have been taken. Cousins writes of the film:*

> *I am Belfast* was filmed by walking the streets of the city, every one of them. I wanted to avoid various points of view – those of the policy-maker, journalist, tourist, sectarian, Hollywood filmmaker or historian. Instead, the film should feel more like people-watching or, to use Virginia Woolf's nice phrase, "street haunting." The main character, a ten-thousand-year-old woman played by Helena Bereen, drifts through the city like the ghost of a wise woman.
>
> Filming on ordinary streets means that you don't photograph too many famous places. Belfast has some buildings and places that are conventionally beautiful and cinematic, but our film hopes to find beauty, emotion and meaning in smaller, less obviously pretty things: the grisailles of mud flats and a bird's wing; the glint of new buildings; the *mano no aware* as they say in Japan, the sadness of time passing; and the baroque swearing of two lively women.

This portfolio is published courtesy of the British Film Institute, from which I am Belfast *can be purchased in dual format (DVD and Blu Ray). Founded in 1933, the BFI is a charitable film organization which promotes and preserves filmmaking and television in the United Kingdom. It was granted a Royal Charter in 1983.*

Airborne

"Softly, softly come to me ..."

A salt hill, near the Shore Road

"This place could sink a ship ..."

A street's shining wall

"Come with me, let's get lost. Someone painted a wall golden, so I go to it. The warm morning sun on my face, and on the back of my neck — the wall reflects it. It's so nice here — let's wait a bit. And listen. Let's listen first, and then look, and then walk."

Buoy sculptures

"When I now look at myself, I see colour … a riot of colour …
softer than satin was the light."

Jennymount Linen Mill, Shore Road

"A study in brick-red and white … an Italian palazzo built in the late 1800s —
we made more linen than anywhere in the world."

Gantries

"And also with my new eyes, I notice how theatrical we are. Boy, do we put on a show. This is a proscenium, a stage. So much of what I, Belfast, am is a stage – or frame … We're very good at framing ourselves, aren't we?"

The Crown Bar

"A crime scene; a rhyme scene; a time scene."

Estuary, Belfast Lough

"The name of my one rivers means where the sweet water meets the salt. *That's how I started. Here, where the river meets the sea, sweet meets salt — is that what I am, is that what we are? Salt and sweet, like hard and soft?"*

City Hall at dusk

"And we thought. *Right here in 17 and 92, we paraded to support the French Revolution, the Fall of the Bastille, and Poland's resistance against Russia. (We're quite good at parades.) Resolutions were passed by a lawyer named Theobald Wolfe Tone. We drank to political solidarity between Catholics and Protestants, to universal suffrage, the influence of Thomas Paine whom I knew — those were the days, my friend."*

Street near Belfast City Hall

"When I looked at myself in the mirror back then, what did I see? A city that was brilliant, friendly, volcanic, inward, outward, homophobic, creative, loquacious, feminine, déclassé, romantic, sentimental, pious and edgy ... And have you ever noticed, that we're surreal too ..."

Construction of the *Titanic*, vintage footage

"And then like a tracking shot, the iceberg hit. We fought each other. Is now a good time to talk about it? Is ever a good time? … Did we judder to the Troubles, to our latest war which still troubles us? Or do we glide there – over decades or days, for good reasons and bad, we peered over the top of things and down into the depths. Salt and sweet. Nationalist and unionist. The two sides in our war went wild."

Troubles patrol, walking backwards

"People like us came here — like they did in the 1600s. They came with guns and accents. They were new blood. There was a lotta walking. And salt and sweet forced each other apart. In a few months in one area alone, 1505 Catholic and 315 Protestant families were made to move — the largest enforced movement of people since WWII."

Cave Hill

"Things that couldn't happen did. Cave Hill – the mountain behind me, where people had lived since the Iron Age, where Charles Dickens walked when he visited Belfast – turned on its head. The tenth of March, 19 and 71, three Scottish soldiers were drinking in a bar in town – they were grabbed and taken up the Hill. Maybe they walked the same route as Dickens had 113 years earlier. Whilst they were having a piss, the soldiers were shot in the head. They spouted two liquids: blood and piss at the same time. Do you continue to piss when a hole has been blown in your brain? The soldiers were 17, 18 and 25. Two days later, 4,000 dockers downed their tools in the shipyards and marched in protest."

Underpass, on site of the bombing of McGurk's Bar in 1971

"On the evening of the fourth of December 19 and 71, it was busy. Christmas was coming. The bar's owner, Paddy McGurk, was serving drinks. He was proud of his place. He didn't allow swearing: there was a swear-box on the counter. At 8.45 pm, a bomb exploded in the bar, killing 15 people, and wounding 17 more. McGurk's wife and daughter both died, and he and his three sons were injured. A few hours later, he went on TV to say that he prayed for the bombers, and asking that his family's deaths should not be avenged … The pub was destroyed, yet it's visually here – a trompe l'oeil, a creative response to destruction."

A seagull's wing

"I dream that I am flying over Belfast like a seagull. I look down at myself — in my dream, it's that day [Bloody Friday, 21 July 1972]*, the sea-clouds of smoke — and dive and eat. We were just food for the seagulls, just meat. Were we also just meat for each other? In all our fighting, have we scavenged on each other? The seagulls knew no better — do we? Or was that detached — that aloft?"*

Two Ceasefires

"But things got better. At our listening walls, our wailing walls, we heard news":

> "It's just been announced … at a few minutes past 11 o'clock this morning, the waiting and the speculation ended … a statement from the IRA leadership had finally materialized and its key clause read: 'the leadership of the IRA have decided that as of midnight August 31st there will be a complete cessation of military operations…'"

> "In all sincerity – in all sincerity – we offer to the loved ones of all innocent victims of the past 25 years abject and true remorse. No words of ours will compensate for the intolerable suffering they have undergone during this conflict. Let us firmly resolve, therefore, to respect our differing views of freedom, culture and aspiration – and never again permit our political circumstances to degenerate into bloody warfare."

"Abject and true remorse – what words! It's like we woke up. What did we see when the storm passed? We saw that we'd been blasted sideways. We saw good things … And on sunny days, doors darted light-beams. That old luminosity was still there."

Palestine Street

"In old streets that we always called the Holy Land — Palestine Street, Jerusalem Street — people from Asia and the Middle East moved in, and lived their lives their ways."

Immigrants, the New Lodge flats

"*Let's stop at this famous place – the New Lodge. Built not very well, to house as many people as possible. But they were poor people, so they didn't matter. There's what you'd expect: razor-wire on the bottom right, messages about the IRA Hunger Strikers on the top of the flats. Because of drive-by shootings and other things, this was the most dangerous place to stand during the Troubles. And yet – look – there's magic here. Suddenly among this crane, it rises; and like a seagull flying up around the flats, and a camera on a crane in a Hollywood movie, filming a dance routine … Shall we make a musical about the New Lodge? Someone coming to live here, from Poland or Lithuania?*"

Torc

"And after the storm passed, we noticed other good things. We made ships and linen and music and war and peace here. But people too — people from Hopewell and the New Lodge, the Antrim Road and the Holy Land, the Ormeau and Orangefield."

Pietà

"*A man's lying in the hot afternoon sun today — a pietà. He's going to burn: he's us, he's me. Two women see him. One in turquoise tells her friend to leave him alone. But the one in black can't help herself — she has to help.*"

Shadow-play

"*When the storm cleared, it also left something bad: walls. Our Berlin walls. Today we have more walls keeping salt and sweet apart than I can ever remember ... Fornenst each other, this split in me seems as solid as concrete, as tarmac. I wish it were shadow-play. I wish my walls had electric shadows on them, or movies ... I wish my walls grew things; I wish those things — ivy, wall flowers — would break open the walls. I wish our walls were gold.*"

Mural, Shankill Road

"And what about Lord Arthur Chichester who sort of founded me, Belfast — or so the history books say — in the 1600s. Look at his eyebrows — Marlene Dietrich eyebrows! Salt and sweet, man and woman, day and night — they should all merge. That's what I want to say to you. Don't just look at Belfast; imagine Belfast — me *... That's what the painter of this mural did — it's a dreamscape. The Giant's Causeway on the left,* Titanic, *the cranes all coming out of the water — the real world pushed to the far right. And then this man in blue — the things his eyes have seen ... "*

The Funeral of the Last Bigot

"Imagine — some October morning in the future, when the walls are down and the Creature from the Black Lagoon is gone — imagine that there is only one bigot left. He's an old man and he dies":

"… I looked into their eyes and all I saw was fading death of me and mine, of God and wine, and all that we purveyed. And so I knew — their eyes told me — the engine of my days, a braveheart locomotive that set our pulses racing; that showed that blood and soil are never self-effacing; that anger, power and loyalty are the duty of our days. So bury me today — and with me — what kept us apart. And sing your song of harmony for all ye like, and from the heart: I *was* the Belfast you all knew; and with me that's now dying, something new is born today — a transgression, a trying."

PORTFOLIO

is generously supported by Nicholson & Bass Ltd, Belfast.

native descendants will change the whole religious-national-ethnic-sectarian dynamic that has so scarred the city for at least a century and a half – and, in fact, have already done so.

So part of my unexpected destiny, strange or not, is to have become an immigrant, nationally-ambiguous and, even, exilic writer. In recent years, I have come to view this as an *almost* unqualified creative positive. For there is a sense in which a writer's true homeland is language. Within English, the global *lingua franca*, the interplay of the national and transnational is now acute. For the poet as immigrant, it becomes fruitful, as in my case, to inhabit double perspectives within a single language – to be a "tinker of the spirit," shifting between various cultures, seeing what I can make out of looking both ways from the threshold of expatriate life.

In the new Age of the Refugee that is now upon us, it is perhaps no bad thing for a writer to be disabused somewhat of the enchantments of "roots," and to feel in himself, as a distant echo, the fragility of the insular in face of the global upheavals. In a critical or reputational sense, the danger is that you might seem to fall between two stools. In a creative sense, the bifocal award is that you are bound by neither.

What is a city? Not, surely, simply the material urban culture at a named spot.

A moment's reflection makes clear that it is equally something quite immaterial: a general atmosphere, a cultural ambience, a civic timbre, an embodied *zeitgeist*, a psycho-social pattern – the angles are legion. What is adumbrated, in short, by the classical term *civitas*, the cumulative ethos or values, or prevailing *leitmotif* of self-definition or collective self-consciousness, that binds together a city or a state (e.g., Athens or Sparta, Hong Kong or Jerusalem), especially in relation to common purpose, shared responsibility, and/or "imagined community." The apparently anodyne slogan, *People Make Glasgow,* gets the classical idea in exact demotic.

Cities, of course, never stay static. Like consciousness, they must evolve, morph, segue, metamorphose. A fixed city is a fantastical dystopia, like the frozen stopwatch episode of "The Twilight Zone." But the rate at which the material and immaterial cultures of any city change can vary dramatically. With some cities, especially ancient ones, these can proceed together in slow and stately tandem, under the aegis of tradition. In others – subject to war, natural catastrophe, or urban planning – the two are razed, then reborn, together. In still others, the material and the immaterial move rapidly out of sync, with the latter often moving much more swiftly. Such has been the fate of many Eastern European and Balkan cities after the fall of communism. As the Polish dissident Adam Michnik remarked, surveying the East's dismal perspectives, "The worst thing about communism is what comes after."

Since my arrival in Belfast, the material culture of the city has changed not quite beyond all recognition – but profoundly for the better. Large swathes of the old industrial working-class districts have been renewed or redeveloped, including many tragically wrecked by the Troubles (bombings, rioting, arson, flight, dereliction). Much of this task of reconstruction during the Troubles fell to the Northern Ireland Housing Executive, whose slow transformation of Belfast despite the troubled mayhem was widely viewed as a rare early triumph of non-sectarian, municipal socialism. It learnt from the brutalist excesses of housing redevelopment in Britain, and returned (often quite aesthetically) to the scale of the city's traditionally terraced streets.

Discrimination against Catholics in the allocation of housing had been a key grievance that led to the formation of the Civil Rights Movement in the run-up to the outbreak of the Troubles. The whole political pH of the city began to change as progressive urban renewal kicked in from the early eighties. Nonetheless, a huge, rich, highly distinctive urban heritage was lost. In her extraordinarily evocative book, *Byker* (Cape, 1983), the Finnish photographer Sirkka-Liisa Konttinen provides a visual record of a cognate North-of-England working-class community on the eve of its destruction, not by communal violence, but wholesale redevelopment.

In the case of Belfast, this double palimpsest – the material and the immaterial, both past and present – parses in a different form. Since the Belfast Agreement (as it is formally known), indeed long before, I would not be alone in seeing the immaterial lagging well *behind* the material. The paramilitary cessations of violence, the removal of the Army from the streets, the full functioning of devolution, the overall economic improvement, indeed the totality of the new constitutional and social dispensation – all this transformed the tone of the city and wider polity. Above all, the funereal, tense, leaden, insular, super-bitter atmosphere of the Troubles that lay like a psychic slab over the population has been magicked away.

Yet few here would dissent from the view that the native territory remains deeply toxic in the immaterial dimension. One prime source, of course, is the poisonous legacy of the vanished violence. The British and Irish states, as well as all the major Northern political parties, may have reached a durable accommodation – but deeper down, on the communal and attitudinal level, "the antique quarrel" of ethno-religious, national and sectarian division is largely intact and highly unmoderated, still bedevilling Belfast and Ulster as it has done since Partition. This is the lurking iceberg, instinct says, that could yet sink the New Belfast and the New North. On the eve of his departure from the North (1972), Heaney wrote: "we must uproot or petrify." That choice still faces the immaterial city in respect of its troubled past.

To a city's blend of the material and immaterial, there must be added a further ingredient: the subjective onlooker, yourself. Just as that blend must change over time, so do you, its interpreter. You must search for a city: it does not simply present its meshed palimpsest and subjective mnemonics *in vacuo*. That context is your own shifting, evolving, seguing, metamorphosing self. If that self changes dramatically, through whatever combination of inner and outer experience, so may your view of what lies before you. What was discounted, for instance, might now be cherished. You might walk the same streets, pass the same buildings, meet some of the same people as decades before. But are you "in the same place," as a therapist might put it?

The city's blend has evolved. You have evolved. The perspectival relationship between you and it must, perforce, have evolved. Perhaps this is often why, when I am abroad on Belfast's troubled palimpsest, I feel at home – in a new city – on the same streets of recessional cities I no longer inhabit.

———

To understand fully the Northern polity and thus Belfast's place within it, a comprehensive historical definition of "Northern Ireland" is always seasonable. The series of events between 1916 and 1922 – leading to a new "Irish Free State" and the retention of six Ulster counties within the newly named "The United Kingdom of Great Britain and Northern Ireland" (the "Northern" now added) – is but the basic historical description.

And a description, of course, is never quite the same as an explanation. Together, these constitute a historical narrative – and the narratives about the North, however divergent, have tended over time, in my view, to become detached from a *third* but essential historical context. They first congealed, then petrified, into the two contending, predominant Irish-

British perspectives, both in politics and historiography, the pan-European context of Partition, I have long thought, has generally fallen from view even in the most scholarly narratives.

I have already alluded to Butler in the context of the Succession States, of which the Irish Free State was formally the last (1922). With regard to Irish parallels, the wider European situation in the immediate aftermath of the Great War merits the closest scrutiny. The four great intra-European empires (the Austro-Hungarian, the German, the Ottoman, the Russian) had comprehensively collapsed; and the Treaty of Versailles and many others (Brest-Litvosk, St Germain, Neuilly, Trianon, Sèvres, Lausanne, Rapallo, including several British imperial agreements vis-à-vis the carve-up of the post-Ottoman Middle East) brought into being a dramatically new, post-imperial state system in interwar Europe.

In retrospect, this period 1918-1922 seems a gigantic interregnum for organized-legitimate power and cartography, much as the collapse of communism would be for the decade from 1989. The reconfigured and reconfiguring continent was not only characterized by new, expanded and/or revolutionary states; but nationally-ambiguous territories, condominiums, annexations, Free Cities, minority rights, non-state armed formations, uprisings, putsches, population "transfers," and much else of post-colonial descent amid the rise of the "nation-state." Even in Ireland, as Heinrich Böll would later write in his masterly *Irish Journal* (1957), referring to the direct writerly participation in the events of Easter Monday 1916, "eighteen months before Lenin took over the remains of an empire, the Irish poets were scraping away the first stone from the pedestal of that other empire which was regarded as indestructible but has since turned out to be far from it."

Once the formation of Northern Ireland is contextualized in this period, it immediately ceases to be a process confined simply to the historical umbilicus between the two islands, and assumes its proper pan-European nexus as well. That nexus is, first of all historically, the aforementioned Plantation of Ireland and its Siamese twin, the Reformation in Ireland. Both are what French historiography calls "la longue durée" — those deep structures that move glacially through history. In addition to "civilizing" and commercial motivations, the Plantation was conceived explicitly as a means of making "English-speaking" and "Protestant" the Gaelic and Catholic fastness of Ulster, where the power of the English crown had been historically weak. Through various historical knock-ons, it could be said to have succeeded with the first aim, but failed partly with the second.

One of the main architects of this policy of dispossession and colonization, the English Viceroy of Ireland, Sir Arthur Chichester, was also instrumental in the founding of Belfast, which remained a largely Protestant city until the mid-nineteenth century. Even if it is maintained that the subsequent communal polarization in Ulster had more to do with further waves of Scottish immigration than the original plantation in the early seventeenth century, there is also a thesis in cultural geography, known as "First Effective Settlement," that holds that the original successful settlement of an empty or (as we would say today) "ethnically-cleansed" or dispossessed territory is of crucial significance to later social and cultural development, no matter how small the original group of settlers may have been.

Indeed, this very principle was deployed, intuitively, by the aforementioned European empires for centuries. All over Europe, populations considered "loyal" by the imperial authorities were "planted" in territories, especially borderlands or frontiers, which needed to be "secured." Such were the Serbs of the Krajina, the Saxons of Transylvania, the Russians of Novorossiya – and the Protestants of Ulster.

Four centuries later, the irony is that what began as an anabasis of the migrant into the native has ended in the ostensibly autochthonous and immutable divisions of Northern society and (lo and alas) of our Troubled Belfast. Here I will re-join my own narrative in an earlier essay, "The New North" (2008):

> If the emergence of Northern Ireland was the long-distance descendant of the Plantation, it can also be understood as the terminus to a great swathe of lands shaped by the Reformation, arcing from Central and Northern Europe, into the British-and-Irish archipelago. Likewise, the cognate independence of the South belongs to a much later pan-European cultural pattern; namely, the small nations of Europe, the so-called Succession States, that emerged out of the imperial aftermath of the First World War ... In this European perspective, the creation of Northern Ireland eighty-six years ago was, willy-nilly, the product of the very same ascendant continental pattern that brought into existence the Succession States. Even if the North

was not itself, properly speaking, one of those states, remaining a loyal remnant of an older multinational Union, it was nonetheless a new constitutional European jurisdiction and, in this sense, one of the new small succession "countries" of post-Versailles Europe ... If such dynamics are amenable to grand theories, it might be said that Northern Ireland had emerged out of the historical equivalent of two colliding tectonic plates, one foundational, one contemporary: the Reformation in Ireland, and the disintegration of internal European empires.

Though not much frequented by standard historiography, the implicit Eastern trope here, that there are parallels between modern Ireland (and its Partition) and the other post-Versailles Succession States of Eastern Europe – and *their* successors – has some pedigree in Irish writing. Heaney often uses Polish experience as a trope for his native ground (Ireland and Poland, he says, "have their historical roofs off," unlike England, where no shot has been fired in political anger since the Civil War); whilst the ever-prescient Butler (1900-1991), Ireland's Orwell, wrote extensively on the close parallels between religious, national and ethnic loyalties and tensions within Ireland (especially the North) and the Balkans (especially Yugoslavia).

———

In early 1996 I visited Sarajevo right at the end of its long siege. Through a journalist friend, an invitation reached me from the Sarajevo Winter Festival, which was celebrating its own resurrection and the city's multi-ethnic survival after nearly four years of encirclement by the war criminals in the hills. It was inviting many of the writers, artists and actors who had actively supported, from the outside, the survival of what Bosnia had come to represent.

I had written and edited some journalism; joined solidarity groups in Ireland and Britain; and, with the Irish-language poet Nuala Ní Dhomhnaill, spoke out at a number of literary events and public meetings concerning "the scandal of Sarajevo." As I wrote in one essay, Bosnia was the Spanish Civil War of our time, representing "a clash between the open and closed society, a modern polity aspiring to pluralism and democracy, and one predicated on hatred and 'purity' – between the ideals of the Enlightenment and the dark cult of chauvinism." Susan Sontag, who visited Sarajevo 11 times during the war, risking her life each time, was the best-known plenipotentiary of this global republic of conscience – whose "embassies" (in the words of Heaney's famous poem for Amnesty International) "were everywhere/but operated independently/and no ambassador would ever be relieved." I had been recalled to Sarajevo for my first first-hand briefing.

It was one of the key moments of my life – the beginning, in fact, of a third narrative, and eventual subject of an essay to which I am especially attached, "A Week in Sarajevo" (1996). Like the Pope's day in Dublin, it would be a decisive swerve into an utterly unexpected course in life. By the end of the nineties, I had edited the first post-war anthology of Bosnian writing, *Scar on the Stone: Contemporary Poetry from Bosnia* (Bloodaxe, 1998), and bought and renovated a house on the Dalmatian coast, not far from Dubrovnik. I have since spent long periods in both Bosnia and Croatia. To the bifocal perspectives of those first two narratives, I managed to add a trifocal extra, with a growing influence (I would soon discern) on the evolution of my writing, especially poetry.

Comparisons between Belfast and Sarajevo have for me proved very fertile. In the case of pre-war Sarajevo, for instance, Muslims, Catholics, Orthodox and Jews were entirely intermingled, with no trace of necessitated segregation. Religious intermarriage was widespread and normal; and although non-Yugoslav national sentiment did of course exist before the break-up of Yugoslavia, the various Bosnian denominations were not dangerously "nationalized" until Milosevic's virulent Serbian chauvinism appeared in 1987, triggering a rapid chain reaction throughout the federation that caught up with even this most cosmopolitan of cities. Bosnia had been the most ethically diverse of the six constituent republics; but what it tragically lacked, as the authoritarian structures of Yugo-communism fell away, was any ready theory of state that could secure its actually-existing ethnic and religious diversity. It fell to a multi-ethnic citizen mobilization to defend the city for most of the first year of the siege.

That Balkan contrast could not be starker. Since the arrival of Catholic mass immigration to the mills from the countryside in the mid-nineteenth century, Belfast has been a profoundly segregated city. There have been intercommunal riots, including over Home Rule, every decade since the 1850s. It is often claimed that the city had proportionately one of the largest working-classes in post-war Western Europe; even now, these traditional districts are almost completely segregated on sectarian grounds. One the first districts where Catholics settled, Ardoyne (from the Irish, *Ard Eoin*,

"Eoin's height"), remains a huge nationalist ghetto in a sea of loyalist estates, in North Belfast, currently the most fractured and turbulent area of the city. Working-class and rural intermarriage across communal boundaries is still unusual.

The euphemistic "peace walls" – the city's homespun version of the Berlin wall – snake half-visibly through various districts, "interfaces" and flashpoints where intercommunal violence has long flared. Some hold, half-jokingly, that Belfast is not so much a single unified *urbs* as a series of contiguous sectarian villages – and there is a certain metaphorical truth in that. Everywhere in working-class areas there are curbstones painted in the contending national colours, marking (to the foot) the communal boundaries – over which, if you are someone from "the other side," it was (and very often still is) high danger to cross. Nor is leafy middle-class Belfast fully immune from all this – the divisions are simply more "civilized" behind the façade of the genteel.

What saved Northern Ireland after 1969 from anything like a Bosnian fate was, of course, the huge power of the British state, with its long history of Irish statecraft. After Partition in 1922, the locus of that power moved symbolically from Dublin Castle to Belfast Castle; but the Westminster Parliament and its London bureaucracy, however amnesiac over the next half-century, never quite forgot the lessons of the previous two centuries. The essential British-London metropolitan mistake was, however, to allow Northern Ireland to become what might be called in Eastern Europe an "autonomous region," outwith many of the norms, laws, developments, common narratives and principles of Great Britain proper.

The little one-party state soon become, *de facto*, a Protestant-Unionist bastion, with its own internally powerful Parliament (prorogued by Westminster in 1972), civil service, police and auxiliary special forces; its unrelenting sectarian ethos and authoritarian *modus operandi* made it, in the classic phrase, "a cold house for Catholics." Meanwhile, down South, a second political monolith took shape, sustained by Irish Catholicism. One might easily argue that the Northern Troubles from 1969 were a kind of time-lag peregrination of violence out of the earlier "interregnum" period that led to the establishment of the Irish Free State.

Early in the millennium, owing to my time in the Balkans, I was asked to teach a course at Queen's University Belfast on post-communism in Central Europe and the Balkans. I had to read up, especially, on an unfamiliar but fascinating academic literature: the theory and practice of "state formation." I learnt that there are essentially only four types of states characterizing the whole of Europe and North America in the post-war period: the nation state (centred on a predominant ethnic group, or "people"); the ethno-religious federation (e.g., the USSR, Yugoslavia, and Czechoslovakia); the true confederation (Switzerland); and the federal nation (the US and Canada).

After the fall of communism, only two true federations had survived: the Russian Federation and, in effect – though usually not quite seen in this light – the monarchical multinational "union" of the United Kingdom, held together by the glue of "Britishness." Whilst recent events suggested the former might be fragile in the longer term, why – I wondered (and still wonder) – had the latter been so enduringly successful, even in the face of Irish violence? Just the tensile strength of an evolved, self-correcting democracy?

Westminster often pays lip service to "the four nations of the United Kingdom." But, in truth, this phrase is almost never heard in Northern Ireland; it is a self-defining catch-phrase in Great Britain for the whole of Ukania that has near-zero traction in Northern Ireland. Indeed, I have never once heard the word *nation* naturally, spontaneously or even ideologically applied to our Lilliputian state. It is simply not a word, concept or belief that feels right, ironically, to the culture *as a whole*.

"Occam's razor" will clarify. For the unionist or loyalist, the *nation* is nearly always "Britain," the overall "state formation," within which, perhaps, "Ulster" is at best a subordinate quasi-formation. For the Irish nationalist or republican, the Irish nation is by definition the whole of Ireland and its peoples – so that, *ipso facto*, one of its cardinal parts can never contain its geographical whole. *Northern Ireland* is a kind of linguistic limbo which strikes neither side as the actual serious *nation* to which they give *final* assent.

To repeat: Northern Ireland has never been, *is not*, and will not likely be any time soon a fully "imagined" nation. That is because – to crib the title of Benedict Anderson's classic book of the same name – Northern Ireland has not one, but two highly divergent *imagined communities* inhabiting the same territory. These constitute two narratives, two "Ulsters of the mind" (Heaney) – shades of Israel and Palestine! – in long-term historical contention.

As an illustration, one might cite the high proportion of the North's population that already possesses an Irish passport by dint of the Republic's constitution. In one of those strange historical twists that one would never have expected, the Belfast Agreement actually guarantees (via subsequent law) every child born in Northern Ireland after 2005 both British and Irish citizenship. Strange destiny, indeed – the North may be the only jurisdiction in the world that is, *de jure*, in the matter of citizenship, automatically *multinational*.

If Northern Ireland itself is not a nation, then what is it? The search for even loose parallels in Europe yields few pickings. There are now two miserable Slav gangster para-states descending from imperial plantations – Transnistria in Moldova, Republika Srpska in Bosnia (the latter much larger than the North). My own joke – that if Scotland secedes, the North risks becoming "Kaliningrad on the Irish Sea," an actual exclave – is not much appreciated here when the allusion is twigged. Both new Kosova (tensions of religion and language) and old Belgium (tensions of language and culture) contain contending "imagined communities" within a single state. The ethno-religious divisions, the subsequent partition, and the current unrecognized union of the island's north with Turkey make Cyprus an interesting parallel. The Basque country too has real resonances.

But perhaps it is better to take a leaf out of the lexicon of the recent Nobel Laureate, Svetlana Alexievich, when she remarked that her "small" country, Belarus, had been caught up in the "grinder" of history. That image for the six truncated Ulster counties somehow seems right – albeit in a much less catastrophic way.

So my bifocal credo for the Belfast home-place has become: *Look east, but then west.* Fruitful as the Eastern trope can be, it has no meaning, needless to say, shorn of the North's actual Western European context. In the Balkans, what historians call "the pre-national period" in the Ottoman lands lasted well into the second half of the nineteenth century; for example, neither the national idea nor even the word for the state now known as *Macedonia* existed in the 1850s. In contrast, "an idea of Ireland" had already been in existence for centuries.

By the late eighteenth century, the Irish Parliament had legislative independence within a Kingdom of Ireland separate from the Kingdom of Great Britain, though sharing the same monarchy and under the administrative control of the British executive power. Inspired by the American and French Revolutions, and led mainly by *Belfast* Presbyterians, the Irish Rebellion of 1798 sought, through arms, full nationhood and a clean break with Britain. It failed; and the union of the Irish and British

Parliaments that created the *first* "United Kingdom" followed swiftly, and in fear, in 1801. Even during that Union, importantly, Ireland remained a single constitutional polity, with a strong sense of its cultural distinctiveness – and with most of the population speaking Irish until the Great Famine.

Ireland, then, joins England, Scotland, France, Spain and Portugal in a very antique sense of itself as a "nation". "What ish my nation?" asks the drunken Irishman, MacMorris, in Shakespeare's *Henry V* (c. 1599). The island is, in this sense, and several others – for instance, the efflorescence of early Christian monastic and manuscript culture – a core Western European country.

So that when Partition came, within living memory of the Famine, the shock might be likened to the screaming roots of a mandrake – a deep cultural and political trauma. And yes, the depth and felt injustice of that all-island trauma since 1969 added a certain Irish revolutionary and martyred glamour (the British Left was particularly susceptible) to the intense bitterness and extreme ugliness of violence everywhere. It is also why neither "imagined community" – though scarred – will wither on the vine anytime soon. Bereavement, it becomes ever clearer this century, is a world-historical political force. In short, Northern Ireland was quite unique in the post-war West.

To *description* and *explanation* must be added *actuality*. What are we left with? A very small polity. Six counties only. "A place apart" (Dervla Murphy), a narrow ground, a *provincia*? In my own mind I would, now, often think of it naturally – if a bit ironically – as simply "the native territory."

We have got our Lilliput and must make it work, *faute de mieux*. A *work-in-progress* – capital, Belfast. The constitutional dispensation is settled, human rights fully guaranteed, whatever the latest sound-and-fury emanating from the Stormont Parliament might be. *For the time being*, anyway. And after nearly four decades and three narratives, I do often marvel at the fact that I have somehow transitioned from the West's largest English-speaking polity to its smallest – from the über-metropolitan to the ultra-peripheral.

Then I remind myself that living in a *provincia* was the common human condition for most of Europe before the First World War. Was Bukovina really, by definition, any less "cosmopolitan" than Vienna, the imperial capital? People lived, loved and died in "provinces" whose boundaries have now vanished without trace into those of other polities. Often these "native territories" and their capitals produced artists and, especially, writers of enormous talent – like Joseph Roth, Paul Celan, Czeslaw Miłosz, Herta Müller. Or, come to think of it, Seamus Heaney. In this light, Northern Ireland might be seen as a kind of "modern throwback" … To a post-globalized future?

In the wake of nearly 30 years of civil disturbance, terrorism and counter-terrorism – and after nearly four years of arduous negotiations – the politically miraculous occurred. A settlement was reached and signed on the same day – and a moment of all-Ireland euphoria swept the fractured island over the Easter weekend of 1998. It would take another decade for the envisioned institutions to operate fully, but the die was cast.

Although the whole process is now filed in Westminster under the rubric "devolution," the reality was, and is, much more supple and subtle, constitutionally speaking. In effect, in retrospect, the core negotiation centred on none other than a new "state formation" for the devolved polity – one that could accommodate the perspectives of the constitutional-monarchical (the North) and the constitutional-republican (the South). My own earlier narrative again:

> But what exactly was this [new] state? For the polity that exited the Troubles was profoundly different from the vanished unionist bastion of four decades earlier … Is it a permanent remnant of an older Union, the lost province of a future unified Irish nation, or one of the small countries of Europe? In according various degrees of formal legitimacy to each of these perspectives, the Belfast Agreement consciously foreclosed on the possibility of a single constitutional answer. "All" or "none" might easily be construed as more plausible answers … The natural tendency of any polity to bolster the autonomy of its own civic life is, however, well under way. In the current period of dramatic cultural and economic transformation, Northern Ireland can often seem akin to a "city state" – Belfast, and all its hinterland within easy driving distance – or even a kind of "anti-state," where classic sovereignty has been diluted in the name of the native ground, or common good.

Hallelujah! …To which might be added that the Agreement, *as a process*, is surely a global model for other intractable conflicts.

As I wander through the stalls at St George's Market on a Saturday morning, I am bound to dwell on the civic meaning of the new diversity. Even here, in a corner of Europe, the waves of globalization and its cousins – migration and the re-imagining of nations – are lapping strongly. I am struck, especially, by how well Belfast has managed its immigration. Bar an occasional incident, the overwhelming response of the city's inhabitants to the newcomers seems to have ranged from the nonplussed to the genuinely welcoming.

You might wonder, in light of a sectarian past and present, why such "easygoingness" has so easily materialized. Perhaps it has something to do with the assumption that even large-scale immigration poses no risk to the blesséd divisions of "the antique quarrel." Perhaps it has something to do with a subliminal belief that this new infusion of people will, thankfully, give relief to those very divisions. Or, precisely, perhaps both.

For myself, I tend to the idea that the city's *laissez-faire* response to its new human element has a great deal to do with Ireland's own experience of immigration. As the trilingual Irish novelist Hugo Hamilton once remarked (his mother was German), "Here in Ireland, we understand the emptiness of migrancy perhaps better than anyone else." Not only because of the historical trauma – the island lost half its population in the nineteenth century – but because so many living Irish people, North and South, have worked for summers, years and decades in the multicultural cities of North America, Britain and the Continent before returning to the island. If Belfast's diversity suddenly begins to resemble that of Boston or London – and then feels quite natural – *so what?* And – my thought continues – if Troubled Belfast itself is so deeply divided on the national question, what's the point of getting hysterical about some imagined "existential threat" to one or another "imagined community" – the single possibility of which, even the dogs in the streets know by now, is *kaput* ...

But Belfast being Belfast, the first decade of the Agreement hardly ran smoothly. A series of provincial "culture wars," especially in and around the city, immediately bubbled up from the communal mantle underlying the new dispensation. Slowly it became clear that Belfast was even more deeply troubled than one might have imagined when focussing solely on political and governmental solutions. Most of these local conflicts centred on holding or extending "cultural territory"; many were sparked off by Orange marches (like the stereophonic one at Drumcree) in proximity to Catholic communities.

What soon could not be gainsaid is that *integral* to each of the "two traditions" is a deep element of antagonism to the *other*. Put another way, each "tradition" or "identity" has to decommission something *within itself*, if anything like real civic-civil co-existence can be secured; to that end, *if desired*, each "side" has also to shift the collective focus from self-exculpatory "prevention of the other" to self-affirming "transformation of the inherited." That, of course, is a cultural archetype stretching right across the globe; writ very large, it might even be called "the clash of civilisations." But it is also what makes Belfast's very narrow ground so utterly intractable.

There are the old tensions, the old narratives, a new diversity – and the complex psycho-cultural currents that carry it all along. There are offsets, too, flowing from the city's tradition of tough politics: the struggle for gay rights, the revival of Irish, the widespread hostility to Great Power thinking, the urge to escape a mantle of dreadful provincialism. Yet the real puppet-master of the body politic must be, it often seems to me, *the very space of the place* – the intense cabin fever of the polity, as it were. Fed up with the whole scene? You cannot simply take a bus to Florida or Los Angeles and start afresh. If you wish to escape the atmosphere of the North, you must leave it altogether.

That the Belfast ground is still deeply narrow is, then, taken as read. Triumphalist Orangeism, republican martyrology, "Biblical" Protestantism, and severe deprivation continue to weave much of its urban warp and woof. I would say that the degree to which Northern society is equidistant from much in Great Britain and the Republic is barely appreciated outside "the Province." Yeats once remarked that the North was "half-Scotch" – and a certain "tidy-mindedness," a certain Protestant work ethic, a certain British-imperial industrial culture set down in an Irish landscape, does permeate the very grain of Belfast. But the wider bifurcated polity and its intractable psychodynamics lack utterly the common civil society and culture of Scotland – well reflected in its civic, rather ethnic, nationalism – which may soon take it altogether out of fractured Britain.

What then for the city-state's republican-monarchical Lilliput? An English dependency? The Republic's foundling? To what will it stay loyal? Itself divided?

———

Not so long ago I was "driving Lilliput," criss-crossing those same streets of former cities. I was thinking about what a young poet had said to me earlier from a sofa in my office: *Ireland, you know, is a literary superpower.* I had paused a moment before I agreed, ticking off in my mind a first quick roster of distinction: Shaw, Yeats, O'Casey, Beckett, Bowen, Heaney, Butler, Tóibín… before trailing off into many others. It's something of a mystery – we concluded weakly, adjourning till the next *reprise* of the theme – that such a small culture had produced such literary magnificence over the past century.

A moment later I was stopped at traffic lights and an amplifying image sprang to mind: *a gigantic microcosm.* Ireland, that is. Not that the trope was new to me. But the phrase was. Ireland (East, West, South, North) seemed large enough to contain "epigrammatic" multitudes. But small enough to retain a human scale in the age of anthills – the megapolitan cities, the authoritarian Eurasian federations, the failed states, the neo-liberal malls. Butler's first book, after all, was entitled *Escape from the Anthill* (Lilliput Press, 1985).

As with some of the other small ancient countries of Europe, it could be said of Ireland: *small size, big space.* To the metropolitan with a map, those counties, provinces and cardinal spaces might seem a "limited" territory. But cultural space does not exist in proportion to geographical size. Even less its global relevance. Heaney, towards the end of his life, proffered that the world was becoming "a big Ulster." From Ukraine to Bahrain, Thailand to the Central African Republic, the truth of that metaphor now seems borne home daily on the magic carpet of the global media.

Small cultures have energies, strengths and insights that are often invisible or largely inaccessible to the larger psycho-spatial territories of classic "metropolitan" cultures. Precisely because the beast's lair is often so close, a *provincia* can have a special feel for the extremist political seductions of "borderland/borderline identities." The North, once thought to be Western Europe's great aberration, seems less so now – and, indeed, more of a canary in the global coalmine.

Revving up from those lights, I recalled for the umpteenth time something said by the very fine Shetlandic poet, Robert Alan Jamieson. At a reading in Glasgow, he observed that whereas the so-called "peripheral" culture could see straight to the centre of its "metropolitan" capital, the reverse was hardly the case. As it happened, his remarks occurred just before I attended a "Reception for Contemporary British Poetry" at Buckingham Palace. Since I am not even a British citizen, the invitation was perhaps a tiny example of why the "British" Monarchy has been so successful for so long.

It was fun to cross the Palace's gravelled moonlit courtyard and process up the Soviet-style plush of the grand staircases. Soon the Royals were circulating with their equerries though the Picture Gallery hung with masterpieces. Prince Phillip approached one group of us waiting poets and critics, champagne in hand, and asked: "In your readings, does the poet read his own work?" He evidently had never attended a common-or-garden "poetry reading." Trapped at the glittering centre, the distant gossamer was occluded. No wonder those Belfast Presbyterians had once led the campaign to break with the remote centre.

Hence the desire to stay close to *small size, big space* seems instinct in many Irish writers. Perhaps this only reflects the inspirational need of most literary artists for the precise images and small details of known worlds. *Never stray too far from your first style* was Orwell's parallel dictum. Heaney held that his creative course was always locked into "Irish airspace." Beckett never left his mastery of the Dublin demotic. Bowen, who remained in black-out London during its Churchillian hour (see under: "Mysterious Kôr"!), had an unsurpassed grasp of her Anglo-Irish native territory. Swift created his Lilliput. Butler, who attended Charterhouse (which he loathed) and Oxford, gets the cultural logic of the smaller-scale exactly, in his second volume *The Children of Drancy* (Lilliput Press, 1988):

> Yeats deliberately chose the small community, moving his heart and his body and as much as he could of his mind from London to Ireland, his birthplace. For him and a dozen other well-known Irish writers Ireland had been a larger Brook Farm, a refuge whose walls were built not by some transcendental theory but by history and geography. For a few years our most parochial period became also our most creative.

I never left – I guess – the alternative grain of that first narrative.

This essay was delivered at the John Hewitt International Summer School on 27 July 2016. It was written before the film I am Belfast *was seen by the author.*

Chris Agee is the Editor of this journal. His third collection of poems, Next to Nothing *(2009), was shortlisted in Britain for the Ted Hughes Award for New Work in Poetry, funded by the British Poet Laureate. He recently edited* Balkan Essays *(The Irish Pages Press, 2016), the sixth volume of Hubert Butler's essays. His fourth collection of poems,* Blue Sandbar Moon, *is forthcoming. He divides his time between Ireland, Scotland and Croatia.*